A Voyage
to the Northwest Coast
of America

GABRIEL FRANCHÈRE

Painted by Joseph Charles Franchère. Reproduced by courtesy of The Antiquarian and Numismatic Society of Montreal. Chateau de Ramezay, Montreal.

The Lakeside Classics

A VOYAGE TO THE NORTHWEST COAST OF AMERICA

By Gabriel Franchère

EDITED BY

MILO MILTON QUAIFE

The Lakeside Press

R. R. DONNELLEY & SONS COMPANY

CHICAGO

Christmas, 1954

PUBLISHERS' PREFACE

FOLLOWING their custom of selecting material for the Lakeside Classics without regard to continuity of time and place, the Publishers have again left the Plains States and gone back another fifty years and to the Pacific Northwest for the scene of this year's volume.

Gabriel Franchère, the author of this narrative, was a fellow member of the same expedition as Alexander Ross whose reminiscences furnished the subject matter for the 1923 volume. But his experiences were different, enough so to make his story a fresh one even to those familiar with Ross's account; and Franchère's return journey through the country north of the Canadian border, a country with which many of our readers are no doubt familiar, adds a new interest. With the historical introduction and the maps as background we hope our readers will find much pleasure in what we offer.

To Dr. Quaife and to those who in turn were helpful to him we are indebted for the excellent historical introduction and notes; and to The Newberry Library for the loan of their copy of the original edition for use as copy.

The enthusiastic reception given the changes made last year in the typography, paper and color of binding has been very gratifying and we hope will continue in favor as each new volume is added during this third quarter century of the Lakeside Classics. We send this new title with our best wishes for Christmas and the New Year.

THE PUBLISHERS

Christmas, 1954

CONTENTS

ix

ILLUSTRATIONS

HISTORICAL INTRODUCTION

THE extent to which individuals influence the course of history affords food for perennial debate. How different, for example, would the course of subsequent history have been if Napoleon Bonaparte had been slain at the bridge of Lodi? Or what would the further course of American history have been if one of the bullets which pierced young George Washington's clothing at Braddock's defeat on the Monongahela had pierced his brain instead? Or, again, if a German immigrant youth named John Jacob Astor, coming to America in 1784, had not chanced to encounter on shipboard a fellow passenger who told him about the opportunities afforded by the American fur trade, would the Stars and Stripes or the banner of Britain or of Russia today float over the Valley of the Columbia and marvelous California?

Our immediate concern is with the career of Astor, a youth of humble birth and rearing, who lived to become a man of immense wealth and one of the most daring and successful merchants of all time. Before the ship which brought him to America made land he had pumped his fellow-passenger dry of information concerning the fur-trade and had fixed upon his occupation in the

New World which lay before him. So successful was he that by the year 1800 he had acquired a fortune of a quarter-million dollars and had become one of the leading figures in the American fur trade.

Two events of the period—the evacuation by the British in 1796 of the line of Great Lakes posts and the purchase of Louisiana in 1803—enlarged immensely the opportunities for expansion of the trade. Already Astor had made his initial venture to the Orient by dispatching a ship to Canton, from whose single voyage he gained a profit of $50,000. The Lewis and Clark exploration of 1803–1806 served to sharpen his vision of a world-wide trade and no general of an army ever moved more decisively to achieve his objectives than Astor. On April 6, 1808 he incorporated in New York State the American Fur Company with a capital of $1,000,000 supplied wholly by himself, and through this agency began his projected advance across the Continent.

As an initial measure, an agreement was reached with the Canadian North West and Michilimackinac companies for a division of the trade of the Great Lakes area, whereby the three parties joined hands to create the South West Company, which was to operate in the area lying south of the Canadian border. The War of 1812, which affected materially the normal operations of the fur trade, played into Astor's hands. In 1816 Congress, quite probably instigated by Astor, passed an act excluding foreigners from trading within the United States and a year later Astor bought out his Canadian partners at a very low price. By further steps which we do not pause to narrate, within another decade the American Fur Company obtained a virtual monopoly of the fur trade of the United States.

Oddly enough, the War of 1812 which facilitated Astor's dominance of the trade of the Great Lakes and Upper Mississippi area had the contrary effect of defeating the most daring and far-reaching of all his projects. Open to the world at the beginning of the nineteenth century was the alluring prize of America's trans-Rocky Mountain Pacific Coast, whose control was fast slipping from the grasp of decrepit Spain. Three great nations—Russia, Great Britain, and the United States—competed for the prize. For the latter, German-born John Jacob Astor assumed the leading role. His far-flung project for controlling the trade of the Continent contemplated the establishment of a central depot at the mouth of the Columbia, to which the furs from dependent interior posts should be brought and where the supplies required for the further prosecution of the trade should be kept. Meanwhile, vessels plying the Northwest Coast would harvest the skins of the sea otters, upon which the Chinese placed a fabulous valuation, and a fleet of ships would carry the entire output of furs to Canton for sale in the Chinese market. Returning thence to Europe and New York, they would supply the western world with the tea and other Oriental products which were in demand there. As the final link in the extensive trading chain, a vessel would sail annually from New York for Cape Horn and the mouth of the Columbia laden with the trade goods and other supplies which were required there.[1]

To forestall the competition of the Montreal North West Company, Astor invited it to join him in the trade of the Columbia, offering a one-

---

[1]Lakeside Classics readers who are familiar with *Alexander Henry's Travels and Adventures* (the Classics volume for 1921) will note with interest that the idea of establishing a post at the mouth of the Columbia was not original with Astor. Instead, "much of the credit belongs to Astor's friend, patron, and occasional partner," Alexander Henry of Montreal. Kenneth Porter, *John Jacob Astor Business Man* (Cambridge, 1931), I, 170. As early as March 5, 1786, Henry wrote to William Edgar, long-time Detroit merchant who had recently removed to New York, advising the establishment of trading posts on the rivers of the Northwest Coast, which he described as "my favorite plan." Almost inevitably, Porter observes, Henry expounded this project in his conversations with Astor. Pertinent also is the fact that Edgar, his correspondent of 1786, was one of the Commissioners appointed by the Act of Incorporation of Astor's American Fur Company to receive subscriptions for its stock.

third interest in the enterprise. The astute and aggressive Northwesters declined the proffer, however, and instead instituted their own plans for a swift descent upon the Columbia. Although a Northwester, Alexander Mackenzie, in 1793 had been the first white man to cross the continent north of Mexico,[2] the Northwesters had no establishment on the Pacific, and their trade was conducted over the long and arduous overland route to Montreal, whence their furs were dispatched to the European and other world markets. Astor's plan of supplying his Pacific station by ship from New York and sending the furs obtained by sea to the Oriental market possessed an advantage which the Northwesters would have found difficult, if not impossible, to overcome.

However, the Northwesters and their working force of humble Canadian voyageurs were postgraduate masters of the lore of the American wilderness, a fact which no one appreciated more keenly than Astor. To insure the success of his new venture, therefore, he persuaded several prominent Northwesters to join his organization and in addition to these leaders he enlisted the services of a considerable number

[2]His journal was published as the Lakeside Classics volume for 1931, entitled *Alexander Mackenzie's Voyage to the Pacific Ocean in 1793.*

of Canadian clerks and voyageurs. All of these
assembled at New York in the summer of 1810,
where the ship *Tonquin* was in readiness to convey them around Cape Horn to the mouth of the
Columbia. Meanwhile, an overland party was
dispatched from Saint Louis to traverse the
route which Lewis and Clark had blazed across
the continent half a dozen years earlier. Upon
completing the journey its members were to join
hands with the voyagers who had come by sea
in the undertaking which has ever since been
known as the Astorian enterprise.

If the information supplied by a somewhat
remote descendant may be trusted the American
ancestor of Gabriel Franchère came from Vitre
in Brittainy to Canada at an "early day." Gabriel's father (also named Gabriel) was born at
Quebec, March 4, 1752, where about the year
1779 he married Felicite Miron. In characteristic
French-Canadian fashion nineteen children were
born to them during the period 1780–1804,
eleven of whom died in early childhood, and it
is perhaps not surprising to learn that the mother
died in 1807 at the comparatively early age of
forty-seven.

Gabriel Franchère Sr. was a merchant in Montreal where Gabriel Franchère Jr., his seventh
child, was born November 3, 1786. Although detailed information concerning his early life is

lacking, it is evident that he obtained a fair education. He himself relates that he had seldom ventured outside his native city when in 1810 he eagerly embraced the proffered opportunity to exchange the humdrum life of a clerk in his father's establishment for the exciting career of a fur trader on the Northwest Coast of America.

From this point Franchère may be left to narrate his own story of his four-years' adventure by sea and land, from which he returned to Montreal in early September, 1814 to be greeted by his family as one risen from the dead. Since his departure from New York they had received no word from him, and they had long since concluded that he had been killed by the Indians at the destruction of the *Tonquin*. Awaiting him, also, was the patient sweetheart, Sophie Routhier, whom he had left behind. They were married in 1815, and the union lasted until her death in 1837.

From 1810 onward Franchère's entire career was associated with the fur trade. For several years following his return from the Astorian enterprise he served as Astor's Montreal agent. Later he became a resident of Sault Sainte Marie, Michigan, where for several years during the thirties he managed the local American Fur Company establishment. The Company failed in 1842 (Astor had sold his interest eight years earlier) and Franchère joined the Saint Louis concern which in 1834 had purchased the Western Department from Astor, and which now (1842) had become known as Pierre Chouteau Jr. and Company. Still later, Franchère removed to New York, where he established his own fur business and prior to his death was the senior partner in the firm of Gabriel Franchère and Company. His outspoken devotion to his adopted country did not prevent him from retaining a lively interest in his native city and land. One consequence of the Patriot Rebellion of 1837 was the migration of many French-Canadian refugees to the United States, many of them to New York City. To succor the destitute and to promote the welfare of his compatriots generally Franchère assumed the leadership in establishing the Society of St. John the Baptist, patterned after the association of the same name which was devoted to the preservation of the French language and culture. Numerous other societies throughout the United States (more than 100 according to one statement) looked upon Franchère as their founder. When he visited Montreal in 1853 the parent Society tendered him a public reception "in his character of a distinguished compatriot and the President of the National Society in New York." A subscription was taken to provide his portrait for the Canadian Institute, then the representative literary association in Montreal.[3]

Ten or more children were born to Franchère and his wife in the years from 1817 to 1837. Several of them died in the years 1822–38, and in 1837 the mother followed her children in death. Two years later, on a visit to Detroit Franchère "chanced to get introduced to a widow lady, Mrs. Prince, a niece of Colonel Mack, and being in want of a person to be a second mother to my little daughter I concluded it was best to marry at once."[4]

Although there is no hint of romance in the bridegroom's prosaic report of the event, the union seems to have been a fortunate one for both parties. Family information discloses that the Prince family came from England to Cincinnati, where a son, John S. Prince, was born,

[3]Statements adapted from a typed copy in Minnesota Historical Society Library of an unidentified source, apparently a contemporary publication. Efforts to determine the present location of the portrait have proved unavailing. The Canadian Institute ceased its existence in 1885.

[4]Franchère to Henry H. Sibley, Feb. 22, 1839, in Sibley Papers, Minnesota Historical Society Library. Information concerning the number of children and dates of their birth and deaths is found in an old-age report (ms.) of a descendant in possession of the Minnesota Historical Society. Additional information has been received from Dr. Frederick W. Franchère of Lake Crystal, Minnesota, a great-grandson of the author.

May 7, 1821, the father dying soon afterward. What circumstance may have brought Mrs. Prince to Detroit remains unknown, save for the clue supplied by the statement in Franchère's letter that she was a niece of Colonel Stephen Mack. The latter was for a generation one of Detroit's leading citizens, and a co-founder of the city of Pontiac. His memory is preserved in the name of Mack Avenue, one of Detroit's important streets. John S. Prince, who thus became Franchère's stepson, was destined in his turn to become one of Saint Paul's leading citizens. In Franchère's declining years he paid numerous visits to his stepson and on the last one died in his home, April 12, 1863.

His long-time friend and admirer, Benjamin P. Avery, himself a prominent journalist and editor, wrote an obituary appreciation which was published subsequently in Volume VI of the *Minnesota Historical Collections* under the title "Death of a Remarkable Man." The writer characterized him as "a man below the medium stature, of very simple and correct habits, which insured him good health and cheerful spirits. He possessed a blithe disposition, veined with a kindly humor, true to his adopted country, and had a firm faith in the Christian religion."

Avery stated further that upon the failure of the American Fur Company in 1848 Franchère had sacrificed his fortune "in an extremely honorable manner" to assist in meeting the liabilities of the firm. This seems to imply that instead of being a mere employee, Franchère had become one of the members of the firm.

Franchère was one of the last survivors of the Astorians. Avery in 1863 supposed him to be the last. Franchère himself in 1854 listed four survivors—himself, Ramsay Crooks, Alfred Seton of New York, and Benjamin Pillet of Canada. Crooks died in 1859. No record of the death of Seton or Pillet has been found.[5]

Efforts made to trace the descendants of Franchère, now many and widely scattered, have met with but limited success. Five daughters and one son are reported to have died young, leaving one son and four daughters who lived to maturity. Henriette, the eldest, married at Sault Sainte Marie in February 1838 and Matilda (the second daughter bearing the name) married at Detroit in January, 1840. The uncertain memory of an old-age descendant of Franchère reports the marriages of all four daughters, with some uncertainty concerning the names of two of the bridegrooms. Of their

[5]The later lives of most of the obscure members of the expedition remain, of course, unknown. One of them, Charles Boucher, lived on Grosse Ile, below Detroit, from about 1829 until his death in 1865. He was buried at Wyandotte, Michigan, June 21, 1865.

further lives and careers no information has been obtained.

A grandson[6] of Evariste, the son of Franchère who grew to manhood, has supplied ample information concerning his career and descendants.

Born at Montreal, July 14, 1820, at the age of 12 he became a cabin boy on the Great Lakes. After some eight years of freshwater service he became a salt-water sailor with his headquarters more or less of the time at New York. In 1849 he joined in the Gold Rush, sailing around Cape Horn to California, where he remained for twenty years. His prospecting for gold having proved unprofitable, about the year 1851 he established a drugstore in Marysville, which he continued until he left California.

Another Forty-niner was Martha Mary Cross, a seventeen-year-old Michigan girl who accompanied her Uncle and Aunt to California by the overland prairie-schooner route. Several years later (the date uncertain) she married Evariste Franchère. Martha was a Protestant, and when her husband reported their marriage to his father, the latter disowned and disinherited him.

Eventually both Evariste and Martha became homesick for the East and about the year 1869 they returned on one of the early overland trains

[6]Dr. Frederick W. Franchère of Lake Crystal, Minnesota.

to cross the Continent. Mrs. Franchère had a sister who was married to the proprietor of a general store in Lake Crystal, Minnesota, and after some visiting around Franchère settled there, where he conducted a drug and general store until his death in 1892.

Evariste Franchère had two sons, Gabriel William and Frederick E. Franchère. Gabriel William, the older one, was a partner in his father's business, which he continued to conduct until his own death in January, 1902. He had four children: Harold, a dentist of Lake Crystal, who died in 1945; Frederick William, a physician of Lake Crystal, who has only recently retired from active practice; Evariste Gabriel, a jeweler of Los Angeles; and Lucille Franchère Tinder, a nurse in World War I, who lives in Yucaipa, California.

Frederick E. Franchère, Evariste and Martha Franchère's second son, was born in California and reared to manhood in Lake Crystal. He became a physician of Sioux City, Iowa, about the year 1902, where he died about 1942. One daughter, a teacher, resides in Sioux City; another lives in Raleigh, North Carolina; and a son in Oswego, Oregon.

Of Astor's Astorian enterprise, Chittenden, one of the ablest historians of the fur trade, wrote: "The general plan upon which it was based stands above criticism. It was a project no less feasible than magnificent. Although its course was one of almost uniform diaster, its very failures showed that under normal conditions its success would have exceeded the anticipations of its great promoter. He had proposed well, but God and man, with tempest and war, had disposed in a way which he could scarcely have imagined possible."[7]

Fortunately for posterity, three of the young men whom Astor employed as clerks possessed both the industry and the ability to keep contemporary journals and subsequently to publish narratives of their observations and experiences. These were Alexander Ross, Ross Cox, and Franchère. Earliest in the field was Franchère, whose narrative was first published in French at Montreal in 1820. Cox's *Adventures on the Columbia River* was published at New York in 1832. It is a book of over 300 finely-printed pages which recite the story of the Astorian expedition and in addition the experiences of the author during several subsequent years in the Columbia River region. Although it is a valuable work, no reprint edition seems ever to have been issued.

Last of the series of original narratives of the expedition to appear was Alexander Ross's *Ad-*

[7]Hiram M. Chittenden, *The American Fur Trade of the Far West* (New York, 1902), Vol. I, 228.

ventures of the First Settlers on the Oregon or Columbia River, which was first published in London in 1849. It has since been twice reprinted: by Reuben Gold Thwaites in 1904 as Volume VII of his extensive compilation of *Early Western Travels;* and more recently as the Lakeside Classics volume for 1923.

Ross Cox is reputed to have been an Irishman, concerning whom comparatively little is known beyond the information he himself has provided in his narrative of *Adventures on the Columbia River.*[8] Alexander Ross was a Scot who throughout life remained a British subject. The North West Company was dominated by Scotsmen, and both national and racial affiliations inclined Ross to deal leniently with Astor's Scots-Canadian partners, whose loyalty still remains debatable. Franchère, on the contrary, became an American citizen, loyally attached to his adopted country. This fact may have lent edge to the sharpness with which, in the Appendix to his narrative, written in 1854, he criticized their conduct.

The steps by which the narrative now before us was developed invite our careful attention. Franchère was one of the "scribbling" clerks who excited the ire of Captain Thorn during the

[8]Franchère gives his full name as Rossenberg Cox, a curious name for an Irishman.

voyage of the *Tonquin* from New York to the mouth of the Columbia. When he returned to Montreal four years later he brought with him a journal of his travels which evidently was kept industriously, frequently under trying circumstances of hardship and danger. In the preface to the 1820 edition of his book he related that his only motive for keeping the journal was to provide his family and friends with a more accurate account of his experiences than a mere oral recital would permit. In response to the urging of friends who read it, he was finally persuaded to undertake its publication.

In or about the year 1819, therefore, Franchère procured a large-leaf notebook and set about the unwonted task of fashioning his four years' record into a narrative suitable for publication. At its head he wrote in a forthright hand.

Journal
d'un Voyage sur la Côte du Nord ouest de L'Amerique Septentrionale pendant les Années 1811–12, 13 & 1814.

When it was completed the 220-page record was turned over to Michel Bibaud for publication. What became of the original journal we have no knowledge. There are many ways of checking the accuracy of the narrative, however, which leave no room for doubt that it is a conscientious and painstaking factual recital.

Although Franchère had evidently received a fair education he was a stranger to the literary art and it was fortunate that in Bibaud he obtained an editor who knew how to produce an eminently readable narrative. Michel Bibaud was an industrious teacher, poet, and journalist, who devoted a long life-time to the promotion of French-Canadian culture and literature. Under his editorial guidance the book was published at Montreal in 1820 with but one slight change in the title Franchère had employed:

Relation d'un Voyage a la Côte du Nord-Ouest de L'Amerique Septentrionale, dan les-Années 1810, 11, 12, 13 et 14.
Par G. Franchère Fils.

Long after the two principals in the undertaking had departed to the other world confusion concerning their respective roles in it arose, accompanied by some rather sweeping imputations against the honor of Franchère. This confusion still exists and our further commentary will undertake the task of clarifying it. The issue, simply stated, concerns the respective contributions of Franchère and Bibaud to the production of the published book. It is the function of an editor to edit, and there is no room for doubt that Bibaud performed his task in thorough-going fashion. It is quite another

matter to claim for him the authorship of the narrative, and to accuse Franchère of concealing this agency when the second edition was published in English translation at New York in 1854. Yet such are the charges which in recent decades have gained widespread currency.

What seems to be the most substantial biography of Bibaud, published in 1908 by Judge L. W. Sicotte in the *Canadian Antiquarian and Numismatic Journal*, makes these statements. "In 1820 he published an account of the travels of Gabriel Franchère. His narrative is written in a pleasing style more like fiction, and there are passages in this volume that compare favorably with the best French works. The following description of the Saskatchewan is a good example [here follows Bibaud's description which begins with the last paragraph of page 248 of our present reprint]. I could thus quote page after page of such descriptions of true literary merit. On the other hand the book is written in a simplicity of style which recalls that of Defoe and which may be perused with great interest and pleasure. This volume, which is very rare, was translated into English, and in 1854 a second edition was published in the United States by M. Gabriel Franchère himself, who, having become an American citizen, seems

to have forgotten that Bibaud was the author
of the narrative, for Mr. J. V. Huntington, his
publisher and translator, praised its good qualities without appearing to realize that the feathers
which he places in Franchère's cap really belonged to another."

Professor W. Stewart Wallace, compiler of a
widely-known Dictionary of Canadian Biography, relying upon Judge Sicotte's statements,
in his sketch of Bibaud repeats them substantially
as follows: "This volume which is now very
rare was published also in an English translation;
and in 1854 a second edition of the translation
was brought out in New York by Franchère
himself, though without acknowledgment of
Bibaud's authorship." [9]

A review of Judge Sicotte's statements discloses certain errors which call for correction.
Perhaps it is a matter of judgment, over which
men may reasonably disagree, to say that the
book reads "like fiction." With the exception of
a few literary flights (most notably the one about
the Saskatchewan, which Judge Sicotte quotes)
in which Bibaud indulged, it does not seem to
me to read like fiction; on the contrary it im-

[9] In the sketch devoted to Franchère's career, however,
Professor Wallace clearly credits Franchère as author of
the book, making no mention of Bibaud's supposed re-
sponsibility for it.

presses me as an unusually well-written narrative of sober facts.

Passing this matter, and the minor error that an English translation was published prior to 1854 (this seems to be the reasonable interpretation of Judge Sicotte's somewhat ambiguous statement), we come to his major charge that Bibaud was the author of the work, and that Franchère conveniently "forgot" this fact when the 1854 edition was published. Yet it is clear that Bibaud himself never claimed to be the author. Instead, he published the narrative in 1820 giving this distinction to Franchère; and this representation was repeated, in effect, by his son who in 1857, when Bibaud was still living, published the earliest dictionary of Canadian biography, in which the sketch of his Father's career lists him simply as the *rédacteur* (editor) of Franchère's narrative.[10]

Gerald E. Hart, formerly a well-known Canadian historian and collector, whose many ac-

---

[10]Concerning Franchère, Bibaud Jr. wrote: "*Mr. Franchère a donna de ce voyage une relation que, depourvue de l'apparat scientifique, ne laisse pas de se faire lire avec un grand interet,*" adding that the French edition was out of print and that an edition in English had been recently published. *Dictionnaire Historiques des Hommes Illustres du Canada et de L'Amerique* (Montreal, 1857), 120. If Bibaud senior was in fact the author of the book, his son could not conceivably have published such a statement as this.

quisitions of literary treasures included the Franchère Manuscript, apparently took the trouble to examine it, with this resultant verdict written in pencil on the first page immediately below the title: "This ms. is the original in the Author's hand-writing of Franchère's 'Narrative of a Voyage to the Northwest Coast of America in the years 1811–14,' first printed in French at Montreal in 1820 from this copy, revised and considerably altered by Mr. Bibaud the Historian and Poet. . . . The text as shown herein is so different to the published version, it should be reprinted verbatim, inasmuch as Mr. Bibaud has embellished the language considerably."

Our own extensive examination of the Manuscript serves to confirm and amplify Hart's comment. Although Bibaud was evidently a conscientious editor, he treated Franchère's copy with a degree of freedom which would not meet the approval of present-day historical scholars. In particular he subjected it to an enormous number of transpositions, ranging from single sentences to entire chapters. In passing, it may be noted that Franchère made no division into chapters; those found in the printed book are the work of Bibaud. Transpositions and minor revisions of sentences or longer passages apart, Bibaud "embellished"—to use

Hart's word—the copy with a number of footnotes and other additions of his own composition, with no indication to the reader that these
were not the output of Franchère's pen. These
additions can commonly be recognized without
too great difficulty by the reader who bears in
mind the difference between Bibaud's extensive
literary background and experience and the relatively meager store of learning possessed by
Franchère.

On the matter of literary style something further remains to be said. We have already learned
from Judge Sicotte's indictment that Huntington, who translated the 1854 edition, praised the
"Defoe-like" quality of the narrative, for which he
ascribed credit to Franchère. With no desire to
deprecate Bibaud's editorial contribution, it seems
to me that in ascribing the Defoe-like simplicity
of style to Franchère Huntington came nearer to
the truth than does Judge Sicotte, who derides
him for doing so. In the main, Bibaud adheres
closely to Franchère's factual recital, whose simplicity Huntington praised, while it is precisely
those poetic flights with which Bibaud occasionally embellished the narrative which are conspic-
uously lacking in simplicity.

Between 1820 and 1854, when the second edition of Franchère's *Narrative* was published, two
developments which demand our notice occurred.

John Jacob Astor was not unmindful of the historical importance of his Astorian enterprise and in the early thirties he enlisted the interest of Washington Irving in writing its history. Irving was one of the most renowned Americans of his time, and he was Astor's personal friend. Supplied with journals, diaries, letters, and other records he fell to work, and as the result of his labor *Astoria; or Anecdotes of an Enterprise Beyond the Rocky Mountains* was published at Philadelphia in 1836. The book has ever since been regarded as a classic, whose literary charm and artistry is unquestioned. It has undergone many reprintings, and it still remains by far the best-known account of the Astorian enterprise.

Historians, however, have long been less enthusiastic concerning the scholarly quality of *Astoria*, and some of them have criticized it more or less sharply. One of the earliest critics was Franchère himself, whose narrative, among others, Irving had utilized in writing his book. When it was published in 1836, and for years thereafter, Franchère was living at Sault Sainte Marie and Saint Louis and in no position to reply to Irving's presentation. In 1846, when the controversy with Great Britain over the Oregon country was at its height, Senator Benton of Missouri established contact with him and both quoted from his book in the course of his im-

portant speech on the Oregon question and introduced him to his Senatorial colleagues.
Franchère's pride was stirred by this attention,
and to it he attributes the origin of his desire to
have his book published in English to become a
part of the literature of his adopted country.

A more important consideration was the resentment aroused by a reperusal of Irving's
Astoria. Other shortcomings aside, he deplored
the misrepresentations of the character of some
of the young clerks (himself among the number)
which he found in the book. These considera-
tions were responsible for the publication at New
York in 1854 of an English translation of the
1820 edition of the narrative. The translator,
J. V. Huntington, was a widely-known literary
figure of the time. However excellent his translation may be, his historical competence was but
slight and his editorial footnotes added nothing to
the value of the narrative. The additions made by
Franchère, however, found in the closing pages
of the book, supply useful pertinent information.

Although Mr. Hart expressed the opinion
that in view of the changes introduced by Bibaud,
Franchère's original manuscript should be
published verbatim, it seems unlikely that this
will soon, if ever, be done. Consequently, in my
own editing of the 1854 edition I have sought to
inform the reader of the changes introduced
by Bibaud, and to acquaint him, in so far as

practicable, with the narrative as it left the hands
of Franchère. Dr. R. G. Thwaites, who in 1904
included a reprinting of the 1854 edition in his
Early Western Travels series, reproduced it,
errors and all, virtually verbatim. In the present
edition I have exercised entire freedom to edit
the copy, commonly excising the footnotes and
on frequent occasions substituting my own
rendering of Franchère's manuscript for the
text as presented by Huntington and Bibaud.
Thus, although the present book is basically a
reprint of the 1854 edition, it makes no pretense
of being a verbatim copy of it; instead, I have
frequently departed from it, in ways and places
to which, when readily practicable, attention is
directed in the footnotes.

Two further explanations should be made.
Believing the spelling of geographical names
followed by Franchère to be of greater historical
value than the forms used by Bibaud and Huntington, I have followed the usage of the Manuscript whenever this was noted by me. But since
the time at my disposal did not permit a complete checking of the place names, in many in-
stances I have followed the spelling employed
by Huntington (based in turn upon Bibaud's
rendering). This procedure is not ideally de-
sirable; its excuse is the one already noted. The
other explanation concerns the frequent citation
of "Manuscript" in the footnotes. This, of

course, means Franchère's manuscript narrative, which Bibaud edited for the 1820 book.

To recapitulate:

Franchère kept a contemporary journal (which has disappeared) of his four-year travels from 1810 to 1814. About the year 1819 he composed from it his narrative, designed for publication, which, after editing by Bibaud, was published in French at Montreal in 1820.

This was translated into English by J. V. Huntington and along with some additional matter by Franchère was published at New York in 1854. It was reprinted verbatim by R. G. Thwaites as Volume 6 of the *Early Western Travels* Series. The Franchère Manuscript, used by Bibaud as editorial copy, subsequently came into possession of Gerald E. Hart by whom it was sold at auction in the disposal of his collection at Boston, April 15–19, 1890. It was there purchased by Librarian James Bain for the Toronto Public Library, in whose possession it still remains. The present volume reprints the 1854 edition, subject to numerous changes, based in large part upon a study of the Manuscript, introduced by the present Editor.

Before concluding I wish to express my renewed obligation to my Publishers for affording me unrestricted liberty to investigate and edit the volume; to express in like manner my continued obligation to my permanent secretary, Letitia M. Quaife for the performance of much routine service; to Mrs. Elleine Stones and her corps of assistants of the Burton Historical Collection, Detroit Public Library, for their continued helpfulness to a troublesome patron; to Professor W. Stewart Wallace, Librarian of the University of Toronto, for helpful information; to Charles R. Sanderson, Chief Librarian of the Toronto Public Libraries, for permission to study and utilize the Franchère manuscript; to Miss Laura Lober, Chief of the Reference Division of the Library, and her staff for competent service cordially rendered; to Mrs. Karl F.F. Kurth of Detroit for information concerning her grandfather, Charles Boucher, a member of the Astorian expedition; to Miss Alice Clapp, Librarian of the Sault Sainte Marie Public Library, for helpful assistance in the use of the Franchère Papers in her custody; finally, to Dr. Frederick W. Franchère of Lake Crystal, Minnesota and to Secretary Harold D. Cater of the Minnesota Historical Society and the members of his staff for pictures and information concerning Gabriel Franchère and his descendants. I am again indebted to Mrs. Lucille R. Wyant for preparing the maps which show the route followed by Franchère in 1814 from Astoria to Montreal.

M. M. Quaife
Detroit, May 1, 1954

NARRATIVE

OF A

VOYAGE

TO

THE NORTHWEST COAST OF AMERICA

IN THE YEARS 1811, 1812, 1813, AND 1814

OR THE

FIRST AMERICAN SETTLEMENT ON THE PACIFIC

By GABRIEL FRANCHERE

TRANSLATED AND EDITED BY J. V. HUNTINGTON

REDFIELD

110 AND 112 NASSAU STREET, NEW YORK

1854.

PREFACE TO
THE SECOND EDITION

IN 1846, when the boundary question (that of the Oregon Territory in particular) was at its height, the Hon. Thomas H. Benton delivered in the United States Senate a decisive speech, of which the following is an extract:

"Now for the proof of all I have said. I happen to have in my possession the book of all others which gives the fullest and most authentic details on all the points I have mentioned—a book written at a time and under circumstances when the author (himself a British subject and familiar on the Columbia) had no more idea that the British would lay claim to that river than Mr. Harmon, the American writer whom I quoted, ever thought of our claiming New Caledonia.[1] It

[1]Daniel W. Harmon (1778–1845) was an uncle of Daniel Harmon Brush, whose life story, entitled *Growing Up With Southern Illinois*, was published as the Lakeside Classics volume for 1944. Harmon's narrative, alluded to by Senator Benton, entitled *Journal of Voyages and Travels in the Interior of North America*, was published at Andover, New Hampshire, in 1820.

"New Caledonia" was the name applied by Harmon and other contemporaries to the Fraser River Valley, whose first descent by white men was made by Alexander Mackenzie in 1793. His narrative, entitled *Alexander Mackenzie's Voyage to the Pacific Ocean in 1793*, was published as the Lakeside Classics volume for 1931.

is the work of Mr. Franchère, a gentleman of Montreal, with whom I have the pleasure to be personally acquainted, and one of those employed by Mr. Astor in founding his colony. He was at the founding of Astoria, at its sale to the North West Company, saw the place seized as a British conquest, and continued there after its seizure. He wrote in French: his work has not been done into English, though it well deserves it; and I read from the French text. He gives a brief and true account of the discovery of the Columbia."[2]

I felt justly proud of this notice of my unpretending work, especially that the latter should have contributed, as it did, to the amicable settlement of the then pending difficulties. I have flattered myself ever since that it belonged to the historical literature of the great country which by adoption has become mine.

The re-perusal of *Astoria* by Washington Irving (1836) inspired me with an additional motive for giving my book in an English dress. Without disparagement to Mr. Irving's literary fame, I may venture to say that I found in his work inaccuracies, misstatements (unintentional of course), and a want of chronological order which struck forcibly one so familiar with the events themselves. I

[2]Benton's speech, delivered May 25, 1846 is printed in the *Congressional Globe*, 29th Cong. 1st Sess., 857–62.

thought I could show—or rather that my simple narration, of itself plainly discovered—that some of the young men embarked in that expedition (which founded our Pacific empire), did not merit the ridicule and contempt which Captain Thorn attempted to throw upon them, and which perhaps, through the genius of Mr. Irving, might otherwise remain as a lasting stigma on their characters.

But the consideration which, before all others, prompts me to offer this narrative to the American reading public is my desire to place before them, therein, a simple and connected account (which at this time ought to be interesting) of the early settlement of the Oregon Territory by one of our adopted citizens, the enterprising merchant John Jacob Astor. The importance of a vast territory, which at no distant day may add two more bright stars to our national banner, is a guarantee that my humble effort will be appreciated.[3]

NOTE BY THE EDITOR

It has been the editor's wish to let Mr. Franchère speak for himself. To preserve in the translation the Defoe-like simplicity of the original narrative of the young French Canadian has been

[3]Oregon became a State in 1869. Washington, after long delay, in 1889.

his chief care. Having read many narratives of travel and adventure in our northwestern wilderness, he may be permitted to say that he has met with none that gives a more vivid and picturesque description of it, or in which the personal adventures of the narrator and the varying fortunes of a great enterprise mingle more happily, and one may say more dramatically, with the itinerary. The clerkly minuteness of the details is not without its charm either, and their fidelity speaks for itself. Take it altogether, it must be regarded as a fragment of our colonial history saved from oblivion; it fills up a vacuity which Mr. Irving's classic work does not quite supply; it is, in fact, the only account by an eye-witness and a participator in the enterprise, of the first attempt to form a settlement on the Pacific under the Stars and Stripes.[4]

The Editor has thought it would be interesting to add Mr. Franchère's Preface to the original French edition, which will be found on the next page.

BALTIMORE, *February* 6, 1854.

[4]Apparently Mr. Huntington did not know of Ross Cox's *Adventures on the Columbia River*, published at New York in 1832, and Alexander Ross's *Adventures of the First Settlers on the Oregon or Columbia River*, published at London in 1849, both of which were accounts by participants in the Astorian enterprise. The latter, which was reprinted as the Lakeside Classics volume for 1923, will be cited hereafter as Ross, *First Settlers on the Oregon*.

PREFACE TO
THE FRENCH EDITION

WHEN I was writing my journal on the vessel which carried me to the Northwest Coast of North America, or in the wild regions of this continent, I was far from thinking that it would be placed one day before the public eye. I had no other end in writing but to procure to my family and my friends a more exact and more connected detail of what I had seen or learned in the course of my travels than it would have been possible for me to give them in a *viva voce* narration. Since my return to my native city, my manuscript has passed into various hands and has been read by different persons: several of my friends immediately advised me to print it; but it is only quite lately that I have allowed myself to be persuaded that without being a learned naturalist, a skilful geographer, or a profound moralist, a traveller may yet interest by the faithful and succinct account of the situations in which he has found himself, the adventures which have happened to him, and the incidents of which he has been a witness; that if a simple ingenuous narrative, stripped of the merit of science and the graces of diction, must needs be less enjoyed by the man of letters or by the savant, it would have, in compensation, the advantage of being at the level of a greater number of readers; in fine, that the desire of affording an entertainment to his countrymen, according to his capacity, and without any mixture of the author's vanity or of pecuniary interest, would be a well-founded title to their indulgence. Whether I have done well or ill in yielding to these suggestions, which I am bound to regard as those of friendship or of goodwill, it belongs to the impartial and disinterested reader to decide.

MONTREAL, 1819.

INTRODUCTION

SINCE the independence of the United States of America, the merchants of that industrious and enterprising nation have carried on an extremely advantageous commerce on the Northwest Coast of this continent. In the course of their voyages they have made a great number of discoveries which they have not thought proper to make public; no doubt to avoid competition in a lucrative business.

In 1792 Captain Gray, commanding the ship *Columbia* of Boston, discovered in latitude 46° 19″ north, the entrance of a great bay on the Pacific Coast.[5] He sailed into it, and having perceived that it was the outlet or estuary of a large river, by the fresh water which he found at a little distance from the entrance, he continued his course upward some eighteen miles, and dropped anchor on the left bank, at the opening of a deep

[5]Captain Robert Gray was the commander of a small sailing ship dispatched by a group of Boston merchants to engage in the trade of the Northwest Coast and China. The Columbia was discovered and entered by him on May 11, 1792. Prior to this voyage he had visited the Northwest Coast, and sailing thence to China, was the first mariner to carry the Stars and Stripes around the Globe (1787–90). For a more detailed account of his voyages see M. M. Quaife, *The Flag of the United States* (New York, 1942), Chap. 9.

bay. There he made a map or rough sketch of
what he had seen of this river (accompanied by
a written description of the soundings, bearings,
&c.) ; and having finished his traffic with the natives (the object of his voyage to these parts), he
put out to sea, and soon after fell in with Captain
Vancouver, who was cruising by order of the
British government, to seek new discoveries. Mr.
Gray acquainted him with the one he had just
made, and even gave him a copy of the chart he
had drawn up. Vancouver, who had just driven
off a colony of Spaniards established on the coast,
under the command of Señor Quadra (England
and Spain being then at war), despatched his first-
lieutenant Broughton, who ascended the river in
boats some one hundred and twenty or one hundred and fifty miles, took possession of the country in the name of his Britannic Majesty, giving
the river the name of the *Columbia*, and to the
bay where the American captain stopped, that of
Gray's Bay. Since that period the country had
been seldom visited (till 1811) and chiefly by
American ships.[6]

[6]Two errors in the author's sketch should be noted. It
was Gray himself who named the Columbia; nor were the
Spaniards driven off by Vancouver. Instead, by a Con-
vention between Great Britain and Spain entered upon in
1794 it was agreed that neither should claim exclusive
jurisdiction at Nootka, and they should jointly oppose any
attempt by another power to do so.

Sir Alexander Mackenzie, in his second overland voyage, tried to reach the western ocean
by the Columbia River, and thought he had succeeded when he came out six degrees farther
north, at the bottom of Puget's Sound, by another river.[7]

In 1805 the American government sent Captains Lewis and Clark with about thirty men including some Kentucky hunters, on an overland
journey to the mouth of the Columbia. They
ascended the Missouri, crossed the mountains at
the source of that river, and following the course
of the Columbia, reached the shores of the Pacific,
where they were forced to winter. The report
which they made of their expedition to the United
States Government created a lively sensation.

Mr. John Jacob Astor, a New York merchant,
who conducted almost alone the trade in furs
south of the great lakes Huron and Superior, and
who had acquired by that commerce a prodigious
fortune, thought to augment it by forming on the
banks of the Columbia an establishment of which
the principal or supply factory should be at the

---

[7]Alexander Mackenzie's first "overland voyage" re-
sulted in the discovery of the Mackenzie River, which
empties into the Arctic Ocean. The second voyage, performed in 1793, led him to the Pacific Ocean, being the
first crossing of the American Continent north of Mexico.
For it, see *Alexander Mackenzie's Voyage to the Pacific Ocean
in 1793*, the Lakeside Classics volume for 1931.

mouth of that river. He communicated his views
to the agents of the North West Company; he
was even desirous of forming the proposed establishment in concert with them; but after some
negotiations, the inland or wintering partners of
that association of fur-traders having rejected the
plan, Mr. Astor determined to make the attempt
alone. He needed for the success of his enterprise
men long versed in the Indian trade, and he soon
found them. Mr. Alexander McKay (the same who
had accompanied Sir Alexander Mackenzie in his
travels overland), a bold and enterprising man,
left the North West Company to join him; and
soon after, Messrs. Duncan McDougall and Donald McKenzie (also in the service of the Company), and Messrs. David Stuart and Robert
Stuart, all of Canada, did the same. At length,
in the winter of 1810 a Mr. Wilson Price Hunt of
St. Louis on the Mississippi having also joined
them, they determined that the expedition should
be set on foot in the following spring.

It was in the course of that winter that one of
my friends made me acquainted in confidence
with the plan of these gentlemen, under the in-
junction of strictest secrecy. The desire of seeing
strange countries, joined to that of acquiring a
fortune, determined me to solicit employment of
the new Association; on the 20th of May I had
an interview with Mr. A. McKay, with whom the

preliminaries were arranged; and on the 24th of the same month I signed an agreement as an apprenticed clerk for the term of five years.

When the Associates had engaged a sufficient number of Canadian boatmen they equipped a bark canoe under charge of Messrs. Hunt and McKenzie, with a Mr. Perrault as clerk and a crew of fourteen men. These gentlemen were to proceed to Mackinac and thence to St. Louis, hiring on the way as many men as they could to man the canoes, in which, from the last-mentioned port, they were to ascend the Missouri to its source, and there, diverging from the route followed by Lewis and Clark, reach the mouth of the Columbia to form a junction with another party who were to go round by way of Cape Horn. In the course of my narrative I shall have occasion to speak of the success of both these expeditions.

A Voyage
to the Northwest Coast
of America

Depuis l'indépendance des États Unis, de ~~l'amérique~~
Les commerçants de cette nation entreprenante, ont
fait sur la côte du Nord Ouest de l'amérique Septentrionale un trafic ~~très~~ ᶜᵉᵗᵗᵉ ᵍᵒᵘᵛᵉʳⁿᵉᵐᵉⁿᵗ avantageux, Ils
ont dans le cours de leurs voyages, fait beaucoup
de découvertes, ~~desquels~~ ᵈᵒⁿᵗ ils n'ont point fait ~~de~~ part
au public, Sans doute dans l'appréhension d'une
concurrence. En 1792,[2] Le Capitaine Gray, Com-
mandant le navire Columbia de Boston, décou-
vrit l'entrée d'une grande ~~rivière~~ ᵇᵃʸᵉ par le 46°
19" de latitude ~~Nord~~ ˢᵉᵖᵗᵉⁿᵗʳⁱᵒⁿᵃˡᵉ — Il y entra, Et S'étant
assuré que c'était une grande rivière, par l'eau
douce qu'il trouvât à peu de distance de son
embouchure, il remonta environ dixhuit milles,
Et mouilla Son vaisseau à l'entrée d'une baye
assez profonde au Nord de cette rivière — ~~en~~
Et en fit une Carte ; après avoir fait Son Commerce (l'objet pour lequel il était dans ces parages
avec les Naturels — il reportât, Et rencontra bientôt
Le Capt Vancouver, qui par ordre des Gouverne-
ment britanniques, était alors en voyage de découvertes
Il lui

FIRST PAGE OF FRANCHÈRE'S JOURNAL

A Voyage
to the Northwest Coast
of America

Chapter I
From Montreal to New York

WE remained in Montreal the rest of the spring and a part of the summer. At last, having completed our arrangements for the journey, we received orders to proceed, and on the 26th of July, accompanied by my father and brothers and a few friends, I repaired to the place of embarkation, where was prepared a birch bark canoe manned by nine Canadians, having Mr. A. McKay as commander, and a Mr. A. Fisher as passenger. The sentiments which I experienced at that moment would be as difficult for me to describe as they were painful to support; for the first time in my life I quitted the place of my birth, and was separated from beloved parents and intimate friends, having for my whole consolation the faint hope of seeing them again. We embarked at about five P. M. and arrived at La Prairie de la Madeleine (on the opposite side of the St. Law-

3

rence) toward eight o'clock. We slept at this village and the next morning very early, having
secured the canoe on a wagon, we got in motion
again and reached St. John's on the river Riche-
lieu a little before noon. Here we relaunched our
canoe (after having well calked the seams), crossed
or rather traversed the length of Lake Champlain,
and arrived at Whitehall on the 30th. There
we were overtaken by Mr. Ovide de Montigny
and a Mr. P. D. Jeremie, who were to be of the
expedition.

Having again placed our canoe on a wagon, we
pursued our journey and arrived on the 1st of
August at Lansingburg, a little village situated
on the bank of the river Hudson. Here we got
our canoe once more afloat, passed by Troy and
by Albany, everywhere hospitably received, our
Canadian boatmen, having their hats decorated
with parti-colored ribbons and feathers, being
taken by the Americans for so many wild Indians,
and arrived at New York on the 3d at eleven
o'clock in the evening.

We had landed at the north end of the city,
and the next day, being Sunday, we re-embarked,
and were obliged to make a course round the city,
in order to arrive at our lodgings on Long Island.
We sang as we rowed; which, joined to the un-
usual sight of a birch-bark canoe impelled by nine
stout Canadians, dark as Indians and as gayly

adorned, attracted a crowd upon the wharves to gaze at us as we glided along. We found on Long Island (in the village of Brooklyn) those young gentlemen engaged in the service of the new company who had left Canada in advance of our party.

The vessel in which we were to sail not being ready, I should have found myself quite isolated and a stranger in the great city of New York, but for a letter of introduction to Mr. G——, given me on my setting out by Madame his sister. I had formed the acquaintance of this gentleman during a stay which he had made at Montreal in 1801; but as I was then very young he would probably have had some difficulty in recognising me without his sister's letter. He introduced me to several of his friends, and I passed in an agreeable manner the five weeks which elapsed between my arrival in New York and the departure of the ship.

I shall not undertake to describe New York; I will only say that the elegance of the buildings, public and private, the cleanliness of the streets, the shade of the poplars which border them, the public walks, the markets always abundantly provided with all sorts of commodities, the activity of its commerce, then in a flourishing condition, the vast number of ships of all nations which crowded the quays; all, in a word, conspired to make me feel the difference between this great maritime city and my native town, of whose steeples I had never lost sight before, and which was by no means at that time what it is now.

New York was not then, and indeed is not at this time a fortified town; still, there were several batteries and military works, the most consider-able of which were seen on the Narrows, or chan-nel which forms the principal mouth of the Hud-son. The isles called Governor's Island, and Bedloe or Gibbet Island were also well fortified. On the first, situated to the west of the city and about a mile from it, there were barracks sufficiently capacious for several thousand sol-diers, and a Moro, or castle, with three tiers of guns, all bomb-proof. These works have been strengthened during the last war.[8]

The market-places are eight in number; the most considerable is called Fly-Market.

The Park, the Battery, and Vauxhall Garden, are the principal promenades. There were, in 1810, thirty-two churches, two of which were de-voted to the Catholic worship; and the popula-tion was estimated at ninety thousand souls, of whom ten thousand were French. It is thought

[8]In 1698 Governor's Island was set aside as a rustic re-treat for the colonial governors; hence the name, which still persists. In 1800 it was ceded to the United States Government by the State of New York and Castle William and Fort Jay were subsequently erected on it. In 1821 Fort Jay was made military headquarters for the New York area.

that this population has since been augmented (1819) by some thirty thousand souls.

During my sojourn at New York, I lodged in Brooklyn, on Long Island. This island is separated from the city by a sound, or narrow arm of the sea. There is here a pretty village, not far from which is a basin, where some gun-boats were hauled up and a few war vessels were on the stocks. Some barracks had been constructed here and a guard was maintained.

Before leaving New York, it is well to observe that during our stay in that city, Mr. McKay thought it the part of prudence to have an interview with the minister plenipotentiary of his Britannic Majesty, Mr. Jackson, to inform him of the object of our voyage and get his views in regard to the line of conduct we ought to follow in case of war breaking out between the two powers; intimating to him that we were all British subjects, and were about to trade under the American flag. After some moments of reflection Mr. Jackson told him "that we were going on a very hazardous enterprise; that he saw our object was purely commercial, and that all he could promise us was, that in case of a war we should be respected as British subjects and traders."

This reply appeared satisfactory, and Mr. McKay thought we had nothing to apprehend on that side.

The vessel in which we were to sail was called the *Tonquin*, of about 300 tons burden, commanded by Captain Thorn (a first lieutenant of the American navy, on furlough for this purpose) with a crew of twenty-one men. The number of passengers was thirty-three. Here follow the names of both.

PASSENGERS.

PARTNERS { Messrs. Alexander McKay
        "   Duncan McDougall,
        "   David Stuart,
        "   Robert Stuart, } all of Canada.

CLERKS {
James Lewis of New York.
Russell Farnham of Massachusetts.
William W. Matthews of New York.
Alexander Ross,
Donald McGillis,
Ovide de Montigny,
Francis B. Pillet,
Donald McLennan,
William Wallace,
Thomas McKay,
Gabriel Franchère, } all from Canada.

BOATMEN, ETC. {
Oliver Roy Lapensée,
Ignace Lapensée
Basile Lapensée,
Jacques Lafantaisie,
Benjamin Roussel,
Michel Laframboise,
Giles Leclerc,

Joseph Lapierre,
Joseph Nadeau,
J. B'te. Belleau,
Antoine Belleau,
Louis Bruslé,
P. D. Jeremie,
all of Canada.

Johann Koaster, ship-carpenter, a Russian,
George Bell, cooper, New York,
Job Aitken, rigger and calker, from Scotland,
Augustus Roussil, blacksmith, Canada,
Guilleaume Perreault, a boy. These last were all
mechanics, &c., destined for the establishment.

CREW.

Jonathan Thorn, captain, New York State.
Ebenezer D. Fox, 1st mate, of Boston.
John M. Mumford, 2d mate, of Massachusetts.
James Thorn, brother of the captain, New York.
John Anderson, boatswain, foreigner.
Egbert Vanderhuff, tailor, New York.
John Weeks, carpenter, New York.
Stephen Weeks, armorer, New York.
John Coles, New York, } sailmakers.
John Martin, a Frenchman, }

SAILORS {
John White, New York.
Adam Fisher, New York.
Peter Verbel, New York.
Edward Aymes, New York.
Robert Hill, Albany, New York.
John Adams, New York.
Joseph Johnson, Englishman,
Charles Roberts, New York,
}

A colored man as cook,
A mulatto steward,
And three or four others whose names I have
forgotten.[9]

[9]The Manuscript lists the names of 17 members of the
crew, which totaled 21. An open space follows, to fill
which the Editor has supplied the line "and three or four
others whose names I have forgotten."

Chapter II

From New York to the Falklands

ALL being ready for our departure, we went on board ship and weighed anchor on the 6th of September, in the morning. The wind soon fell off, and the first day was spent in drifting down to Staten Island, where we came to anchor for the night. The next day we weighed anchor again; but there came on another dead calm, and we were forced to cast anchor near the lighthouse at Sandy Hook. On the 8th we weighed anchor for the third time, and by the help of a fresh breeze from the southwest we succeeded in passing the bar; the pilot quitted us at about eleven o'clock, and soon after we lost sight of the coast.

One must have experienced it one's self, to be able to conceive the melancholy which takes possession of the soul of a man of sensibility at the instant that he leaves his country and the civilized world to go to inhabit with strangers in wild and unknown lands. I should in vain endeavor to give my readers an idea, even faintly correct, of the painful sinking of heart that I suddenly felt, and of the sad glance which I involuntarily cast toward a future so much the more frightful to me as it offered nothing but what was perfectly confused and uncertain. A new scene of life was unfolded before me, but how monotonous, and ill suited to diminish the dejection with which my mind was overwhelmed! For the first time in my life, I found myself under way upon the main sea, with nothing to fix my regards and arrest my attention but the frail machine which bore me between the abyss of waters and the immensity of the skies. I remained for a long time with my eyes fixed in the direction of that land which I no longer saw, and almost despaired of ever seeing again; I made serious reflections on the nature and consequences of the enterprise in which I had so rashly embarked; and I confess that if at that moment the offer had been made to release me from my engagement, I should have accepted the proposal with all my heart. It is true that the hopeless confusion and incumberment of the vessel's deck, the great number of strangers among whom I found myself, the brutal style which the Captain and his subalterns used toward our young Canadians; all, in a word, conspired to make me augur a vexatious and disagreeable voyage. The sequel will show that I did not deceive myself in that.[10]

---

[10]Captain Thorn was a hard-bitten naval officer, a furious disciplinarian, and wholly lacking in tact. That his land-lubber passengers sorely tried his seaman's soul is clear; it is equally clear that his treatment of them passed

We perceived very soon in the S. W., which was our weather side, a vessel that bore directly toward us; she made a signal that was understood by our captain; we hove to, and stood on her bow. It turned out to be the American frigate *Constitution*. We sent our boat on board of her, and sailed in company till toward five o'clock, when, our papers having been sent back to us, we separated.[11]

the boundary of common sense and even of normal humanity. Alexander Ross at this point gives a detailed recital of Thorn's mistreatment of the Canadians which provoked a quarrel with Alexander McKay (who protested against it) and the threat by Captain Thorn to blow out the brains of any one who should venture to disobey his orders. From the outset of the voyage until its close, months later, relations between Captain Thorn and the fur-trade partners and clerks were exceedingly frigid. Ross, *First Settlers on the Oregon*, Chap. 2.

[11]The *Constitution* became famous in American history for her roles in the Tripolitan War of 1803–1805 and in the War of 1812. In 1830 her destruction was ordered by the Secretary of the Navy, whereupon Oliver W. Holmes, a Boston youth barely twenty-one years old, achieved public renown for himself and added fame for the *Constitution* by dashing off (in pencil, on a scrap of paper) the ballad "Old Ironsides" which is still treasured in memory by millions of Americans. Its publication led to the cancellation of the order for razing the *Constitution*, which continued in service for another generation, and which is still preserved in Boston Harbor. The reason for escorting the *Tonquin* was to protect the latter from interference by a British naval vessel which was reported to be lying off New York on the mission of "impressing" seamen into the British service.

The wind having increased, the motion of the vessel made us sea-sick, those of us, I mean, who were for the first time at sea. The weather was fine, however; the vessel, which at first sailing was lumbered in such a manner that we could hardly get in or out of our berths, and scarcely work ship, by little and little got into order, so that we soon found ourselves more at ease.

On the 14th we commenced to take flying fish. The 24th, we saw a great quantity of dolphins. We prepared lines and took two of the latter, which we cooked. The flesh of this fish appeared to me excellent.

After leaving New York, till the 4th of October we headed southeast. On that day we struck the trade winds and bore S. S. E.; being, according to our observations, in latitude 17° 43″ and longitude 22° 39″.

On the 5th, in the morning, we came in sight of the Cape Verde Islands, bearing W. N. W. and distant about eight or nine miles, having the coast of Africa to the E. S. E. We should have been very glad to touch at these islands to take in water; but as our vessel was an American bottom, and had on board a number of British subjects, our captain did not think fit to expose himself to meet the English ships-of-war cruising on these coasts, who certainly would not have failed to make a strict search, and to take from us the best part of our crew; which would infallibly have proved disastrous to the object for which we had shipped them.

Speaking of water, I may mention that the rule was to serve it out in rations of a quart a day; but that we were now reduced to a pint and a half. For the rest, our fare consisted of fourteen ounces of hard bread, a pound and a quarter of salt beef or one of pork per day, and half a pint of Souchong tea, with sugar, per man. The pork and beef were served alternately: rice and beans, each once a week; cornmeal pudding with molasses, ditto; on Sundays the steerage passengers were allowed a bottle of Teneriffe wine. All except the four partners, Mr. Lewis, acting as captain's clerk, and Mr. T. McKay, were in the steerage; the cabin containing but six berths, besides the captain's and first mate's state-rooms.[12]

As long as we were near the coast of Africa we had light and variable winds and extremely hot weather; on the 8th we had a dead calm, and saw several sharks round the vessel; we took one, which we ate. I found the taste to resemble sturgeon. We experienced on that day an excessive heat, the mercury being at 94° of Fahrenheit.

[12]This long paragraph is not found in this place in the Manuscript. Because of the very frequent transpositions of sections of the narrative made by Bibaud, the original Editor, it is perhaps hazardous to affirm that it does not occur at some other place.

From the 8th to the 11th we had on board a
canary bird, which we treated with the greatest
care and kindness, but which nevertheless
quitted us, probably for a certain death.

The nearer we approached to the equator the
more we perceived the heat to increase: on the
16th, in latitude 6°, longitude 22° west from
Greenwich, the mercury stood at 108°. We discovered on that day a sail bearing down upon
us. The next morning she reappeared, and approached within gun-shot. She was a large brig,
carrying about twenty guns: we sailed in company all day by a good breeze, all sail spread;
but toward evening she dropped astern and
altered her course to the S. S. E.

On the 18th, at daybreak, the watch alarmed
us by announcing that the same brig which had
followed us the day before was under our lee, a
cable's length off, and seemed desirous of knowing who we were, without showing her own
colors. Our Captain appeared to be in some
alarm; and admitting that she was a better sailer
than we, he called all the passengers and crew on
deck, the drum beat to quarters, and we feigned
to make preparations for combat.

It is well to observe that our vessel mounted
ten pieces of cannon and was pierced for twenty;
the forward port-holes were adorned with sham
guns. Whether it was our formidable appearance

or no, at about ten A. M. the stranger again
changed her course, and we soon lost sight of
her entirely.

Nothing further remarkable occurred to us till
the 22d, when we passed the line in longitude 25°
9″. According to an ancient custom the crew
baptized those of their number who had never
before crossed the equator; it was a holiday for
them on board. About two o'clock in the afternoon we perceived a sail in the S. S. W. We were
not a little alarmed, believing that it was the
same brig which we had seen some days before;
for it was lying to, as if awaiting our approach.
We soon drew near, and to our great joy discovered that she was a Portuguese; we hailed her,
and learned that she came from some part of
South America, and was bound to Pernambuco,
on the coast of Brazil. Very soon after, we began
to see what navigators call the Clouds of Magellan: they are three little white spots that one
perceives in the sky almost as soon as one passes
the equator: they were situated in the S. S. W.

The 1st November, we began to see great
numbers of aquatic birds. Toward three o'clock
P. M., we discovered a sail on our larboard, but
did not approach sufficiently near to speak her.
The 3d, we saw two more sails making to the
S. E. We passed the Tropic of Capricorn on the
4th, with a fine breeze, and in longitude 33° 27″.

We lost the trade winds, and as we advanced south the weather became cold and rainy. The 11th, we had a calm, although the swell was heavy. We saw several turtles, and the Captain having sent out the small boat, we captured two of them. During the night of the 11th and 12th the wind changed to the N. E. and raised a terrible tempest, in which the gale, the rain, the lightning, and thunder seemed to have sworn our destruction; the sea appeared all a-fire, while our little vessel was the sport of winds and waves. We kept the hatches closed, which did not prevent us from passing very uncomfortable nights while the storm lasted; for the great heats that we had experienced between the tropics had so opened the seams of the deck that every time the waves passed over, the water rushed down in quantities upon our hammocks. The 14th, the wind shifted to the S. S. W., which compelled us to beat to windward. During the night we were struck by a tremendous sea; the helm was seized beyond control, and the man at the wheel was thrown from one side of the ship to the other, breaking two of his ribs, which confined him to his berth for a week.

In latitude 35° 19″, longitude 40°, the sea appeared to be covered with marine plants, and the change that we observed in the color of the water, as well as the immense number of gulls and other aquatic birds that we saw, proved to us that we were not far from the mouth of the Rio de la Plata. The wind continued to blow furiously till the 21st, when it subsided a little and the weather cleared up. On the 25th, being in the 46th degree and 30 minutes of latitude, we saw a penguin.

We began to feel sensibly the want of water. Since passing the Tropic of Capricorn the daily allowance had been always diminishing, till we were reduced to three gills a day, a slender modicum considering that we had only salt provisions. We had, indeed, a still, which we used to render the sea-water drinkable; but we distilled merely what sufficed for the daily use of the kitchen, as to do more would have required a great quantity of wood or coal. As we were not more than one hundred and fifty leagues from the Falkland Isles, we determined to put in there and endeavor to replenish our casks, and the captain caused the anchors to be got ready.

We had contrary winds from the 27th of November to the 3d December. On the evening of that day we heard one of the officers, who was at the mast head, cry "Land! Land!" Nevertheless, the night coming on and the barren rocks which we had before us being little elevated above the ocean, we hove to.

CHAPTER III

Around Cape Horn

O N the 4th (Dec.) in the morning, I was not the last to mount on deck to feast my eyes with the sight of land; for it is only those who have been three or four months at sea who know how to appreciate the pleasure which one then feels even at sight of such barren and bristling rocks as form the Falkland Isles. We drew near these rocks very soon, and entered between two of the islands, where we anchored on a good ground. The first mate being sent ashore to look for water, several of our gentlemen accompanied him. They returned in the evening with the disappointing intelligence that they had not been able to find fresh water.[13] They brought us, to compensate for this, a number of wild geese and two seals.

The weather appearing to threaten, we weighed anchor and put out to sea. The night was tempestuous, and in the morning of the 5th we had

[13] Alexander Ross states that Captain Thorn "not liking the place, changed his resolution of taking in water there." He also narrates a near-tragedy occasioned by Captain Thorn's threat to abandon one of the sailors (Joseph Johnson) who had fallen asleep while on shore and thus had failed to regain the ship with the remaining members of the shore party. *First Settlers on the Oregon*, 24–25.

lost sight of the first islands. The wind blowing off land, it was necessary to beat up all that day; in the evening we found ourselves sufficiently near the shore, and hove to for the night. The 6th brought us a clear sky, and with a fresh breeze we succeeded in gaining a good anchorage, which we took to be Port Egmont, and where we found good water.

On the 7th, we sent ashore the water casks, as well as the cooper to superintend filling them, and the blacksmiths who were occupied in some repairs required by the ship. For our part, having erected a tent near the springs, we passed the time while they were taking in water, in coursing over the isles: we had a boat for our accommodation, and killed every day a great many wild geese and ducks. These birds differ in plumage from those which are seen in Canada. We also killed a great many seals. These animals ordinarily keep upon the rocks. We also saw several foxes of the species called Virginia fox: they were shy and yet fierce, barking like dogs and then flying precipitately. Penguins are also numerous on the Falkland Isles. These birds have a fine plumage, and resemble the loon: but they do not fly, having only little stumps of wings which they use to help themselves in waddling along. The rocks were covered with them. It being their setting season we found them on their nests, from which they would not stir. They are not wild or timid: far from flying at our approach, they attacked us with their bill, which is very sharp, and with their short wings. The flesh of the penguin is black and leathery, with a strong fishy taste, and one must be very hungry to make up one's mind to eat it. We got a great quantity of eggs by dislodging them from their nests.

As the French and English[14] had both attempted to form establishments on these rocks, we endeavored to find some vestige of them; the tracks which we met everywhere made us hope to find goats also: but all our researches were vain: all that we discovered was an old fishing cabin, constructed of whale bone, and some seal-skin moccasins; for these rocks offer not a single tree to the view, and are frequented solely by the vessels which pursue the whale fishery in the southern seas. We found, however, two head-boards with inscriptions in English, marking the spot where two men had been interred: as the letters were nearly obliterated, we carved new ones on fresh pieces of board procured from the ship. This pious attention to two dead men nearly proved fatal to a greater number of the living; for all the casks having been filled and sent on board, the Captain gave orders to re-em-

[14]The Manuscript reads "Portuguese" instead of "French and English."

bark, and without troubling himself to inquire if this order had been executed or not, caused the anchor to be weighed on the morning of the 11th, while I and some of my companions were engaged in erecting the inscriptions of which I have spoken, others were cutting grass for the hogs, and Messrs. McDougall and D. Stuart had gone to the south side of the isle to look for game. The roaring of the sea against the rock-bound shore prevented them from hearing the gun, and they did not rejoin us till the vessel was already at sea. We then lost no time, but pushed off, being eight in number, with our little boat, only twenty feet keel. We rowed with all our might, but gained nothing upon the vessel. We were losing sight of the islands at last, and our case seemed desperate. While we paused, and were debating what course to pursue, as we had no compass, we observed the ship tacking and stand-ing toward us. In fine, after rowing for three hours and a half in an excited state of feeling not easily described, we succeeded in regaining the vessel and were taken on board at about three o'clock P. M.

Having related this trait of malice on the part of our Captain, I shall be permitted to make some remarks on his character. Jonathan Thorn was brought up in the naval service of his country, and had distinguished himself in a battle fought

VIEW OF THE FALKLAND ISLES

Boat and five passengers pulling after Ship Tonquin

between the Americans and the Turks at Tripoli,
some years before: he held the rank of first lieutenant. He was a strict disciplinarian, of a quick
and passionate temper, accustomed to exact obe-
dience, considering nothing but duty, and giving
himself no trouble about the murmurs of his
crew, taking counsel of nobody, and following
Mr. Astor's instructions to the letter. Such was
the man who had been selected to command our
ship. His haughty manners, his rough and over-
bearing disposition, had lost him the affection
of most of the crew and of all the passengers:
he knew it, and in consequence sought every
opportunity to mortify us. It is true that the
passengers had some reason to reproach themselves; they were not free from blame; but he
had been the aggressor; and nothing could excuse the act of cruelty and barbarity of which
he was guilty, in intending to leave us upon those
barren rocks of the Falkland Isles, where we
must inevitably have perished. This lot was reserved for us, but for the bold interference of
Mr. R. Stuart, whose uncle was of our party, and
who, seeing that the Captain, far from waiting for
us, coolly continued his course, threatened to
blow his brains out unless he hove to and took
us on board.[15]

[15]Alexander Ross relates that in consequence of the renewed hatred of the passengers for Captain Thorn, when

We pursued our course, bearing S. S. W., and
on the 14th, in latitude 54° 1′, longitude 64° 13′,
we found bottom at sixty-five fathoms and saw
a sail to the south. On the 15th, in the morning,
we discovered before us the high mountains of
Tierra del Fuego, which we continued to see till
evening: the weather then thickened, and we
lost sight of them. We encountered a furious
storm, which drove us to the 56th degree and
18′ of latitude. On the 18th, we were only fifteen
leagues from Cape Horn. A dead calm followed,
but the current carried us within sight of the
cape, five or six leagues distant. This Cape, which
forms the southern extremity of the American
continent, has always been an object of terror
to the navigators who have to pass from one sea
to the other; several of whom, to avoid doubling
it, have exposed themselves to the long and dangerous passage of the Straits of Magellan, especially when about entering the Pacific Ocean.
When we saw ourselves under the stupendous
rocks of the Cape, we felt no other desire but
to get away from them as soon as possible, so
little agreeable were those rocks to the view,
even in the case of people who had been some

in his hearing the partners conversed only in the Scottish
dialect and the Canadians in French. This conduct led
Captain Thorn to infer that they were plotting a mutiny.
First Settlers on the Oregon, 25–30.

months at sea! And by the help of a land breeze we succeeded in gaining an offing. While becalmed here, we measured the velocity of the current setting east, which we found to be about three miles an hour.

The wind soon changed again to the S. S. W., and blew a gale. We had to beat. We passed in sight of the islands of Diego Ramires, and saw a large schooner under their lee. The distance that we had run from New York, was about 9,165 miles. We had frightful weather till the 24th, when we found ourselves in 58° 16' of south latitude. Although it was the height of summer in that hemisphere, and the days as long as they are at Quebec on the 21st of June (we could read on deck at midnight without artificial light) the cold was nevertheless very great and the air very humid: the mercury for several days was but fourteen degrees above freezing point, by Fahrenheit's thermometer. If such is the temperature in these latitudes at the end of December, corresponding to our June, what must it be in the shortest days of the year, and where can the Patagonians then take refuge, and the inhabitants of the islands so improperly named the Land of Fire!

The wind, which till the 24th had been contrary, hauled round to the south, and we ran westward. The next day being Christmas, we had

the satisfaction to learn by our noon-day observation that we had weathered the Cape, and
were, consequently, now in the Pacific Ocean.
Up to that date we had but one man attacked
with scurvy, a malady to which those who make
long voyages are subject, and which is occasioned
by the constant use of salt provisions, by the
humidity of the vessel, and the inaction.

From the 25th of December till the 1st of January, we were favored with a fair wind and ran
eighteen degrees to the north in that short space
of time. Though cold yet, the weather was nevertheless very agreeable. On the 17th in latitude
10° S., and longitude 110° 50' W. we took several
bonitas, an excellent fish. We passed the equator
on the 23d in 128° 14' of west longitude. A great
many porpoises came round the vessel. On the
25th arose a tempest, which lasted till the 28th.
The wind then shifted to the E. S. E. and carried
us two hundred and twenty-four miles on our
course in twenty-four hours. Then we had several days of contrary winds; on the 8th of February it hauled to the S. E., and on the 11th we
saw the peak of a mountain covered with snow,
which the first mate, who was familiar with these
seas, told me was the summit of Mona Roah, a
high mountain on the island of Owhyhi, one of
those which the circumnavigator Cook named
the Sandwich Isles, and where he met his death

in 1779.[16] We headed to the land all day, and although we made eight or nine knots an hour it was not till evening that we were near enough to distinguish the huts of the Islanders: which is sufficient to prove the prodigious elevation of Mona Roah above the level of the sea.

[16]Owhyhi, more commonly spelled Owyhee, was an alternative name for Hawaii, largest of the group which Captain Cook named the Sandwich Islands. Mauna Loa is an active volcano whose eruptions are notable for the great quantities of lava discharged.

Chapter IV
Sojourn at Hawaii

WE were ranging along the coast with the aid of a fine breeze when the boy Perrault, who had mounted the fore-rigging to enjoy the scenery, lost his hold, and being to windward where the shrouds were taut, rebounded from them like a ball some twenty feet from the ship's side into the ocean. We perceived his fall and threw over to him chairs, barrels, benches, hen-coops, in a word everything we could lay hands on; then the Captain gave the orders to heave to; in the twinkling of an eye the lashings of one of the quarter-boats were cut apart, the boat lowered and manned: by this time the boy was considerably a-stern. He would have been lost undoubtedly but for a wide pair of canvas overalls full of tar and grease, which operated like a life-preserver. His head, however, was under when he was picked up, and he was brought on board lifeless about a quarter of an hour after he fell into the sea. We succeeded, notwithstanding, in a short time in bringing him to, and in a few hours he was able to run upon the deck.

The coast of the island, viewed from the sea, offers the most picturesque *coup d'oeil*, and the loveliest prospect; from the beach to the moun-

tains the land rises amphitheatrically, all along
which is a border of lower country covered with
cocoa-trees and bananas, through the thick foliage whereof you perceive the huts of the islanders; the valleys which divide the hills that lie
beyond appear well cultivated, and the mountains themselves, though extremely high, are
covered with wood to their summits, except those
few peaks which glitter with perpetual snow.

As we ran along the coast some canoes left the
beach and came alongside with vegetables and
cocoa-nuts; but as we wished to profit by the
breeze to gain the anchorage, we did not think
fit to stop. We coasted along during a part of the
night; but a calm came on which lasted till the
morrow. As we were opposite the bay of Karaka-
koua,[17] the natives came out again in greater
numbers, bringing us cabbages, yams, taro, bananas, bread-fruit, water-melons, poultry, &c.,
for which we traded in the way of exchange.
Toward evening, by the aid of a sea breeze that
rose as day declined, we got inside the harbor,
where we anchored on a coral bottom in fourteen
fathoms water.

The next day the Islanders visited the vessel
in great numbers all day long, bringing, as on
the day before, fruits, vegetables, and some pigs,

[17]Now called Kealalekan Bay, on the southwest coast
of Hawaii Island.

in exchange for which we gave them glass beads, iron rings, needles, cotton cloth, &c.

Some of our gentlemen went ashore and were astonished to find a native occupied in building a small sloop of about thirty tons: the tools of which he made use consisted of a half worn-out axe, an adze, about two-inch blade, made out of a paring chisel, a saw, and an iron rod which he heated red hot and made it serve the purpose of an auger. It required no little patience and dexterity to achieve anything with such instruments: he was apparently not deficient in these qualities, for his work was tolerably well advanced. Our people took him on board with them, and we supplied him with suitable tools, for which he appeared extremely grateful.

On the 14th, in the morning, while the ship's carpenter was engaged in replacing one of the cat-heads, two composition sheaves fell into the sea; as we had no others on board, the Captain proposed to the Islanders, who are excellent swimmers, to dive for them, promising a reward; and immediately two offered themselves. They plunged several times, and each time brought up shells as a proof that they had been to the bottom. We had the curiosity to hold our watches while they dove, and were astonished to find that they remained four minutes under the water. That exertion appeared to me, however, to fa-

tigue them a great deal, to such a degree that
the blood streamed from their nostrils and ears.
At last one of them brought up the sheaves and
received the promised recompense, which consisted of four yards of cotton.

Karaka-koua Bay, where we lay, may be three-
quarters of a mile deep and a mile and a half
wide at the entrance: the latter is formed by two
low points of rock which appear to have run
down from the mountains in the form of lava,
after a volcanic eruption. On each point is situated a village of moderate size; that is to say, a
small group of the low huts of the Islanders. The
bottom of the bay terminates in a bold escarp-
ment of rock, some four hundred feet high, on
the top of which is seen a solitary cocoa-tree.

On the evening of the 14th I went ashore with
some other passengers, and we landed at the
group of cabins on the western point of those
which I have described. The inhabitants entertained us with a dance executed by nineteen
young women and one man, all singing together,
and in pretty good time. An old man showed us
the spot where Captain Cook was killed, on the
14th of February, 1779, with the cocoa-nut trees
pierced by the balls from the boats which the
unfortunate navigator commanded. This old
man, whether it were feigned or real sensibility,
seemed extremely affected and even shed tears,

in showing us these objects. As for me, I could
not help finding it a little singular to be thus, by
mere chance, upon this spot on the 14th of February, 1811; that is to say, thirty-two years after,
on the anniversary of the catastrophe which has
rendered it forever celebrated. I drew no sinister
augury from the coincidence, however, and returned to the ship with my companions as gay as
I left it. When I say with my companions, I ought
to except the boatswain, John Anderson, who,
having had several altercations with the Captain
on the passage, now deserted the ship, preferring
to live with the natives rather than obey any
longer so uncourteous a superior. A sailor also
deserted; but the Islanders brought him back, at
the request of the Captain. They offered to bring
back Anderson, but the Captain preferred leaving
him behind.

We found no good water near Karaka-koua
Bay: what the natives brought us in gourds was
brackish. We were also in great want of fresh
meat, but could not obtain it: the King of these
islands having expressly forbidden his subjects to
supply any to the vessels which touched there.
One of the chiefs sent a canoe to Toeaie Bay to
get from the Governor of the island, who resided
there, permission to sell us some pigs. The messengers returned the next day and brought us a
letter, in which the Governor ordered us to pro-

ceed without delay to the isle of Owahou, where the King lives; assuring us that we should there find good water and everything else we needed.

We got under way on the 16th, and with a light wind coasted the island as far as Toeaie Bay. The wind then dropped away entirely, the Captain, accompanied by Messrs. McKay and McDougall, went ashore to pay a visit to the Governor aforesaid. He was not a native, but a Scotchman named John Young, who came hither some years after the death of Captain Cook. This man had married a native woman, and had so gained the friendship and confidence of the King as to be raised to the rank of chief, and after the conquest of Owahou by King Tamehameha, was made Governor of Owhyé, the most considerable of the Sandwich Islands, both by its extent and population. His Excellency explained to our gentlemen the reason why the King had interdicted the trade in hogs to the inhabitants of all the islands: this reason being that His Majesty wished to reserve to himself the monopoly of that branch of commerce, for the augmentation of his royal revenue by its exclusive profits. The Governor also informed them that no rain had fallen on the south part of Hawaii for three years; which explained why we found so little fresh water: he added that the north part of the island was more fertile than the south, where we were:

but that there was no good anchorage: that part
of the coast being defended by sunken rocks
which form heavy breakers. In fine, the Governor
dismissed our gentlemen with a present of four
fine fat hogs; and we, in return, sent him some
tea, coffee, and chocolate and a keg of Madeira
wine.

The night was nearly a perfect calm, and on
the 17th we found ourselves abreast of Mona
Wororaie a snow-capped mountain, like Mona
Roah, but which appeared to me less lofty than
the latter.[18] A number of Islanders came to visit
us as before, with some objects of curiosity and
some small fresh fish. The wind rising on the
18th, we soon passed the western extremity of
Hawaii and sailed by Mowhee and Tahouraha,
two more islands of this group, and said to be,
like the rest, thickly inhabited. The first presents
a highly picturesque aspect, being composed of
hills rising in the shape of a sugar loaf and completely covered with cocoa-nut and bread-fruit
trees.

At last, on the 21st, we approached Owahou,
and came to anchor opposite the bay of Uhytiti,
outside the bar, at a distance of some two miles
from the land.

[18]The Manuscript reads "Mont Kea" in place of "Mona
Roah."

CHAPTER V

Domain of King Tamehameha

THERE is no good anchorage in the Bay of Uhytiti,[19] inside the bar or coral reef: the holding-ground is bad: so that in case of a storm the safety of the ship would have been endangered. Moreover, with a contrary wind it would have been difficult to get out of the inner harbor; for which reasons, our Captain preferred to remain in the road. For the rest, the country surrounding the bay is even more lovely in aspect than that of Karaka-koua; the mountains rise to a less elevation in the back-ground, and the soil has an appearance of greater fertility.

Taméaméah, whom all the Sandwich Isles obeyed when we were there in 1811, was neither the son nor the relative of Tierroboo, who reigned in Owyhee (Hawaii) in 1779, when Captain Cook and some of his people were massacred. He was at that date but a chief of moderate power; but being skilful, intriguing, and full of ambition, he succeeded in gaining a numerous party and finally possessed himself of the sovereignty. As soon as he saw himself master of Owyhee, his native island, he meditated the conquest of the leeward islands, and in a few years

[19]Honolulu Harbor.

he accomplished it. He even passed into Atouay, the most remote of all, and vanquished the ruler of it, but contented himself with imposing on him an annual tribute. He had fixed his residence at Owahou because of all the Sandwich Isles it was the most fertile, the most picturesque—in a word, the most worthy of the residence of the sovereign.

As soon as we arrived, we were visited by a canoe manned by three white men, Davis and Wadsworth, Americans, and Manini, a Spaniard. The last offered to be our interpreter during our stay; which was agreed to. Taméaméa presently sent to us his prime-minister, Crainocou, to whom the Americans have given the name of Pitt, on account of his skill in the affairs of government. Our Captain, accompanied by some of our gentlemen, went ashore immediately to be presented to Taméaméa. About four o'clock P.M. we saw them returning, accompanied by a double pirogue conveying the King and his suite. We ran up our colors and received His Majesty with a salute of four guns.

Taméaméa was above the middle height, well made, robust and inclined to corpulency, and had a majestic carriage. He appeared to me from fifty to sixty years old. He was clothed in the European style and wore a sword. He walked a long time on the deck, asking explanations in

regard to those things which he had not seen on
other vessels, and which were found on ours. A
thing which appeared to surprise him was to see
that we could render the water of the sea fresh
by means of the still attached to our caboose; he
could not imagine how that could be done. We
invited him into the cabin, and having regaled him with some glasses of wine, began to
talk of business matters: we offered him merchandise in exchange for hogs, but were not
able to conclude the bargain that day. His Majesty
re-embarked in his double pirogue at about six
o'clock in the evening. It was manned by twenty-
four men. A great chest containing firearms was
lashed over the center of the two canoes forming
the pirogue; and it was there that Taméaméa
sat, with his prime-minister at his side.

In the morning, on the 22d, we sent our water-
casks ashore and filled them with excellent water.
At about noon His Sable Majesty paid us another
visit, accompanied by his three wives and his
favorite minister. These females were of an extraordinary corpulence and of unmeasured size.
They were dressed in the fashion of the country,
having nothing but a piece of tappa, or bark-cloth,
about two yards long, passed round the hips and
falling to the knees.[20] We resumed the negotia-

[20]While the King was in the cabin his three "queens,"
who had remained on deck, unconcernedly disrobed and

tions of the day before and were more successful. I remarked that when the bargain was concluded he insisted with great pertinacity that part of the payment should be in Spanish dollars. We asked the reason, and he made answer that he wished to buy a frigate of his brother, King George, meaning the King of England. The bargain concluded, we prayed His Majesty and his suite to dine with us; they consented, and toward evening retired, apparently well satisfied with their visit and our reception of them.

In the meantime, the natives surrounded the ship in great numbers with hundreds of canoes, offering us their goods, in the shape of eatables and the rude manufactures of the island, in exchange for merchandise; but as they had also brought intoxicating liquors in gourds, some of the crew got drunk; the Captain was, consequently, obliged to suspend the trade, and forbade any one to traffic with the Islanders except through the first mate, who was intrusted with that business.

I landed on the 22d with Messrs. Pillet and McGillis: we passed the night ashore, spending that day and the next morning in rambling over the environs of the bay, followed by a crowd of men, women, and children.

---

plunged overboard for a swim; after which, they dressed and joined the King in the cabin. Ross, *First Settlers on the Oregon*, 39.

Uhytiti, where Taméaméa resides, and which, consequently, may be regarded as the capital of his kingdom, is—or at least was at that time— a moderate-sized city, or rather a large village. Besides the private houses, of which there were perhaps two hundred, constructed of poles planted in the ground and covered over with matting, there were the royal palace, which was not magnificent by any means: a public store, of two stories, one of stone and the other of wood; two *morais,* or idol temples, and a wharf. At the latter we found an old vessel, the *Lilly Bird,* which some American nagivators had given in exchange for a schooner; it was the only large vessel which King Taméaméa possessed; and, besides, was worth nothing. As for schooners, he had forty of them, of from twenty to thirty tons burden: these vessels served to transport the tributes in kind paid by his vassals in the other islands. Before the Europeans arrived among these savages, the latter had no means of communication between one isle and another but their canoes, and as some of the islands are not in sight of each other, these voyages must have been dangerous. Near the palace I found an Indian from Bombay, occupied in making a twelve-inch cable, for the use of the ship which I have described.

Taméaméa kept constantly round his house a guard of twenty-four men. These soldiers wore,

by way of uniform, a long blue coat with yellow;
and each was armed with a musket. In front of
the house, on an open square, were placed fourteen four-pounders, mounted on their carriages.

The King was absolute, and judged in person
the differences between his subjects. We had an
opportunity of witnessing a proof of it the day
after our landing. A Portuguese, having had a
quarrel with a native who was intoxicated, struck
him: immediately the friends of the latter, who
had been the aggressor after all, gathered in a
crowd to beat down the poor foreigner with
stones; he fled as fast as he could to the house of
the King, followed by a mob of enraged natives,
who, nevertheless, stopped at some distance from
the guards, while the Portuguese, all breathless,
crouched in a corner. We were on the esplanade
in front of the palace royal, and curiosity to see
the trial led us into the presence of His Majesty,
who having caused the quarrel to be explained
to him, and heard the witnesses on both sides,
condemned the native to work four days in the
garden of the Portuguese and to give him a hog.
A young Frenchman from Bordeaux, preceptor
of the King's sons, whom he taught to read, and
who understood the language, acted as interpreter to the Portuguese and explained to us the
sentence. I can not say whether our presence in-
fluenced the decision, or whether, under other

circumstances, the Portuguese would have been less favorably treated. We were given to understand that Taméaméa was pleased to see whites establish themselves in his dominions, but that he esteemed only people with some useful trade and despised idlers, and especially drunkards. We saw at Owahou about thirty of these white inhabitants, for the most part people of no character, and who had remained on the islands either from indolence or from drunkenness and licentiousness. Some had taken wives in the country, in which case the king gave them a portion of land to cultivate for themselves. But two of the worst sort had found means to procure a small still, wherewith they manufactured rum and supplied it to the natives.

The first navigators found only four sorts of quadrupeds on the Sandwich Islands: dogs, swine, lizards, and rats. Since then sheep have been carried there, goats, horned cattle, and even horses, and these animals have multiplied.

The chief vegetable productions of these isles are the sugar cane, the bread-fruit tree, the banana, the water melon, the musk melon, the taro, the ava, the pandanus, the mulberry, &c. The bread-fruit tree is about the size of a large apple tree; the fruit resembles an apple and is about twelve or fourteen inches in circumference; the rind is thick and rough like a melon: when cut transversely it is found to be full of sacs, like the inside of an orange; the pulp has the consistence of water melon, and is cooked before it is eaten. We saw orchards of bread-fruit trees and bananas, and fields of sugar cane, back of Uhy-titi.

The taro grows in low situations and demands a great deal of care. It is not unlike a white turnip, and as it constitutes the principal food of the natives, it is not to be wondered at that they bestow so much attention on its culture. Wherever a spring of pure water is found issuing out of the side of a hill the gardener marks out on the declivity the size of the field he intends to plant. The ground is levelled and surrounded with a mud or stone wall, not exceeding eighteen inches in height and having a flood gate above and below. Into this enclosure the water of the spring is conducted, or is suffered to escape from it, according to the dryness of the season. When the root has acquired a sufficient size it is pulled up for immediate use. This esculent is very bad to eat raw, but boiled it is better than the yam. Cut in slices, dried, pounded, and reduced to a farina, it forms with bread fruit the principal food of the natives. Sometimes they boil it to the consistence of porridge, which they put into gourds and allow to ferment; it will then keep a long time. They also use to mix with it, fish, which they commonly eat raw with the addition of a little salt, obtained by evaporation.

The ava is a plant more injurious than useful to the inhabitants of these isles; since they only make use of it to obtain a dangerous and intoxicating drink, which they also call *ava*. The mode of preparing this beverage is as follows: they chew the root, and spit out the result into a basin; the juice thus expressed is exposed to the sun to undergo fermentation; after which they decant it into a gourd; it is then fit for use, and they drink it on occasions to intoxication. The too frequent use of this disgusting liquor causes loss of sight, and a sort of leprosy, which can only be cured by abstaining from it, and by bathing frequently in the water of the sea. This leprosy turns their skin white: we saw several of the lepers, who were also blind, or nearly so. The natives are also fond of smoking: the tobacco grows in the islands, but I believe it has been introduced from abroad. The bark of the mulberry furnishes the cloth worn by both sexes; of the leaves of the pandanus they make mats. They have also a kind of wax-nut, about the size of a dried plum, of which they make candles by running a stick through several of them. Lighted at one end, they burn like a wax taper, and are the only light they use in their huts at night.

The men are generally well made and tall:
they wear for their entire clothing what they call
a maro; it is a piece of figured or white tappa, two
yards long and a foot wide, which they pass
round the loins and between the legs, tying the
ends in a knot over the left hip. At first sight I
thought they were painted red, but soon perceived that it was the natural color of their skin.
The women wear a petticoat of the same stuff as
the maro but wider and longer, without, however, reaching below the knees. They have sufficiently regular features, and but for the color
may pass, generally speaking, for handsome
women. Some, to heighten their charms, dye
their black hair (cut short for the purpose) with
quick lime, forming round the head a strip of
pure white, which disfigures them monstrously.
Others among the young wear a more becoming
garland of flowers. For other traits, they are very
lascivious, and far from observing a modest reserve, especially toward strangers.[21] In regard to
articles of mere ornament, I was told that they
were not the same in all the Island. I did not see
them either clothed in their war dresses or habits
of ceremony. But I had an opportunity to see

[21]"The women are handsome in person, engaging in
their manner, well-featured, and have countenances full
of joy and tranquility, but chastity is not their virtue."
Ross, *First Settlers on the Oregon*, 51.

them paint or print their tappa, or bark cloth, an
occupation in which they employ a great deal of
care and patience. The pigments they use are
derived from vegetable juices, prepared with the
oil of the cocoa-nut. Their pencils are little reeds
or canes of bamboo, at the extremity of which
they carve out divers sorts of flowers. First they
tinge the cloth they mean to print, yellow, green,
or some other color, which forms the ground:
then they draw upon it perfectly straight lines,
without any other guide but the eye; lastly they
dip the ends of the bamboo sticks in paint of a
different tint from the ground, and apply them
between the dark or bright bars thus formed.
This cloth resembles a good deal our calicoes and
printed cottons; the oils with which it is impregnated renders it impervious to water. It is said
that the natives of Atowy excel all the other
islanders in the art of painting the tappa.

The Sandwich Islanders live in villages of one
or two hundred houses arranged without sym-
metry, or rather grouped together in complete
defiance of it. These houses are constructed (as
I have before said) of posts driven in the ground,
covered with long dry grass, and walled with
matting; the thatched roof gives them a sort of
resemblance to our Canadian barns or granges.
The length of each house varies according to the
number of the family which occupies it: they are

not smoky like the wigwams of our Indians, the fireplace being always outside in the open air, where all the cooking is performed. Hence their dwellings are very clean and neat inside.

Their pirogues or canoes are extremely light and neat: those which are single have an outrigger, consisting of two curved pieces of timber lashed across the bows and touching the water at the distance of five or six feet from the side; another piece, turned up at each extremity, is tied to the end and drags in the water, on which it acts like a skating iron on the ice, and by its weight keeps the canoe in equilibrium: without that contrivance they would infallibly upset. Their paddles are long, with a very broad blade. All these canoes carry a lateen, or sprit-sail, which is made of a mat of grass or leaves, extremely well woven.

I did not remain long enough with these people to acquire very extensive and exact notions of their religion: I know that they recognize a Supreme Being, whom they call Etoway, and a number of inferior divinities. Each village has one or more morais. These morais are enclosures which served for cemeteries; in the middle is a temple, where the priests alone have a right to enter: they contain several idols of wood, rudely sculptured. At the feet of these images are deposited, and left to putrify, the offerings of the people, consisting of dogs, pigs, fowls, vegetables, &c. The respect of these savages for their priests extends almost to adoration; they regard their persons as sacred, and feel the greatest scruple in touching the objects or going near the places which they have declared taboo or forbidden. The taboo has often been useful to European navigators, by freeing them from the importunities of the crowd.[22]

In our rambles we met groups playing at different games. That of draughts appeared the most common. The checker board is very simple, the squares being marked on the ground with a sharp stick: the men are merely shells or pebbles. The game was different from that played in civilized countries, so that we could not understand it.

Although nature has done almost everything for the inhabitants of the Sandwich Islands— though they enjoy a perpetual spring, a clear sky, a salubrious climate, and scarcely any labor is required to produce the necessaries of life— they can not be regarded as generally happy: the artisans and producers, whom they call Tootoos, are nearly in the same situation as the Helots among the Lacedemonians, condemned to labor almost incessantly for their lord, or Eris, without hope of bettering their condition,

[22]The custom of Taboo, widespread among primitive peoples, was abolished by King Kanahemeka II in September, 1819, soon after his accession to the throne. This action prepared the way for the coming of missionaries to the Islands shortly afterward.

and even restricted in the choice of their daily
food.[23] How has it happened[24] that among a
people yet barbarous, where knowledge is nearly
equally distributed, the class which is beyond
comparison the most numerous has voluntarily
submitted to such a humiliating and oppressive
yoke? The Tartars, though infinitely less numerous than the Chinese, have subjected them,
because the former were warlike and the latter
were not. The same thing has happened, no
doubt, at remote periods, in Poland and other
regions of Europe and Asia. If moral causes are
joined to physical ones, the superiority of one
caste and the inferiority of the other will be still
more marked; it is known that the natives of
Hispaniola, when they saw the Spaniards arrive
on their coast in vessels of an astonishing size to
their apprehensions, and heard them imitate the
thunder with their cannon, took them for beings
of a superior nature to their own. Supposing
that this island had been extremely remote from
every other country and that the Spaniards,

[23]The Tootoos and all the women, the wives of the king
and principal chiefs excepted, are eternally condemned to
the use of fruits and vegetables; dogs and pigs being ex-
clusively reserved for the table of the Eris.

[24]All of the remainder of the chapter (including footnotes 23 and 25) is the contribution of Bibaud, who in
editing the 1820 edition of Franchère's narrative occasionally supplied shorter or longer commentaries of his
own. In so far as practicable these are identified in the
present edition.

after conquering it, had held no further communication with any civilized land, at the end of
a century or two the language and the manners
would have assimilated, but there would have
been two castes, one of lords enjoying all the advantages, the other of serfs charged with all the
burdens. This theory seems to have been realized anciently in Hindostan; but if we must
credit the tradition of the Sandwich Islanders,
their country was originally peopled by a man
and woman who came to Owyhee in a canoe.
Unless, then, they mean that this man and
woman came with their slaves, and that the Eris
are descended from the first and the Tootoos from
the last, they ought to attribute to each other the
same origin, and consequently regard each other
as equals and even as brothers, according to the
manner of thinking that prevails among savages.
The cause of the slavery of women among most
barbarous tribes, is more easily explained: the
men have subjected them by the right of the
strongest, if ignorance and superstition have not
caused them to be previously regarded as beings
of an inferior nature, made to be servants and
not companions.[25]

[25]Some Indian tribes think that women have no souls,
but die altogether like the brutes; others assign them a
different paradise from that of men, which indeed they
might have reason to prefer for themselves, unless their
relative condition were to be ameliorated in the next
world.

CHAPTER VI

From Hawaii to the Columbia

HAVING taken on board a hundred head of live hogs, some goats, two sheep, a quantity of poultry, two boat-loads of sugar cane to feed the hogs, as many more of yams, taro, and other vegetables, and all our water-casks being snugly stowed, we weighed anchor on the 28th of February, sixteen days after our arrival at Karakakoua.

We left another man (Edward Aymes) at Owahou. He belonged to a boat's crew which was sent ashore for a load of sugar canes. By the time the boat was loaded by the natives the ebb of the tide had left her aground, and Aymes asked leave of the coxswain to take a stroll, engaging to be back for the flood. Leave was granted him, but during his absence, the tide having come in sufficiently to float the boat, James Thorn, the coxswain, did not wait for the young sailor, who was thus left behind. The captain immediately missed the man, and on being informed that he had strolled away from the boat on leave, flew into a violent passion. Aymes soon made his appearance alongside, having hired some natives to take him on board; on perceiving him, the Captain ordered him to

stay in the long-boat, then lashed to the side with
its load of sugar cane. The Captain then himself
got into the boat, and, taking one of the canes,
beat the poor fellow most unmercifully with it;
after which, not satisfied with this act of brutal-
ity, he seized his victim and threw him overboard! Aymes, however, being an excellent
swimmer, made for the nearest native canoe, of
which there were, as usual, a great number
around the ship. The Islanders, more humane
than our Captain, took in the poor fellow, who,
in spite of his entreaties to be received on board,
could only succeed in getting his clothes, which
were thrown into the canoe. At parting, he told
Captain Thorn that he knew enough of the laws
of his country to obtain redress, should they
ever meet in the territory of the American
Union.[26]

While we were getting under sail, Mr. McKay
pointed out to the Captain that there was one
water-cask empty, and proposed sending it
ashore to be filled, as the great number of live

[26]First Mate Ebenezer D. Fox, more humane than Captain Thorn, on various occasions endeavored to ameliorate
the condition of the victims of the Captain's wrath. On
this one, according to Alexander Ross, Fox signaled to
some natives to take Aymes into their canoe and subsequently contrived to throw overboard the sailor's clothes
and "protection" paper, again signaling to the natives to
convey them to Aymes. *Ross, First Settlers on the Oregon*,
46–47.

animals we had on board required a large quantity of fresh water. The Captain, who feared that some of the men would desert if he sent them ashore, made an observation to that effect in answer to Mr. McKay, who then proposed sending me in a canoe which lay alongside to fill the cask in question: this was agreed to by the Captain, and I took the cask, accordingly, to the nearest spring. Having filled it, not without some difficulty, the Islanders seeking to detain me and I perceiving that they had given me some gourds full of salt water, I was forced also to demand a double pirogue (for the canoe which had brought the empty cask was found inadequate to carry a full one) the ship being already under full sail and gaining an offing. As the natives would not lend a hand to procure what I wanted, I thought it necessary to have recourse to the King, and in fact did so. For seeing the vessel so far at sea, with what I knew of the Captain's disposition, I began to fear that he had formed the plan of leaving me on the Island. My fears, nevertheless, were ill-founded; the vessel made a tack toward the shore, to my great joy; and a double pirogue was furnished me through the good offices of our young friend, the French schoolmaster, to return on board with my cask.

Our deck was now as much encumbered as when we left New York; for we had been obliged to place our live animals at the gangways, and to board over their pens, on which it was necessary to pass, to work ship. Our own numbers were also augmented; for we had taken a dozen Islanders for the service of our intended commercial establishment. Their term of engagement was three years, during which we were to feed and clothe them, and at its expiration they were to receive a hundred dollars in merchandise. The Captain had shipped another dozen as hands on the coasting voyage. These people, who make very good sailors, were eager to be taken into employment and we might easily have carried off a much greater number.

We had contrary winds till the 2d of March, when, having doubled the western extremity of the island, we made northing and lost sight of these smiling and temperate countries, to enter very soon a colder region and less worthy of being inhabited. The winds were variable and nothing extraordinary happened to us till the 16th, when, being arrived at the latitude of 35° 11′ north, and in 138° 16′ of west longitude, the wind shifted all of a sudden to the S.S.W. and blew with such violence that we were forced to strike top-gallant masts and top-sails and run before the gale with a double reef in our foresail. The rolling of the vessel was greater than in all the gales we had experienced previously. Never-

theless, as we made great headway and were
approaching the Continent, the Captain by way
of precaution lay to for two nights successively.
At last, on the 22d, in the morning, we saw the
land. Although we had not been able to take
any observations for several days, nevertheless,
by the appearance of the coast we perceived that
we were near the mouth of the river Columbia,
and were not more than three miles from land.
The breakers formed by the bar at the entrance
of that river, and which we could distinguish
from the ship, left us no room to doubt that we
had arrived at last at the end of our voyage.

The wind was blowing in heavy squalls, and
the sea ran very high: in spite of that, the Captain caused a boat to be lowered, and Mr. Fox
(first mate), Basile Lapensée, Ignace Lapensée,
Jos. Nadeau, and John Martin, got into her, taking some provisions and firearms, with orders to
sound the channel and report themselves on
board as soon as possible.[27] The boat was not
even supplied with a good sail or a mast, but

[27]Alexander Ross characterizes these men as "one sailor,
a very old Frenchman, and three Canadian lads unac-
quainted with sea service—two of them being carters,
from La Chine and the other a Montreal barber." He relates further that Fox protested against being sent upon
the mission with such hands, yielding when Captain
Thorn taunted him with cowardice, saying: "Mr. Fox, if
you are afraid of water you should have remained at
Boston." *First Settlers on the Oregon*, 59–60.

one of the partners gave Mr. Fox a pair of bed
sheets to serve for the former. Messrs. McKay
and McDougall could not help remonstrating
with the Captain on the imprudence of sending
the boat ashore in such weather, but they could
not move his obstinacy. The boat's crew pulled
away from the ship; alas! we were never to see
her again; and we already had a foreboding of
her fate. The next day the wind seemed to
moderate, and we approached very near the
coast. The entrance of the river, which we
plainly distinguished with the naked eye, appeared but a confused and agitated sea: the
waves, impelled by a wind from the offing, broke
upon the bar and left no perceptible passage.
We got no sign of the boat; and toward evening
for our own safety we hauled off to sea, with all
countenances extremely sad, not excepting the
Captain's, who appeared to me as much afflicted
as the rest, and who had reason to be so. During
the night the wind fell, the clouds dispersed,
and the sky became serene. On the morning of
the 24th we found that the current had carried
us near the coast again, and we dropped anchor
in fourteen fathoms water, north of Cape Disappointment.[28] The *coup d'oeil* is not so smiling by

[28]So named by John Meares, who visited the Northwest
Coast in July, 1788. He was familiar with the charts kept
by Bruno Hecata, a Spaniard, who in 1775 had discovered

a great deal at this anchorage as at the Sandwich Islands, the coast offering little to the eye
but a continuous range of high mountains covered with snow.

Although it was calm the sea continued to
break over the reef with violence between Cape
Disappointment and Point Adams.[29] We sent
Mr. Mumford (the second mate) to sound a passage; but having found the breakers too heavy,
he returned on board about mid-day. Messrs.
McKay and D. Stuart offered their services to go
ashore to search for the boat's crew who left on
the 22d; but they could not find a place to land.
They saw Indians who made signs to them to
pull round the Cape, but they deemed it more
prudent to return to the vessel. Soon after their
return a gentle breeze sprang up from the westward, we raised anchor, and approached the
entrance of the river. Mr. Aikin[30] was then dis-

a bay at the mouth of the Columbia, with indications of a
river. Meares now searched for it, but failing to find it he
named the bay "Deception," and the cape "Disappointment." The latter name still persists.

[29]Captain Robert Gray on May 18, 1792 named the
southern headland of the bay "Point Adams" and the
northern, "Point Hancock." Captain George Vancouver
the same summer renamed Point Hancock "Disappointment," but retained the name Gray had given to Point
Adams.

[30]Alexander Ross lists this man as third mate of the
Tonquin, who had been brought out to take command of
the *Dolly. First Settlers on the Oregon*,64,166–67. Franchère

ENTRANCE OF THE COLUMBIA RIVER

Ship Tonquin, crossing the bar, 25th March, 1811

patched in the pinnace, accompanied by John
Coles (sailmaker), Stephen Weeks (armorer) and
two Sandwich Islanders; and we followed under
easy sail. Another boat had been sent out before
this one, but the Captain judging that she bore
too far south, made her a signal to return. Mr.
Aikin not finding less than four fathoms, we
followed him and advanced between the breakers with a favorable wind, so that we passed the
boat on our starboard, within pistol-shot. We
made signs to her to return on board, but she
could not accomplish it; the ebb tide carried her
with such rapidity that in a few minutes we had
lost sight of her amidst the tremendous breakers
that surrounded us. It was near nightfall, the
wind began to give way, and the water was so
low with the ebb that we struck six or seven
times with violence: the breakers broke over the
ship and threatened to submerge her. At last we
passed from two and three-quarters fathoms of
water to seven, where we were obliged to drop
anchor, the wind having entirely failed us. We
were far, however, from being out of danger, and
the darkness came to add to the horror of our
situation: our vessel, though at anchor, threatened to be carried away every moment by the

does not include him as a member of the crew, but instead lists him as a "Rigger and calker, from Scotland."
The name is variously spelled by both writers.

tide; the best bower was let go and it kept two men at the wheel to hold her head in the right direction. However, Providence came to our succor: the flood succeeded to the ebb, and the wind rising out of the offing, we weighed both anchors in spite of the obscurity of the night and succeeded in gaining a little bay or cove, formed at the entrance of the river by Cape Disappointment and called Baker Bay, where we found a good anchorage.[31] It was about midnight, and all retired to take a little rest: the crew, above all, had great need of it. We were fortunate to be in a place of safety for the wind rose higher and higher during the rest of the night, and on the morning of the 25th allowed us to see that this ocean is not always pacific.

Some natives visited us this day, bringing with them beaver-skins; but the inquietude caused in our minds by the loss of two boats' crews, for whom we wished to make search, did not permit us to think of traffic. We tried to make the savages comprehend by signs that we had sent

[31]Baker Bay was so named by Lieutenant W. R. Broughton, a subordinate of Captain Vancouver, by whom he was dispatched in the summer of 1792 to explore the lower course of the Columbia. Upon returning down river from this assignment Broughton encountered an American ship in the bay, at the mouth of the Columbia, commanded by Captain Baker, whose name he gave to the Bay. Broughton also named Mount Coffin, on the Columbia near the mouth of Cowlitz River.

a boat ashore three days previous and that we had no news of her; but they seemed not to understand us. The Captain, accompanied by some of our gentlemen, landed, and they set themselves to search for our missing people in the woods, and along the shore N. W. of the Cape. After a few hours we saw the Captain return with Weeks, one of the crew of the last boat sent out. He was stark naked, and after being clothed and receiving some nourishment gave us an account of his almost miraculous escape from the waves on the preceding night, in nearly the following terms:

"After you had passed our boat," said he, "the breakers caused by the meeting of the wind roll and ebb-tide became a great deal heavier than when we entered the river with the flood. The boat, for want of a rudder, became very hard to manage, and we let her drift at the mercy of the tide till, after having escaped several surges, one struck us midship and capsized us. I lost sight of Mr. Aiken and John Coles: but the two Islanders were close by me; I saw them stripping off their clothes, and I followed their example; and seeing the pinnace within my reach, keel upward, I seized it; the two natives came to my assistance; we righted her, and by sudden jerks threw out so much of the water that she would hold a man: one of the natives jumped in and, bailing with his two hands, succeeded in a short time in emptying her. The other native found the oars and about dark we were all three embarked. The tide having now carried us outside the breakers, I endeavored to persuade my companions in misfortune to row, but they were so benumbed with cold that they absolutely refused. I well knew that without clothing and exposed to the rigor of the air I must keep in constant exercise. Seeing, besides, that the night was advancing, and having no resource but the little strength left me, I set to work sculling and pushed off the bar, but so as not to be carried out too far to sea. About midnight one of my companions died: the other threw himself upon the body of his comrade and I could not persuade him to abandon it. Daylight appeared at last; and being near the shore I headed in for it and arrived, thank God, safe and sound, through the breakers, on a sandy beach. I helped the Islander who yet gave some signs of life to get out of the boat, and we both took to the woods; but seeing that he was not able to follow me, I left him to his bad fortune and, pursuing a beaten path that I perceived, I found myself, to my great astonishment, in the course of a few hours, near the vessel."

The gentlemen who went ashore with the Captain divided themselves into three parties to search for the native whom Weeks had left at the entrance of the forest; but after scouring the woods and the point of the Cape all day, they came on board in the evening without having found him.

Chapter VII
Founding of Astoria

THE narrative of Weeks informed us of the death of three of our companions, and we could not doubt that the five others had met a similar fate. This loss of eight of our number in two days, before we had set foot on shore, was a bad augury and was sensibly felt by all of us. In the course of so long a passage the habit of seeing each other every day, the participation of the same cares and dangers, and confinement to the same narrow limits had formed between all the passengers a connection that could not be broken, above all in a manner so sad and so unlooked for, without making us feel a void like that which is experienced in a well-regulated and loving family when it is suddenly deprived by death of the presence of one of its cherished members. We had left New York for the most part strangers to one another; but arrived at the river Columbia we were all friends, and regarded each other almost as brothers. We regretted especially the two brothers Lapensée and Joseph Nadeau: these young men had been in an especial manner recommended by their respectable parents in Canada to the care of Mr. McKay; and had acquired by their good conduct the esteem of the Captain, of

the crew, and of all the passengers. The brothers
Lapensée were courageous and willing, never
flinching in the hour of danger, and had become
as good seamen as any on board. Messrs. Fox and
Aikin were both highly regarded by all; the loss
of Mr. Fox, above all, who was endeared to every
one by his gentlemanly behavior and affability,
would have been severely regretted at any time,
but it was doubly so in the present conjuncture:
this gentleman, who had already made a voyage
to the Northwest, could have rendered important services to the Captain and to the Company.
The preceding days had been days of apprehension and of uneasiness; this was one of sorrow
and mourning.

The following day the same gentlemen who
had volunteered their services to seek for the
missing Islander resumed their labors, and very
soon after they left us we perceived a great fire
kindled at the verge of the woods, over against
the ship. I was sent in a boat and arrived at the
fire. It was our gentlemen who had kindled it, to
restore animation to the poor Islander, whom
they had at last found under the rocks, half dead
with cold and fatigue, his legs swollen and his
feet bleeding. We clothed him and brought him
on board, where, by our care, we succeeded in
restoring him to life.

Toward evening a number of the Sandwich

Islanders, provided with the necessary utensils, and offerings consisting of biscuit, lard, and tobacco, went ashore to pay the last duties to their compatriot who died in Mr. Aikin's boat on the night of the 24th. Mr. Pillet and I went with them and witnessed the obsequies, which took place in the manner following. Arrived at the spot where the body had been hung upon a tree to preserve it from the wolves, the natives dug a grave in the sand; then, taking down the body and stretching it alongside the pit, they placed the biscuit under one of the arms, a piece of pork beneath the other, and the tobacco beneath the chin and the genital parts. Thus provided for the journey to the other world, the body was deposited in the grave and covered with sand and stones. All the countrymen of the dead man then knelt on either side of the grave in a double row with their faces to the east, except one of them who officiated as priest; the latter went to the margin of the sea, and having filled his hat with water, sprinkled the two rows of Islanders and recited a sort of prayer to which the others responded, nearly as we do in the litanies. That prayer ended, they rose and returned to the vessel, looking neither to the right hand nor to the left. As every one of them appeared to be familiar with the part he performed, it is more than probable that they observed, as far as circumstances permitted, the

ceremonies practised in their country on like occasions. We all returned on board about sundown.

The next day, the 27th, desirous of clearing
the gangways of the live stock, we sent some men
on shore to construct a pen and soon after landed
about fifty hogs, committing them to the care of
one of the hands. On the 30th the long boat was
manned, armed, and provisioned, and the Captain, with Messrs. McKay and D. Stuart and
some of the clerks embarked on it to ascend the
river and choose an eligible spot for our trading
establishment. Messrs. Ross and Pillet left at the
same time, to run down south and try to obtain
intelligence of Mr. Fox and his crew. In the meantime, having reached some of the goods most at
hand, we commenced, with the natives who came
every day to the vessel, a trade for beaver skins,
and sea-otter stones.

Messrs. Ross and Pillet returned on board on
the 1st of April without having learned anything
respecting Mr. Fox and his party. They did not
even perceive along the beach any vestiges of the
boat. The natives who occupy Point Adams, and
who are called Clatsops, received our young gentlemen very amicably and hospitably. The Captain and his companions also returned on the 4th
without having decided on a position for the establishment, finding none which appeared to
them eligible. It was consequently resolved to ex-

plore the south bank, and Messrs. McDougall
and D. Stuart departed on that expedition the
next day, promising to return by the 7th.

The 7th came and these gentlemen did not return. It rained almost all day. The day after, some
natives came on board and reported that Messrs.
McDougall and Stuart had capsized the evening
before in crossing the bay. This news at first
alarmed us; and, if it had been verified, would
have given the finishing blow to our discourage-
ment. Still, as the weather was excessively bad
and we did not repose entire faith in the story of
the natives—whom, moreover, we might not have
perfectly understood—we remained in suspense
till the 10th. On the morning of that day we were
preparing to send some of the people in search of
our two gentlemen when we perceived two large
canoes, full of Indians, coming toward the vessel:
they were of the Chinook village, which was
situated at the foot of a bluff on the north side of
the river, and were bringing back Messrs. McDougall and Stuart. We made known to these gentlemen the report we had heard on the 8th from the
natives, and they informed us that it had been in
fact well founded; that on the 7th, desirous of
reaching the ship agreeably to their promise,
they had quitted Chinouke Point, in spite of the
remonstrances of the chief, Comcomly, who
sought to detain them by pointing out the danger

to which they would expose themselves in crossing the bay in such a heavy sea as it was; that
they had scarcely made more than a mile and a
half before a huge wave broke over their boat and
capsized it; that the Indians, aware of the danger
to which they were exposed, had followed them,
and that, but for their assistance, Mr. McDougall,
who could not swim, would inevitably have been
drowned; that after the Chinooks had kindled a
large fire and dried their clothes they had been
conducted by them back to their village, where
the principal chief had received them with all
imaginable hospitality, regaling them with every
delicacy his wigwam afforded; that, in fine, if
they had got back safe and sound to the vessel, it
was to the timely succor and humane cares of the
Indians whom we saw before us that they owed
it. We liberally rewarded these generous children
of the forest, and they returned home well satisfied.[32]

This last survey was also fruitless, as Messrs.
McDougall and Stuart did not find an advantageous site to build upon. But as the Captain wished
to take advantage of the fine season to pursue his
traffic with the natives along the N. W. Coast, it

[32]Chief Comcomly was a shrewd and enterprising character who played an interesting role in the life of Fort
Astoria. His daughter married Duncan McDougall, who
served as commander of Fort Astoria prior to its transfer
to the North West Company in 1813.

was resolved to establish ourselves on Point George, situated on the south bank about fourteen or fifteen miles from our present anchorage.[33] Accordingly, we embarked on the 12th in the long-boat, to the number of twelve, furnished with tools and with provisions for a week. We landed at the bottom of a small bay, where we formed a sort of encampment. The spring, usually so tardy in this latitude, was already far advanced; the foliage was budding and the earth was clothing itself with verdure; the weather was superb and all nature smiled. We imagined ourselves in the Garden of Eden; the wild forests seemed to us delightful groves, and the leaves transformed to brilliant flowers. No doubt the pleasure of finding ourselves at the end of our voyage and liberated from the ship made things appear to us a great deal more beautiful than they really were. Be that as it may, we set ourselves to work with enthusiasm and cleared, in a few days, a point of land of its under-brush and of the huge trunks of pine trees that covered it, which we rolled, half-burnt, down the bank. The vessel came to moor near our encampment, and the trade went on. The natives visited us constantly and in great numbers; some to trade,

[33]Point George, where the party now proceeded to build Fort Astoria, was on the site of present-day Astoria. The name was given by Vancouver in 1792.

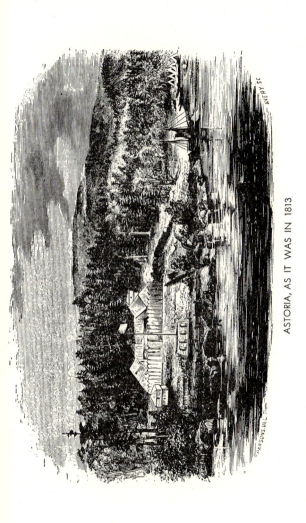

ASTORIA, AS IT WAS IN 1813

others to gratify their curiosity, or to purloin some little articles if they found an opportunity. We landed the frame timbers which we had brought, ready cut for the purpose, in the vessel; and by the end of April, with the aid of the ship-carpenters, John Weeks and Johann Koaster, we had laid the keel of a coasting schooner of about thirty tons.

CHAPTER VIII

Ascending the Columbia

THE Indians having informed us that above certain rapids there was an establishment of white men, we doubted not that it was a trading post of the North West Company; and to make sure of it, we procured a large canoe and a guide and set out on the 2d of May, Messrs. McKay, R. Stuart, Montigny, and I, with a sufficient number of hands. We first passed a lofty headland that seemed at a distance to be detached from the main, and to which we gave the name of Tongue Point. Here the river gains a width of some nine or ten miles and keeps it for about twelve miles up. The left bank, which we were coasting, being concealed by little low islands, we encamped for the night on one of them, at the village of Wakaicum, to which our guide belonged.

We continued our journey on the 3d: the river narrows considerably at about thirty miles from its mouth, and is obstructed with islands which are thickly covered with the willow, poplar, alder, and ash. These islands are, without exception, uninhabited and uninhabitable, being nothing but swamps, and entirely overflowed in the months of June and July; as we understood from

Caalpo, our guide, who appeared to be an intelligent man. In proportion as we advanced, we
saw the high mountains capped with snow which
form the chief and majestic feature, though a
stern one, of the banks of the Columbia for some
distance from its mouth, recede, and give place
to a country of moderate elevation and rising amphitheatrically from the margin of the stream.
The river narrows to a mile or thereabouts; the
forest is less dense, and patches of green prairie
are seen. We passed a large village on the south
bank, called Chreluit, above which is a fine forest
of oaks; and encamped for the night on a low
point, at the foot of an isolated rock about one
hundred and fifty feet high. This rock appeared
to me remarkable on account of its situation, re-
posing in the midst of a low and swampy ground,
as if it had been dropped from the clouds, and
seeming to have no connection with the neighboring mountains. On a cornice or shelving pro-
jection about thirty feet from its base the natives
of the adjacent villages deposit their dead in
canoes; and it is the same rock to which, for this
reason, Lieutenant Broughton gave the name of
Mount Coffin.[34]

[34]"A small rocky height called Coffin Rock, or Mount
Coffin, a receptacle for the dead. All over this rock—top,
sides, and bottom—were placed canoes of all sorts and
sizes containing relics of the dead, the congested dust of
many ages." Ross, *First Settlers on the Oregon*, 113–14.

On the 4th, in the morning, we arrived at a large village of the same name as that which we had passed the evening before, Chreluit, and we landed to obtain information respecting a considerable stream which here discharges into the Columbia, and respecting its resources for the hunter and trader in furs. It comes from the north and is called Kowilitzk by the natives. Mr. McKay embarked with Mr. de Montigny and two Indians in a small canoe to examine the course of this river a certain distance up. On entering the stream they saw a great number of birds which they took at first for turkeys, so much they resembled them, but which were only a kind of carrion eagles, vulgarly called turkey buzzards. We were not a little astonished to see Mr. de Montigny return on foot and alone; he soon informed us of the reason: having ascended the Kowilitzk about a mile and a half, on rounding a bend of the stream they suddenly came in view of about twenty canoes, full of Indians, who had made a rush upon them with the most frightful yells; the two natives and the guide who conducted their little canoe retreated with the utmost precipitancy, but seeing that they would be overtaken they stopped short and begged Mr. McKay to fire upon the approaching savages, which he, being well acquainted with the Indian character from the time he accompanied Sir

Alexander Mackenzie, and having met with similar occurrences before, would by no means do; but displayed a friendly sign to the astonished natives and invited them to land for an amicable talk; to which they immediately assented. Mr. McKay had sent Mr. de Montigny to procure some tobacco and a pipe in order to strike a peace with these barbarians. The latter then returned to Mr. McKay with the necessary articles and in the evening the party came back to our camp, which we had fixed between the villages. We were then informed that the Indians whom Mr. McKay had met were at war with the Chreluits. It was impossible, consequently, to close our eyes all night; the natives passing and repassing continually from one village to the other, making fearful cries, and coming every minute to solicit us to discharge our firearms; all to frighten their enemies and let them see that they were on their guard.

On the 5th, in the morning, we paid a visit to the hostile camp; and those savages, who had never seen white men, regarded us with curiosity and astonishment, lifting the legs of our trousers and opening our shirts to see if the skin of our bodies resembled that of our faces and hands. We remained some time with them to make proposals of peace; and having ascertained that this warlike demonstration originated in a trifling offense on the part of the Chreluits, we found them well disposed to arrange matters in an amicable fashion. After having given them, therefore, some looking-glasses, beads, knives, tobacco, and other trifles, we quitted them and pursued our way.

Having passed a deserted village and then several islands, we came in sight of a noble mountain on the north, about twenty miles distant, all covered with snow, contrasting remarkably with the dark foliage of the forests at its base, and probably the same which was seen by Broughton, and named by him Mount St. Helen. We pulled against a strong current all this day and at evening our guide made us enter a little river, on the bank of which we found a good camping place under a grove of oaks and in the midst of odoriferous wild flowers, where we passed a night more tranquil than that which had preceded it.

On the morning of the 6th we ascended this small stream and soon arrived at a large village called Thlacalama, the chief whereof, who was a young and handsome man, was called Keasseno, and was a relative of our guide. The situation of this village is the most charming that can be, being built on the little river that we had ascended, and indeed at its navigable head, being here but a torrent with numerous cascades leaping from rock to rock in their descent to the deep, limpid water, which then flows through a beautiful prairie enameled with odoriferous flowers of all colors and studded with superb groves of oak. The freshness and beauty of this spot, which Nature seemed to have taken pleasure in adorning and enriching with her most precious gifts, contrasted in a striking manner with the indigence and uncleanliness of its inhabitants; and I regretted that it had not fallen to the lot of civilized men. I was wrong no doubt: it is just that those should be most favored by their common mother who are least disposed to pervert her gifts or to give the preference to advantages which are factitious and often very frivolous. We quitted with regret this charming spot and soon came to another large village which our guide informed us was called Cathlapoutle, and was situated at the confluence of a small stream that seemed to flow down from the mountain covered with snow, which we had seen the day before: this river is called Cowiltk. We coasted a pretty island, well timbered and high enough above the level of the Columbia to escape inundation in the freshets, and arrived at two villages called Maltnaba. We then passed the confluence of the river Wolamat, above which the tide ceases to be felt in the Columbia. Our guide informed us that ascending this river about a day's journey there was a con-

siderable fall, beyond which the country abounded in deer, elk, bear, beaver, and otter. But here
at the spot where we were the oaks and poplar
which line both banks of the river, the green and
flowery prairies discerned through the trees, and
the mountains discovered in the distance offer
to the eye of the observer who loves the beauties
of simple nature a prospect the most lovely and
enchanting. We encamped for the night on the
edge of one of these fine prairies.

On the 7th we passed several low islands and
soon discovered Mount Hood, a high mountain
capped with snow, so named by Lieutenant
Broughton; and Mount Washington,[35] another
snowy summit, so called by Lewis and Clark.
The prospect which the former had before his
eyes at this place appeared to him so charming
that, landing upon a point to take possession of
the country in the name of King George, he
named it Point Belle Vue. At two o'clock we
passed Point Vancouver, the highest reached by
Broughton. The width of the river diminishes
considerably above this point, and we began very
soon to encounter shoals of sand and gravel; a
sure indication that we were nearing the rapids.
We encamped that evening under a ledge of
rocks, descending almost to the water's edge.

[35]Mount Washington is not mentioned in the Manuscript.

The next day, the 8th, we did not proceed far before we encountered a very rapid current. Soon after, we saw a hut of Indians engaged in fishing, where we stopped to breakfast. We found here an old blind man, who gave us a cordial reception. Our guide said that he was a white man, and that his name was Soto. We learned from the mouth of the old man himself that he was the son of a Spaniard who had been wrecked at the mouth of the river; that a part of the crew on this occasion got safe ashore, but were all massacred by the Clatsops with the exception of four, who were spared and who married native women; that these four Spaniards, of whom his father was one, disgusted with the savage life, attempted to reach a settlement of their own nation toward the south, but had never been heard of since; and that when his father, with his companions, left the country, he himself was yet quite young. These good people having regaled us with fresh salmon, we left them and arrived very soon at a rapid opposite an island, named Strawberry Island by Captains Lewis and Clark in 1806. We left our men at a large village to take care of the canoe and baggage; and following our guide, after walking about two hours in a beaten path we came to the foot of the fall, where we amused ourselves for some time with shooting the seals, which were here in abundance, and in

watching the Indians taking salmon below the
cataract in their scoop-nets, from stages erected
for that purpose over the eddies. A chief, a young
man of fine person and a good mien, came to us,
followed by some twenty others, and invited us
to his wigwam: we accompanied him, had roasted
salmon for supper, and some mats were spread
for our night's repose.

The next morning, having ascertained that
there was no trading post near the Falls, and
Caalpo absolutely refusing to proceed farther,
alleging that the natives of the villages beyond
were his enemies and would not fail to kill him
if they had him in their power, we decided to
return to the encampment. Having, therefore,
distributed some presents to our host (I mean
the young chief with whom we had supped and
lodged) and to some of his followers, and procured a supply of fresh salmon for the return
voyage, we re-embarked and reached the camp on
the 14th without accidents or incidents worth
relating.

Chapter IX

Fort Astoria Completed

HAVING built a warehouse (62 feet by 20) to put under cover the articles we were to receive from the ship, we were busily occupied from the 16th to the 30th in stowing away the goods and other effects intended for the establishment.

The ship, which had been detained by circumstances much longer than had been anticipated, left her anchorage at last on the 1st of June and dropped down to Baker Bay, there to wait for a favorable wind to get out of the river. As she was to coast along the north and enter all the harbors in order to procure as many furs as possible, and to touch at the Columbia River before she finally left these seas for the United States, it was unanimously resolved among the partners that Mr. McKay should join the cruise, as well to aid the Captain as to obtain correct information in regard to the commerce with the natives on that coast. Mr. McKay selected Messrs. J. Lewis and O. de Montigny to accompany him; but the latter having represented that the sea made him sick, was excused; and Mr. McKay shipped in his place a young man named Louis Bruslé to serve him in the capacity of domestic, being one of the young

Canadian sailors. I had the good fortune not to
be chosen for this disastrous voyage, thanks to
my having made myself useful at the establishment. Mr. Mumford (the second mate) owed the
same happiness to the incompatibility of his disposition with that of the Captain; he had permission to remain, and engaged with the Company in place of Mr. Aikin as coaster, and in
command of the schooner.[36]

On the 5th of June the ship got out to sea,
with a good wind. We continued in the meantime to labor without intermission at the com-
pletion of the storehouse, and in the erection of
a dwelling for ourselves and a powder magazine.
These buildings were constructed of hewn logs,
and in the absence of boards were tightly covered and roofed with cedar bark. The natives
of both sexes visited us more frequently, and
formed a pretty considerable camp near the
establishment.

On the 15th some natives from up the river
brought us two strange Indians, a man and a
woman. They were not attired like the savages
on the river Columbia, but wore long robes of
dressed deer-skin, with leggings and moccasins

[36]The concluding statement, together with a footnote
(not here reproduced) in the 1854 edition are the work of
Mr. Huntington. They do not appear in Bibaud's 1820
edition, nor in the Manuscript.

in the fashion of the tribes to the east of the Rocky Mountains. We put questions to them in various Indian dialects, but they did not understand us. They showed us a letter addressed to "Mr. John Stuart, Fort Estékatademe, New Caledonia." Mr. Pillet then addressing them in the Knisteneaux language, they answered, although they appeared not to understand it perfectly. Notwithstanding, we learned from them that they had been sent by a Mr. Finnan McDonald, a clerk in the service of the North West Company, and who had a post on a river which they called Spokan; that having lost their way, they had followed the course of the Tacousah-Tesseh[37] (the Indian name of the Columbia) that when they arrived at the Falls the natives made them understand that there were white men at the mouth of the river; and not doubting that the person to whom the letter was addressed would be found there, they had come to deliver it.

We kept these messengers for some days, and having drawn from them important information respecting the country in the interior west of the Mountains, we decided to send an expedition thither under the command of Mr. David Stuart; and the 15th of July was fixed for its departure.

---

[37]In the 1820 edition of Franchère's narrative this name is spelled "Tacousah-Tesse." It does not appear in the Manuscript at all.

All was in fact ready on the appointed day and we were about to load the canoes, when toward midday we saw a large canoe with a flag displayed at her stern rounding the point which we called Tongue Point. We knew not who it could be; for we did not so soon expect our own party, who (as the reader will remember) were to cross the continent by the route which Captains Lewis and Clark had followed in 1805, and to winter for that purpose somewhere on the Missouri. We were soon relieved of our uncertainty by the arrival of the canoe, which touched shore at a little wharf that we had built to facilitate the landing of goods from the vessel. The flag she bore was the British, and her crew was composed of eight Canadian boatmen or voyageurs. A well-dressed man, who appeared to be the commander, was the first to leap ashore, and addressing us without ceremony, said that his name was David Thompson and that he was one of the partners of the North West Company.[38] We in-

[38]David Thompson was a native of London who came to America as an employee of the Hudson's Bay Company in 1789. Although he was employed in the fur trade, his outstanding interest was the pursuit of exploration and geographical discovery. Because the Hudson's Bay Company did not encourage these pursuits, in 1797 Thompson joined the North West Company. He visited the Mandan Indians on the Upper Missouri in 1797–98, half a dozen years in advance of Lewis and Clark, and by 1801 had reached the Rocky Mountains. From 1804 to 1810 he was

vited him to our quarters, which were at one end of the warehouse, the dwelling-house not being yet completed. After the usual civilities had been extended to our visitor, Mr. Thompson said that he had crossed the Continent during the preceding season; but that the desertion of a portion of his men had compelled him to winter at the base of the Rocky Mountains, at the head waters of the Columbia. In the spring he had built a canoe, the materials for which he had brought with him across the mountains, and had come down the river to our establishment. He added that the wintering partners had resolved to abandon all their trading posts west of the mountains, not to enter into competition with us, provided our company would engage not to encroach upon their commerce on the east side: and to support what he said, produced a letter to that effect, addressed by the wintering part-

engaged in trading and establishing posts on the Upper Columbia, whence he now had been sent to forestall the Astorians in occupying the mouth of the Great River. In 1812 he retired from the active pursuit of the fur trade of Lower Canada. From 1816 to 1826 he had charge of the British Commission for surveying the International Boundary from its junction with the Saint Lawrence River westward to Lake of the Woods. Thompson died in poverty and neglect in 1857. For a more adequate sketch of his remarkable career as surveyor and explorer of western Canada and the northwestern United States see *Dict. Am. Biog.*

ners to the chief of their house in Canada, the
Hon. William McGillivray.[39]

Mr. Thompson kept a regular journal, and
traveled, I thought, more like a geographer than
a fur-trader. He was provided with a sextant,
chronometer, and barometer, and during a week's
sojourn which he made at our place had an opportunity to make several astronomical observations. He recognized the two Indians who had
brought the letter addressed to Mr. J. Stuart,
and told us that they were two women, one of
whom had dressed herself as a man to travel with
more security. The description which he gave us
of the interior of the country was not calculated
to give us a very favorable idea of it, and did not
perfectly accord with that of our two Indian
guests. We persevered, however, in the resolution we had taken of sending an expedition
thither; and on the 23d Mr. D. Stuart set out,
accompanied by Messrs. Pillet, Ross, McClellan
and de Montigny, with four Canadian voyageurs
and the two Indian women, and in company with

[39]William McGillivray was a notable figure among the
Northwesters and from 1790 on, one of the wintering
partners. Upon the death of Simon McTavish, McGillivray
became chief agent of the Company at Montreal. Fort
William, for many years famous as the rendezvous of the
Northwesters, was named for McGillivray. For Franchère's
description of it see *post*, Chap. 27.

Mr. Thompson and his crew.[40] The wind being favorable, the little flotilla hoisted sail and was soon out of our sight.[41]

The natives, who till then had surrounded us in great numbers, began to withdraw, and very soon we saw no more of them. At first we attributed their absence to the want of furs to trade with; but we soon learned that they acted in that manner from another motive. One of the secondary chiefs, who had formed a friendship for Mr. R. Stuart, informed him that seeing us reduced in number by the expedition lately sent off, they had formed the design of surprising us, to take our lives and plunder the post. We hastened, therefore, to put ourselves in the best possible

[40]Note 41 below is not found in Franchère's Manuscript nor in the 1820 edition, edited by Bibaud. Although it purports to be the commentary of Franchère it was evidently written by Huntington.

[41]Mr. Thompson had no doubt been sent by the agents of the North West Company, to take possession of an eligible spot at the mouth of the Columbia, with a view of forestalling the plan of Mr. Astor. He would have been there before us, no doubt, but for the desertion of his men. The consequence of this step would have been his taking possession of the country and displaying the British flag as an emblem of that possession and a guarantee of protection hereafter. He found himself too late, however, and the Stars and Stripes floating over Astoria. This note is not intended by the author as an after-thought: as the opinion it conveys was that which we all entertained at the time of that gentleman's visit.

state of defense. The dwelling house was raised, parallel to the warehouse; we cut a great quantity of pickets in the forest and formed a square, with palisades in front and rear, of about 90 feet by 120; the warehouse, built on the edge of a ravine, formed one flank, the dwelling house and shops the other; with a little bastion at each angle north and south, on which were mounted four small cannon. The whole was finished in six days, and had a sufficiently formidable aspect to deter the Indians from attacking us; and for greater surety we organized a guard for day and night.

Toward the end of the month a large assemblage of Indians from the neighborhood of the Strait of Juan de Fuca and Gray's Harbor formed a great camp on Baker Bay for the ostensible object of fishing for sturgeon. It was bruited among these Indians that the *Tonquin* had been destroyed on the Coast, and Mr. McKay (or the chief trader, as they called him) and all the crew massacred by the natives. We did not give credence to this rumor. Some days after, other Indians from Gray's Harbor, called Tchikeylis, confirmed what the first had narrated and even gave us, as far as we could judge by the little we knew of their language, a very circumstantial detail of the affair, so that, without wholly convincing us, it did not fail to make a painful impression on our minds and keep us in an excited state of feeling as to the truth of the report. The Indians of the Bay looked fiercer and more war-like than those of our neighborhood; so we re-doubled our vigilance and performed a regular daily drill to accustom ourselves to the use of arms.

To the necessity of securing ourselves against an attack on the part of the natives was joined that of obtaining a stock of provisions for the winter: those which we had received from the vessel were very quickly exhausted, and from the commencement of the month of July we were forced to depend upon fish. Not having brought hunters with us, we had to rely for venison on the precarious hunt of one of the natives who had not abandoned us when the rest of his country-men retired. This man brought us from time to time a very lean and very dry doe-elk, for which we had to pay, notwithstanding, very dear. The ordinary price of a stag was a blanket, a knife, some tobacco, powder and ball, besides supply-ing our hunter with a musket. This dry meat and smoke-dried fish constituted our daily food, and that in very insufficient quantity for hard-work-ing men. We had no bread, and vegetables, of course, were quite out of the question. In a word, our fare was not sumptuous. Those who accom-modated themselves best to our mode of living were the Sandwich Islanders: salmon and elk were to them exquisite viands.

On the 11th of August a number of Chinoukes visited us, bringing a strange Indian who had, they said, something interesting to communicate. This savage told us, in fact, that he had been engaged with ten more of his countrymen by a Captain Ayres to hunt seals on the islands in Sir Francis Drake's Bay,[42] where these animals are very numerous, with a promise of being taken home and paid for their services; the Captain had left them on the islands to go southwardly and purchase provisions, he said, of the Spaniards of Monterey in California; but he had never returned: and they, believing that he had been wrecked, had embarked in a skiff which he had left them and had reached the main land, from which they were not far distant; but their skiff was shattered to pieces in the surf, and they had saved themselves by swimming. Believing that they were not far from the river Columbia, they had followed the shore, living, on the way, upon shell-fish and frogs; at last they arrived among strange Indians who, far from receiving them kindly, had killed eight of them and made the

[42]Sir Francis Drake's Bay may have been San Francisco Bay, or Bodega Bay in Sonoma County, where the Russians established Fort Ross in 1809, continuing its occupancy until 1841.

rest prisoners; but the Kélémoux, a neighboring tribe to the Clatsops, hearing that they were captives, had ransomed them.

These facts must have occurred in March or April, 1811. The Indian who gave us an account of them appeared to have a great deal of intelligence and knew some words of the English language. He added that he had been at the Russian trading post at Chitka, that he had visited the coast of California, the Sandwich Islands, and even China.

About this time old Comcomly sent to Astoria for Mr. Stuart and me to come and cure him of a swelled throat, which, he said, afflicted him sorely. As it was late in the day we postponed till to-morrow going to cure the chief of the Chinooks; and it was well we did; for the same evening the wife of the Indian who had accompanied us in our voyage to the Falls sent us word that Comcomly was perfectly well, the pretended tonsillitis being only a pretext to get us in his power. This timely advice kept us at home.

Chapter X

Desertion and Pursuit

ON the 26th of September our house was finished, and we took possession of it. The mason work had at first caused us some difficulty; but at last, not being able to make lime for want of lime-stones, we employed blue clay as a substitute for mortar. This dwelling-house was sufficiently spacious to hold all our company, and we had distributed it in the most convenient manner that we could. It comprised a sitting, a dining room, some lodging or sleeping rooms, and an apartment for the men and artificers, all under the same roof. We also completed a shop for the blacksmith, who till that time had worked in the open air.[43]

The schooner, the construction of which had necessarily languished for want of an adequate force at the ship-yard, was finally launched on the 2d of October and named the *Dolly*, with the

[43]Compare Alexander Ross's account in *First Settlers on the Oregon*, Chap. 2. Beginning with a mere "house," the Astorians soon developed a fort, containing several buildings for defense against hostile Indians. For a good account of the subsequent additions, and the final decline of Astoria —renamed Fort George by the North West Company— see Grace P. Morris, "Development of Astoria, 1811–1850" in *Oregon Hist. Quarterly*, XXXVIII, 413–24.

formalities usual on such occasions. I was on that day at Young's Bay, where I saw the ruins of the quarters erected by Captains Lewis and Clark, in 1805–06:[44] they were but piles of rough, unhewn logs, overgrown with parasite creepers.[45]

On the evening of the 5th, Messrs. Pillet and McClellan arrived from the party of Mr. David Stuart in a canoe manned by two of his men. They brought as passengers Mr. Régis Bruguier, whom I had known in Canada as a respectable country merchant, and an Iroquois family. Mr. Bruguier had been a trader among the Indians on the Saskatchewine River, where he had lost his outfit: he had since turned trapper and had come into this region to hunt beaver, being provided with traps and other needful implements. The report which these gentlemen gave of the interior was highly satisfactory: they had found the climate salubrious, and had been well received

[44]Fort Clatsop, occupied by Lewis and Clark from December 24, 1805 to March 23, 1806. In 1901 the site, a short distance up Lewis and Clark River from Young's Bay, was acquired by the Oregon Historical Society. In 1836 John K. Townsend visited the site and reported that the log walls were still perfect, but the bark roof had disappeared and the entire vicinity had become overgrown with thorn and wild currant bushes. *Narrative of Journey Across the Rocky Mountains. . . .* (Philadelphia, 1839), 256. Reprinted in R. G. Thwaites' *Early Western Travels*, XXI, 362.

[45]This statement is not found in the Manuscript, nor in the 1820 edition of the narrative.

by the natives. The latter possessed a great number of horses and Mr. Stuart had purchased several of these animals at a low price. Ascending the river, they had come to a pretty stream, which the natives called Okenakane. Mr. Stuart had resolved to establish his post[46] on the bank of this river, and having erected a log-house he thought best to send back the above named persons, retaining with him for the winter only Messrs. Ross and de Montigny, and two men.*

Meanwhile, the season being come when the Indians quit the seashore and the banks of the Columbia to retire into the woods and establish their winter quarters along the small streams and rivers, we began to find ourselves short of provisions, having received no supplies from them for some time. It was therefore determined that Mr. R. Stuart should set out in the schooner with Mr. Mumford for the threefold purpose of ob-

[46]Fort Okanogan, founded as here described, was on the east bank of the Okanogan River, close to its junction with the Columbia, in present-day Okanogan County, Washington. Upon the acquisition of Astoria by the North West Company, November 12, 1813, Fort Okanogan was made the principal post of deposit for the entire region by the latter. The Hudson's Bay Company, which absorbed the North West Company in 1821, continued to maintain the post until 1859.

*One of these men had been left with him by Mr. Thompson, in exchange for a Sandwich Islander whom that gentleman proposed to take to Canada.

taining all the provisions they could, cutting
oaken staves for the use of the cooper, and trading with the Indians up the river. They left with
this design on the 12th. At the end of five days
Mr. Mumford returned in a canoe of Indians.
This man having wished to assume the command
and to order (in the style of Captain Thorn) the
person who had engaged him to obey, had been
sent back in consequence to Astoria.[47]

On the 10th of November we discovered that
three of our people had absconded, viz., P. D.
Jeremie and the two Belleaux. They had leave to
go out shooting for two days, and carried off with
them firearms and ammunition and a handsome
light Indian canoe. As soon as their flight was
known, having procured a large canoe of the
Chinooks we embarked, Mr. Matthews and I, with
five natives, to pursue them, with orders to proceed as far as the Falls if necessary. On the 11th,
having ascended the river to a place called Oak
Point, we overtook the schooner lying at anchor
while Mr. Stuart was taking in a load of staves

[47]Captain Thorn had frequently quarrelled with Mumford, who was second mate of the *Tonquin*. Upon the departure of the ship from Astoria on its final tragic voyage,
Thorn refused to take Mumford along, an action which
Alexander McKay feelingly deplored. Ross, *First Settlers
on the Oregon*, 88–89. Save for the present comment by
Franchère, only favorable mentions of Mumford have
been noted.

and hoop-poles. Mr. Farnham[48] joined our party, as well as one of the hands, and thus reinforced we pursued our way, journeying day and night and stopping at every Indian village to make inquiries and offer a reward for the apprehension of our runaways. Having reached the Falls without finding any trace of them, and our provisions giving out, we retraced our steps and arrived on the 16th at Oak Point, which we found Mr. Stuart ready to quit.

Meanwhile, the natives of the vicinity informed us that they had seen the marks of shoes imprinted on the sand at the confluence of a small stream in the neighborhood. We got three small

[48]Russell Farnham (1784–1832), for whom see sketch in *Dict. Am. Biog.* He was one of the more active members of the Astorian expedition. Upon the sale of Astoria to the North West Company in November, 1813, Farnham was appointed to carry to Astor the Pacific Fur Company records and funds. On April 3, 1814 he sailed in the *Pedlar* for Kamtchatka, from where he started afoot across Siberia, eventually reaching Saint Petersburg and Copenhagen. In October, 1816 he sailed from Copenhagen for Baltimore and finally delivered the records to Astor, having completed, single-handed, one of the most arduous missions of which we have record. The remainder of his life was spent in Astor's employ, engaged in fur-trade activities chiefly on the Upper Mississippi. He established a home at Portage des Sioux, above Saint Louis, where he died of cholera in 1832. Contemporary acquaintances spoke highly of his character, and Ramsay Crooks, who had ample reason for knowing, stated that he underwent greater hardships "than any half dozen of us."

canoes carrying two persons each, and having ascertained that the information was correct, after searching the environs during a part of the 17th we ascended the small stream as far as some high lands which are seen from Oak Point, and which lie about eight or nine miles south of it. The space between these high lands and the ridge crowned with oaks on the bank of the Columbia is a low and swampy land, cut up by an infinity of little channels. Toward evening we returned on our path to regain the schooner; but instead of taking the circuitous way of the river, by which we had come, we made for Oak Point by the most direct route through these channels; but night coming on, we lost ourselves. Our situation became the most disagreeable that can be imagined. Being unable to find a place where we could land, on account of the morass, we were obliged to continue rowing, or rather turning round, in this species of labyrinth, constantly kneeling in our little canoes, which any unlucky movement would infallibly have caused to upset. It rained in torrents and was dark as pitch. At last, after having wandered about during a considerable part of the night we succeeded in gaining the edge of the mainland. Leaving there our canoes because we could not drag them (as we attempted) through the forest, we crossed the woods in the darkness, tearing ourselves with the brush, and reached the schooner at about two in the morning, benumbed with cold and exhausted with fatigue.

The 18th was spent in getting in the remainder of the lading of the little vessel, and on the morning of the 19th we raised anchor and dropped down abreast of the Kreluit village, where some of the Indians offering to aid us in the search after our deserters, Mr. Stuart put Mr. Farnham and me on shore to make another attempt. We passed that day in drying our clothes and the next day embarked in a canoe with one Kreluit man and a squaw, and ascended the river before described as entering the Columbia at this place. We soon met a canoe of natives who informed us that our runaways had been made prisoners by the chief of a tribe which dwells upon the banks of the Willamet River, and which they called Cathlanaminimin. We kept on and encamped on a beach of sand opposite Deer Island. There we passed a night almost as disagreeable as that of the 17th–18th. We had lighted a fire and contrived a shelter of mats; but there came on presently a violent gust of wind, accompanied with a heavy rain: our fire was put out, our mats were carried away, and we could neither rekindle the one nor find the others: so that we had to remain all night exposed to the fury of the storm. As soon as it was day we re-embarked and set our-

selves to paddling with all our might to warm
ourselves. In the evening we arrived near the
village where our deserters were and saw one of
them on the skirts of it. We proceeded to the hut
of the chief where we found all three, more inclined to follow us than to remain as slaves among
these barbarians. We passed the night in the
chief's lodge, not without some fear and some
precaution; this chief having the reputation of
being a wicked man and capable of violating the
rights of parties. He was a man of high stature
and a good mien, and proud in proportion, as
we discovered by the chilling and haughty manner in which he received us. Farnham and I
agreed to keep watch alternately, but this arrangement was superfluous as neither of us could
sleep a wink for the infernal thumping and singing made by the medicine men all night long by
a dying native. I had an opportunity of seeing
the sick man make his last will and testament:
having caused to be brought to him whatever he
had that was most precious, his bracelets of copper, his bead necklace, his bow and arrows and
quiver, his nets, his lines, his spear, his pipe, &c.,
he distributed the whole to his most intimate
friends, with a promise on their part to restore
them, if he recovered.

On the 22d, after a great deal of talk and infinite quibbling on the part of the chief, we agreed

with him for the ransom of our men. I had visited
every lodge in the village and found but few of
the young men, the greater part having gone on
a fishing excursion; knowing, therefore, that the
chief could not be supported by his warriors, I
was resolved not to be imposed upon, and as I knew
where the firearms of the fugitives had been deposited I would have them at all hazards; but we
were obliged to give him all our blankets, amount-
ing to eight, a brass kettle, a hatchet, a small pis-
tol, much out of order, a powder-horn, and some
rounds of ammunition: with these articles placed
in a pile before him we demanded the men's
clothing, the three fowling-pieces, and their canoe, which he had caused to be hidden in the
woods. Nothing but our firmness compelled him
to accept the articles offered in exchange; but at
last, with great reluctance, he closed the bargain
and suffered us to depart in the evening with the
prisoners and the property.

We all five (including the three deserters) embarked in the large canoe, leaving our Kreluit
and his wife to follow in the other, and proceeded
as far as the Cowlitzk, where we camped. The
next day we pursued our journey homeward,
only stopping at the Kreluit village to get some
provisions, and soon entered the group of islands
which crowd the river above Gray's Bay. On one
of these we stopped to amuse ourselves with

shooting some ducks, and meanwhile a smart breeze springing up, we split open a double-rush mat (which had served as a bag) to make a sail, and having cut a forked sapling for a mast, shipped a few boulders to stay the foot of it and spread our canvass to the wind. We soon arrived in sight of Gray's Bay, at a distance of fourteen or fifteen miles from our establishment. We had, notwithstanding, a long passage across, the river forming in this place, as I have before observed, a sort of lake, by the recession of its shores on either hand: but the wind was fair. We undertook, then, to cross and quitted the island to enter the broad, lake-like expanse just as the sun was going down, hoping to reach Astoria in a couple of hours.

We were not long before we repented of our temerity: for in a short time the sky became overcast, the wind increased till it blew with violence and, meeting with the tide, caused the waves to rise prodigiously, which broke over our wretched canoe and filled it with water. We lightened it as much as we could by throwing overboard the little baggage we had left, and I set the men to baling with our remaining brass kettle. At last, after having been for three hours the sport of the raging billows and threatened every instant with being swallowed up, we had the unexpected happiness of landing in a cove on the north shore of the river. Our first care was to thank the Almighty for having delivered us from so imminent a danger. Then, when we had secured the canoe, we groped our way to the forest, where we made with branches of trees a shelter against the wind—still continuing to blow with violence—and kindled a great fire to warm us and dry our clothes. That did not prevent us from shivering the rest of the night, even in congratulating ourselves on the happiness of setting our foot on shore at the moment when we began quite to despair of saving ourselves at all.

The morning of the 24th brought with it a clear sky, but no abatement in the violence of the wind till toward evening, when we again embarked and arrived with our deserters at the establishment, where they never expected to see us again. Some Indians who had followed us in a canoe up to the moment when we undertook the passage across the evening before, had followed the southern shore and making the portage of the isthmus of Tongue Point had happily arrived at Astoria. These natives, not doubting that we were lost, so reported us to Mr. McDougall; accordingly that gentleman was equally overjoyed and astonished at beholding us safely landed, which procured, not only for us, but for the culprits, our companions, a cordial and hearty reception.

Chapter XI
Arrival of Overland Party

THE natives having given us to understand that beaver was very abundant in the country watered by the Cowlitz, Mr. R. Stuart procured a guide and set out on the 5th of December, accompanied by Messrs. Pillet and McGillis and a few of the men, to ascend that river and ascertain whether or no it would be advisable to establish a trading-post on its banks. Mr. R. Bruguier accompanied them to follow his pursuits as a trapper.

The season at which we expected the return of the *Tonquin* was now past, and we began to regard as too probable the report of the Indians of Gray's Harbor. We still flattered ourselves, notwithstanding, with the hope that perhaps that vessel had sailed for the East Indies without touching at Astoria; but this was at most a conjecture.

The 25th, Christmas Day, passed very agreeably: we treated the men on that day with the best the establishment afforded. Although that was no great affair, they seemed well satisfied; for they had been restricted during the last few months to a very meager diet, living, as one may say, on sun-dried fish. On the 27th, the schooner having returned from her second voyage up the river, we dismantled her and laid her up for the winter at the entrance of a small creek.

The weather, which had been raining almost without interruption from the beginning of October, cleared up on the evening of the 31st; and the 1st of January, 1812, brought us a clear and serene sky. We proclaimed the new year with a discharge of artillery. A small allowance of spirits was served to the men and the day passed in gayety, every one amusing himself as well as he could.

The festival over, our people resumed their ordinary occupations: while some cut timber for building and others made charcoal for the blacksmith the carpenter constructed a barge and the cooper made barrels for the use of the posts we proposed to establish in the interior. On the 18th in the evening two canoes full of white men arrived at the establishment. Mr. McDougall the resident agent, being confined to his room by sickness, the duty of receiving the strangers devolved on me. My astonishment was not slight when one of the party called me by name as he extended his hand, and I recognized Mr. Donald McKenzie, the same who had quitted Montreal with Mr. W. P. Hunt in the month of July, 1810. He was accompanied by a Mr. Robert McClellan,[49]

[49]Robert McClellan (1770–1815) was famous for his feats as a scout under General Anthony Wayne in the

a partner, Mr. John Reed, a clerk, and eight voyageurs, or boatmen. After having reposed themselves a little from their fatigues, these gentlemen recounted to us the history of their journey, of which the following is the substance.

Messrs. Hunt and McKenzie, quitting Canada, proceeded by way of Mackinac and St. Louis and ascended the Missouri in the autumn of 1810 to a place on that river called Nadoway.[50] where they wintered. Here they were joined by Mr. R. McClellan, by a Mr. Crooks[51] and a Mr. Miller,[52]

Northwestern Indian warfare of 1792 to 1794. In company with Ramsay Crooks he was one of the first Americans to embark upon the fur trade of the Upper Missouri (in 1807). Indian hostilities and other misfortunes dogged his career, and he died in obscurity near Saint Louis in 1815. His tombstone, rediscovered in 1875, bears an inscription thought to have been written by Governor William Clark: "Brave, honest and sincere; an intrepid warrior, whose services deserve perpetual remembrance." *Dict. Am. Biog.*

[50]"Nadaoi" in 1820 edition; not found in Manuscript. The Nodaway River takes its rise in several affluent streams in Cass, Adair and Adams counties, Iowa, and flows almost due south to its junction with the Missouri about ten miles north of Saint Joseph, on the boundary between Holt and Andrew counties.

[51]Ramsay Crooks, whose career is noted in Thomas James' *Three Years Among the Indians and Mexicans,* the Lakeside Classics volume for 1953. Born in 1787, Crooks was but 24 years old in 1811, yet he was already a veteran of the Indian trade.

[52]Joseph Miller, formerly a lieutenant in the First U.S. Infantry and associate of Ramsay Crooks and Robert

traders with the Indians of the South, and all having business relations with Mr. Astor.

In the spring of 1811, having procured two large keel-boats, they ascended the Missouri to the country of the Arikaras, or Rés Indians, where they disposed of their boats and a great part of their luggage to a Spanish trader, by name Manuel Lisa.[53] Having purchased of him and among the Indians 130 horses, they resumed their route in the beginning of August to the number of some sixty-five persons, to proceed across the mountains to the river Columbia. Wishing to avoid the Blackfoot Indians, a warlike and ferocious tribe who put to death all the strangers that fall into their hands, they directed their course southwardly until they arrived at the 40th degree of latitude.[54] Thence they turned to the

McClellan in their Upper Missouri trading enterprises. Ross credits Miller's influence as responsible in large degree for the successful organization of Wilson P. Hunt's overland party at Saint Louis in 1810. *First Settlers on the Oregon*, 191. For the misfortunes encountered by Miller following his withdrawal from Astoria see Ross's narrative, Chapter XIV.

[53]For the career of Manuel Lisa see Thomas James' *Three Years Among the Indians and Mexicans*, pp. 10–11. Lisa was one of the first and most active of the Saint Louis merchants who engaged in the Upper Missouri fur trade.

[54]For the origin of the hostility of the Blackfeet toward the whites see Thomas James, *Three Years Among the Indians and Mexicans*, 52. The difficulties with them encountered by the members of General James' party in

northwest, and arrived, by-and-by, at an old fort or trading post on the banks of a little river flowing west. This post, which was then deserted, had been established, as they afterward learned, by a trader named Henry.[55] Our people, not doubting that this stream would conduct them to the Columbia, and finding it navigable, constructed some canoes to descend it. Having left some hunters (or trappers) near the old fort with Mr. Miller, who, dissatisfied with the expedition, was resolved to return to the United States, the party embarked; but very soon finding the river obstructed with rapids and waterfalls, after having upset some of the canoes, lost one man by drowning, and also a part of their baggage, perceiving

1809–10 are recited in subsequent pages of this volume (consult index). Since its leaders and other surviving members had but recently returned to Saint Louis when Hunt arrived to organize his overland party, he, of course, received ample briefing on the character of the Blackfeet.

[55] Andrew Henry, who in 1810–11 wintered on Henry's Fork of Snake River. See Thomas James, *Three Years Among the Indians and Mexicans,* pp. 34–35 and 80–81. Henry's fort was in Fremont County, Idaho, not far from the site of present-day St. Anthony. William P. Hunt's diary of the overland journey was published, oddly enough, at Paris in 1821, the second Astorian narrative to appear in print. An English translation was published by Philip A. Rollins in 1935 as App. A of *The Discovery of the Oregon Trail Robert Stuart's Narratives . . . of his Overland Trip Eastward from Astoria in 1812–13* (New York, 1935).

that the stream was impracticable, they resolved to abandon their canoes and proceed on foot. The enterprise was one of great difficulty, considering the small stock of provisions they had left. Nevertheless, as there was no time to lose in deliberation, after depositing in a cache the superfluous part of their baggage they divided themselves into four companies under the command of Messrs. McKenzie, Hunt, McClellan, and Crooks, and proceeded to follow the course of the stream, which they named Mad River on account of the insurmountable difficulties it presented. Messrs. McKenzie and McLellan took the right bank, and Messrs. Hunt and Crooks the left. They counted on arriving very quickly at the Columbia; but they followed this Mad River for twenty days, finding nothing at all to eat and suffering horribly from thirst. The rocks between which the river flows being so steep and abrupt as to prevent their descending to quench their thirst (so that even their dogs died of it) they suffered the torments of Tantalus, with this difference that he had the water which he could not reach above his head, while our travellers had it beneath their feet. Several, not to die of this raging thirst, drank their own urine: all, to appease the cravings of hunger, ate beaver skins roasted in the evening at the camp-fire. They even were at last constrained to eat their moccasins. Those on the left or southeast bank suffered, however, less than the others, because they occasionally fell in with Indians, utterly wild, indeed, and who fled at their approach, carrying off their horses. According to all appearances these savages had never seen white men. Our travellers, when they arrived in sight of the camp of one of these wandering hordes, approached it with as much precaution and with the same stratagem that they would have used with a troop of wild beasts. Having thus surprised them, they would fire upon the horses, some of which would fall; but they took care to leave some trinkets on the spot to indemnify the owners for what they had taken from them by violence. This resource prevented the party from perishing of hunger.

Mr. McKenzie having overtaken Mr. McClellan, their two companies pursued the journey together. Very soon after this junction they had an opportunity of approaching sufficiently near to Mr. Hunt, who, as I have remarked, was on the other bank, to speak to him and inform him of their distressed state. Mr. Hunt caused a canoe to be made of a horse-hide; it was not, as one may suppose, very large; but they succeeded nevertheless, by that means in conveying a little horse-flesh to the people on the north bank. It was attempted, even, to pass them across, one by one (for the skiff would not hold any more); several had actually crossed to the south side when, unhappily, owing to the impetuosity of the current the canoe capsized, a man was drowned, and the two parties lost all hope of being able to unite. They continued their route, therefore, each on their own side of the river. In a short time those upon the north bank came to a more considerable stream, which they followed down.[56] They also met, very opportunely, some Indians who sold

[56]The river whose descent is so vividly described is the Snake. It rises in the southern part of Yellowstone Park and after a circuitous course southward, westward, and northward, joins the Columbia in the vicinity of Pasco in southeastern Washington. Apart from its tempestuous current, the river flows through canyons 1000 to 4000 feet deep.

The drowned man was a Canadian, Jean Baptiste Prevost. The traveler Bradbury relates that he had become insane through starvation, and on seeing the horse flesh (which Hunt's party had obtained) on the opposite side of the river he was so agitated in crossing in a skin canoe (contrived by the party from a horsehide) that he upset it, and was unfortunately drowned. Bradbury's narrative in Thwaites (Ed.) *Early Western Travels*, V 232-33.

One of the members of the overland party was Charles Boucher of Berthier, Quebec. Born in 1777 and the father of several children, he was a veteran voyageur, long since inured to the hazards of the fur trade. On one of his journeys through the Detroit River he was so captivated by the appearance of Grosse Ile that he determined to make his future home there. About the year 1829 he purchased a farm site (a portion of which is still owned by descendants) and lived on the Island until his death in 1865. Practically illiterate, he kept no journal, but at a subsequent time dictated certain of his recollections ("about half a dozen pages") to a neighbor, and

them a number of horses. They also encountered in these parts a young American who was deranged, but who sometimes recovered his reason. This young man told them, in one of his lucid intervals, that he was from Connecticut and was named Archibald Pelton; that he had come up the Missouri[57] with Mr. Henry; that all the people at the post established by that trader were massacred by the Blackfeet; that he alone had escaped, and had been wandering, for three years since, with the Snake Indians. Our people took this young man with them. Arriving at the confluence with the Columbia, of the river whose banks they were following, they perceived that it was the same which had been called Lewis River by the American captain of that name in 1805. Here, then, they exchanged their remaining horses for canoes and so arrived at the establishment, safe and sound, it is true, but in a pitiable condition to see; their clothes being nothing but fluttering rags.[57]

this record was retained by a granddaughter until recently. One of Boucher's stories, handed down by word of mouth in the family, concerns the tragic crossing of the Snake. Boucher was in a canoe which capsized. He escaped drowning by clinging to a rock, but in the melee one of his fingers was broken and remained crippled until the end of his life. Information supplied by his granddaughter, Mrs. Karl F. F. Kurth of Detroit in interview of April 10, 1954.

[57]For the pathetic story of Archibald Pelton see Thomas James, *Three Years Among the Indians and Mexicans*,

The narrative of these gentlemen interested us very much. They added, that since their separation from Messrs. Hunt and Crooks they had neither seen nor heard aught of them, and believed it impossible that they should arrive at the establishment before spring. They were mistaken, however, for Mr. Hunt arrived on the 15th February with thirty men, one woman, and two children, having left Mr. Crooks with five men among the Snakes. They might have reached Astoria almost as soon as Mr. McKenzie, but they had passed from eight to ten days in the midst of a plain, among some friendly Indians, as well to recruit their strength as to make search for two of the party who had been lost in the woods. Not finding them, they had resumed their journey and struck the banks of the Columbia a little low-

80–81. J. Neilson Barry in an article entitled "Archibald Pelton First Follower of Lewis and Clark," published in *Wash. Hist. Quarterly,* XIX, 199–201, supplies additional interesting information, chiefly derived from Ross Cox's *Adventures on the Columbia River.* Pelton remained at Fort George after the purchase by the North West Company, and is supposed to have been murdered there, while engaged in chopping timber, by two Chinook Indians. The latter were tried for the killing before a jury made up of North West Company members and an equal number of male and female Indian chiefs. Thus it fell to the lot of poor, clownish Pelton to be the first white man to retrace the route of Lewis and Clark and to become the subject of the first murder trial ever held in Oregon.

er down than the mouth of Lewis River, where Mr. McKenzie had come out.

The arrival of so great a number of persons would have embarrassed us had it taken place a month sooner. Happily, at this time the natives were bringing in fresh fish in abundance. Until the 30th of March we were occupied in preparing triplicates of letters and other necessary papers in order to send Mr. Astor the news of our arrival and of the reunion of the two expeditions. The letters were entrusted to Mr. John Reed, who quitted Astoria[58] for St. Louis in company with Mr. McClellan—another discontented partner who wished to disconnect himself with the association—and Mr. R. Stuart, who was conveying two canoe-loads of goods for his Uncle's post on the Okenakan. Messrs. Farnham and McGillis set out at the same time, with a guide, and were instructed to proceed to the cache, where the overland travellers had hidden their goods near old Fort Henry on the Mad River. I profited by this opportunity to write to my family in Canada. Two days after, Messrs. McKenzie and Matthews set out, with five or six men as hunters, to make an excursion up the Willamet River.

[58]Both the Manuscript and the 1820 edition say at this point: "the name we had given our establishment." This is the first time the name is mentioned by Franchère.

CHAPTER XII
Trading and Exploring Activities

FROM the departure of the last outfit under Mr. McKenzie nothing remarkable took place at Astoria till the 9th of May. On that day we descried, to our great surprise and great joy, a sail in the offing opposite the mouth of the river. Forthwith Mr. McDougall was despatched in a boat to the Cape to make the signals. On the morning of the 10th, the weather being fine and the sea smooth, the boat pushed out and arrived safely alongside. Soon after, the wind springing up, the vessel made sail and entered the river, where she dropped anchor in Baker Bay, at about 2 P. M. Toward evening the boat returned to the Fort, with the following passengers: Messrs. John Clarke of Canada (a wintering partner), Alfred Seton, George Ehnainger, a nephew of Mr. Astor (clerks), and two men. We learned from these gentlemen that the vessel was the *Beaver*, Captain Cornelius Sowles, and was consigned to us; that she left New York on the 10th of October and had touched, in the passage, at Massa Fuero and the Sandwich Isles. Mr. Clarke handed me letters from my father and from several of my friends: I thus learned that death had deprived me of a beloved sister.

On the morning of the 11th we were strangely surprised by the return of Messrs. D. Stuart, R. Stuart, R. McClellan, Crooks, Reed, and Farnham. This return, as sudden as unlooked for, was owing to an unfortunate adventure which befell the party, in ascending the river. When they reached the Falls, where the portage is very long, some natives came with their horses to offer their aid in transporting the goods. Mr. R. Stuart, not distrusting them, confided to their care some bales of merchandise which they packed on their horses: but in making the transit they darted up a narrow path among the rocks and fled at full gallop toward the prairie, without its being possible to overtake them. Mr. Stuart had several shots fired over their heads to frighten them but it had no other effect than to increase their speed. Meanwhile our own people continued the transportation of the rest of the goods and of the canoes; but as there was a great number of natives about, whom the success and impunity of those thieves had emboldened, Mr. Stuart thought it prudent to keep watch over the goods at the upper end of the portage while Messrs. McClellan and Reed made the rearguard. The last named gentleman, who carried strapped to his shoulders a tin box containing the letters and despatches for New York with which he was charged, happened to be at some distance from the former,

and the Indians thought it a favorable opportunity to attack him and carry off his box, the
brightness of which no doubt had tempted their
cupidity. They threw themselves upon him so
suddenly that he had no time to place himself on
the defensive. After a short resistance he received
a blow on the head from a war club, which felled
him to the ground, and the Indians seized upon
their booty. Mr. McClellan perceiving what was
done, fired his carbine at one of the robbers and
made him bite the dust; the rest took to flight,
but carried off the box notwithstanding. Mr. Mc-
Clellan immediately ran up to Mr. Reed; but finding the latter motionless and bathed in blood, he
hastened to rejoin Mr. Stuart, urging him to get
away from these robbers and murderers. But Mr.
Stuart being a self-possessed and fearless man,
would not proceed without ascertaining if Mr.
Reed were really dead, or, if he were, without
carrying off his body; and notwithstanding the
remonstrances of Mr. McClellan, taking his way
back to the spot where the latter had left his companion, had not gone two hundred paces when he
met him coming toward them, holding his bleeding head with both hands.[59]

[59]The Manuscript states at this point: "We were informed of this unfortunate affair by natives from up the
river on the 15th of April." To this, the 1820 edition
adds, "but disbelieved it." In the 1854 edition Hunting-

The object of Mr. Reed's journey being defeated by the loss of his papers, he repaired with the other gentlemen to Mr. David Stuart's trading post at Okenakan, whence they had all set out in the beginning of May to return to Astoria. Coming down the river, they fell in with Mr. R. Crooks and a man named John Day.[60] It was observed in the preceding chapter that Mr. Crooks remained with five men among some Indians who were there termed friendly: but this gentleman and his companion were the only members of that party who ever reached the establishment: and they, too, arrived in a most pitiable condition, the savages having stripped them of everything, leaving them but some bits of deerskin to cover their nakedness.[61]

ton indulges in a somewhat lengthy commentary which we do not reprint.

[60]John Day was a Virginian who joined Hunt's party at its winter camp on the Nodaway, above Saint Joseph. In 1813 he joined the party which Robert Stuart led overland to Saint Louis, but becoming insane early on the journey was conducted back to Astoria by friendly Indians. For the experiences of Day and Ramsay Crooks on the outward journey to Astoria see Alexander Ross, *First Settlers on the Oregon,* 202–207. Irving reports that Day died at Astoria the following year. Thwaites, however, states that there is evidence he joined the North West Company and lived until 1819. *Early Western Travels,* V, 181. John Day River in central Oregon preserves his memory.

[61]The tribe with which Crooks and his companions were left had in fact loyally befriended them. The out-

On the 12th the schooner, which had been sent down the river to the *Beaver's* anchorage, returned with a cargo (being the stores intended for Astoria), and the following passengers: to wit, Messrs. B. Clapp, J. C. Halsey, C. A. Nichols, and R. Cox, clerks; five Canadians, seven Americans (all mechanics), and a dozen Sandwich Islanders for the service of the establishment. The captain of the *Beaver* sounded the channel diligently for several days; but finding it scarcely deep enough for so large a vessel, he was unwilling to bring her up to Astoria. It was necessary, in consequence, to use the schooner as a lighter in discharging the ship, and this tedious operation occupied us during the balance of this month and a part of June.

Captain Sowles and Mr. Clarke confirmed the report of the destruction of the *Tonquin;* they had learned it at Owyhee by means of a letter which a certain Captain Ebbetts, in the employ of Mr. Astor, had left there. It was nevertheless resolved that Mr. Hunt should embark upon the *Beaver* to carry out the plan of an exact commercial survey of the coast which Mr. McKay had been sent to accomplish, and in particular to visit for that purpose the Russian establishment at Chitka Sound.

rage to Crooks and Day which Franchère relates was perpetrated by another band living much closer to Astoria.

The necessary papers having been prepared anew, and being now ready to expedite, were confided to Mr. R. Stuart, who was to cross the continent in company with Messrs. Crooks and R. McClellan, partners dissatisfied with the enterprise, and who had made up their minds to return to the United States.[62] Mr. Clarke, accompanied by Messrs. Pillet, Donald, McLennan, Farnham, and Cox, was fitted out at the same time with a considerable assortment of merchandise to form a new establishment on the Spokan or Clarke's River. Mr. McKenzie, with Mr. Seton, was destined for the borders of Lewis River.[63] while Mr. David Stuart, reinforced by Messrs. Matthews and McGillis, was to explore the region lying north of his post at Okenakan. All these outfits being ready, with the canoes, boatmen, and hunters, the flotilla quitted Astoria on the 30th of June in the afternoon, having on board sixty-two persons. The sequel will show the result of the several expeditions.

[62]Stuart's journal of his return journey to Saint Louis, in whose course he traversed, and probably discovered, the South Pass, famous in the subsequent history of the Oregon Trail, was published by Philip A. Rollins (Ed.), *The Discovery of the Oregon Trail . . .*

[63]At the mouth of Payette River according to Thwaites, *Early Western Travels,* VI, 277. The map which accompanies the original edition of Alexander Ross, *First Settlers on the Oregon,* places it at the mouth of Boise River. Both locations are in western Idaho on the Idaho-Oregon boundary.

During the whole month of July the natives (seeing us weakened, no doubt, by these outfits), manifested their hostile intentions so openly that we were obliged to be constantly on our guard. We constructed covered ways inside our palisades and raised our bastions or towers another story. The alarm became so serious toward the latter end of the month that we doubled our sentries day and night, and never allowed more than two or three Indians at a time within our gates.

The *Beaver* was ready to depart on her coasting voyage at the end of June, and on the 1st of July Mr. Hunt went on board: but westerly winds prevailing all that month, it was not till the 4th of August that she was able to get out of the river; being due again by the end of October to leave her surplus goods and take in our furs for market.

The months of August and September were employed in finishing a house forty-five feet by thirty, shingled and perfectly tight, as a hospital for the sick and lodging house for the mechanics.

Experience having taught us that from the beginning of October to the end of January provisions were brought in by the natives in very small quantity, it was thought expedient that I should proceed in the schooner, accompanied by Mr. Clapp, on a trading voyage up the river to secure a cargo of dried fish. We left Astoria on the 1st of October with a small assortment of merchandise. The trip was highly successful: we found the game very abundant, killed a great quantity of swans, ducks, foxes, &c., and returned to Astoria on the 20th with a part of our venison, wild fowl, and bear meat besides seven hundred and fifty smoked salmon, a quantity of the Wapto root (so called by the natives), which is found a good substitute for potatoes, and four hundred and fifty skins of beaver and other animals of the furry tribe.

The encouragement derived from this excursion induced us to try a second, and I set off this time alone, that is, with a crew of five men only and an Indian boy, son of the old chief Comcomly. This second voyage proved anything but agreeable. We experienced continual rains and the game was much less abundant, while the natives had mostly left the river for their wintering grounds. I succeeded, nevertheless, in exchanging my goods for furs and dried fish and a small supply of dried venison: and returned on the 15th of November to Astoria, where the want of fresh provisions began to be severely felt, so that several of the men were attacked with scurvy.

Messrs. Halsey and Wallace having been sent on the 23d with fourteen men to establish a trading post on the Willamet and Mr. McDougall being confined to his room by sickness, Mr.

Clapp and I were left with the entire charge of the post at Astoria, and were each other's only resource for society. Happily Mr. Clapp was a man of amiable character, of a gay, lively humor and agreeable conversation. In the intervals of our daily duties we amused ourselves with music and reading, having some instruments and a choice library. Otherwise we should have passed our time in a state of insufferable ennui at this rainy season, in the midst of the deep mud which surrounded us and which interdicted the pleasure of a promenade outside the buildings.

CHAPTER XIII

War and Confusion

THE months of October, November, and December passed away without any news of the *Beaver* and we began to fear that there had happened to her, as to the *Tonquin,* some disastrous accident. It will be seen in the following chapter why this vessel did not return to Astoria in the autumn of 1812.

On the 15th of January Mr. McKenzie arrived from the interior, having abandoned his trading establishment, after securing his stock of goods in a cache. Before his departure he had paid a visit to Mr. Clarke on the Spokan, and while there had learned the news, which he came to announce to us, that hostilities had actually commenced between Great Britain and the United States. The news had been brought by some gentlemen of the North West Company, who handed to them a copy of the Proclamation of the President to that effect.

When we learned this news all of us at Astoria who were British subjects and Canadians wished ourselves in Canada; but we could not entertain even the thought of transporting ourselves thither, at least immediately; we were separated from our country by an immense space, and the diffi-

culties of the journey at this season were insuper-
able: besides, Mr. Astor's interests had to be
consulted first. We held, therefore, a sort of
council of war, to which the clerks of the factory
were invited *pro formâ,* as they had no voice in
the deliberations. Having maturely weighed our
situation; after having seriously considered that
being almost to a man British subjects we were
trading, notwithstanding, under the American
flag: and foreseeing the improbability, or rather,
to cut the matter short, the impossibility that
Mr. Astor could send us further supplies or rein-
forcements while the war lasted, as most of the
ports of the United States would inevitably be
blockaded by the British; we concluded to abandon the establishment in the ensuing spring or,
at latest, in the beginning of the summer. We did
not communicate these resolutions to the men
lest they should in consequence abandon their
labor: but we discontinued from that moment
our trade with the natives, except for provisions;
as well because we had no longer a large stock
of goods on hand, as for the reason that we had
already more furs than we could carry away
overland.

So long as we expected the return of the vessel
we had served out to the people a regular supply
of bread: we found ourselves, in consequence,
very short of provisions on the arrival of Mr.

McKenzie and his men. This augmentation in
the number of mouths to be fed compelled us to
reduce the ration of each man to four ounces
of flour and half a pound of dried fish per diem:
and even to send a portion of the hands to
pass the rest of the winter with Messrs. Wallace
and Halsey on the Willamet, where game was
plenty.

Meanwhile, the sturgeon having begun to enter the river, I left on the 13th of February to fish
for them; and on the 15th sent the first boat-load
to the establishment; which proved a very timely
succor to the men, who for several days had
broken off work from want of sufficient food. I
formed a camp near Oak Point, whence I continued to despatch canoe after canoe of fine fresh
fish to Astoria, and Mr. McDougall sent to me
thither all the men who were sick of scurvy, for
the re-establishment of their health.

On the 20th of March Messrs. Reed and Seton,
who had led a part of our men to the post on the
Willamet to subsist them, returned to Astoria
with a supply of dried venison. These gentlemen
spoke to us in glowing terms of the country of
the Willamet as charming, and abounding in beaver, elk, and deer; and informed us that Messrs.
Wallace and Halsey had constructed a dwelling
and trading house on a great prairie, about one
hundred and fifty miles from the confluence of

that river with the Columbia. Mr. McKenzie and his party quitted us again on the 31st to make known the resolutions recently adopted at Astoria to the gentlemen who were wintering in the interior.

On the 11th of April two birch-bark canoes, bearing the British flag, arrived at the factory. They were commanded by Messrs. J. G. McTavish and Joseph Larocque,[64] and manned by nineteen Canadian voyageurs. They landed on a point of land under the guns of the fort and formed their camp. We invited these gentlemen to our quarters and learned from them the object of their visit. They had come to await the arrival of the ship *Isaac Todd,* dispatched from Canada by

[64]Joseph Larocque had an elder brother, François, who figures in the narratives of the Lewis and Clark expedition. In the winter of 1804–1805, as a clerk employed by the North West Company he led a party from Fort Assiniboine to the Mandans where Lewis and Clark were wintering, and from June to October, 1805 he was engaged upon a tour to the Rocky Mountains. M. M. Quaife (Ed.), *Journals of Captain Meriwether Lewis and Sergeant John Ordway, Wis. Hist. Colls.,* XXII, 177. Joseph entered the Company's employ as a mere lad of fourteen, becoming proficient in the native languages. He continued in the employ of the North West and (following 1821) Hudson's Bay companies until 1833, when he retired, subsequently spending fourteen years in France. Returning to Canada, he "devoted himself to works of religion and charity" until his death at Ottawa in 1866. An account of his career is included in Joseph Tassé's *Les Canadiens de l'Ouest,* II, 321–38.

the North West Company in October, 1811 with furs, and from England in March, 1812 with a cargo of suitable merchandise for the Indian trade. They had orders to wait at the mouth of the Columbia till the month of July, and then to return, if the vessel did not make her appearance by that time. They also informed us that the natives near Lewis River had shown them fowling-pieces, gun-flints, lead, and powder; and that they had communicated this news to Mr. McKenzie, presuming that the Indians had discovered and plundered his cache; which turned afterward to be the case.

The month of May was occupied in preparations for our departure from the Columbia. On the 25th Messrs. Wallace and Halsey returned from their winter quarters with seventeen packs of furs and thirty-two bales of dried venison. The last article was received with a great deal of pleasure, as it would infallibly be needed for the journey we were about to undertake. Messrs. Clarke, D. Stuart, and McKenzie also arrived in the beginning of June with one hundred and forty packs of furs, the fruit of two years' trade at the post on the Okenakane, and one year on the Spokan.

The wintering partners (that is to say, Messrs. Clarke and David Stuart) dissenting from the proposal to abandon the country as soon as we

intended, the thing being (as they observed) impracticable from the want of provisions for the
journey and horses to transport the goods, the
project was deferred, as to its execution, till the
following April.[65] So these gentlemen, having
taken a new lot of merchandise, set out again for
their trading posts on the 7th of July. But Mr.
McKenzie, whose goods had been pillaged by the
natives (it will be remembered), remained at
Astoria, and was occupied with the care of col-
lecting as great a quantity as possible of dried
salmon from the Indians. He made seven or
eight voyages up the river for that purpose while
we at the Fort were busy in baling the beaver-
skins and other furs in suitable packs for horses
to carry. Mr. Reed, in the meantime, was sent on
to the mountain-passes where Mr. Miller had
been left with the trappers, to winter there and
to procure as many horses as he could from the
natives for our use on the contemplated journey.
He was furnished for this expedition with three
Canadians and a half-breed hunter named Daion,
the latter accompanied by his wife and two children. This man came from the lower Missouri
with Mr. Hunt in 1811–12.[66]

[65]The Manuscript adds: "for we had decided to follow
the route of Lewis and Clark and to descend the Missouri."

[66]Pierre Dorion Jr., whose father, Pierre, figures in the
Lewis and Clark journals. Pierre Dorion Jr.'s mother was

Our object being to provide ourselves, before quitting the country, with the food and horses necessary for the journey; in order to avoid all opposition on the part of the North West Company, we entered into an arrangement with Mr. McTavish.[67] This gentleman having represented to us that he was destitute of the necessary goods to procure wherewith to subsist his party on their way homeward, we supplied him from our warehouse, payment to be made us in the ensuing spring either in furs or in bills of exchange on their house in Canada.

a Sioux woman. For the tragic fate of Dorion and his family see *post,* Chap. 22.

[67]At this juncture "One of our young men, Rossenberg Cox, preferred to engage in the service of the (North West) Company rather than cross the Continent with us." Manuscript.

Chapter XIV

Fate of the Tonquin

ON the 4th of August, contrary to all expectation we saw a sail at the mouth of the river. One of our gentlemen immediately got into the barge to ascertain her nationality and object: but before he had fairly crossed the river we saw her pass the bar and direct her course toward Astoria, as if she were commanded by a captain to whom the intricacies of the channel were familiar. I had stayed at the Fort with Mr. Clapp and four men. As soon as we had recognized the American flag, not doubting any longer that it was a ship destined for the factory we saluted her with three guns. She came to anchor over against the fort, but on the opposite side of the river, and returned our salute. In a short time after we saw, or rather we heard, the oars of a boat (for it was already night) that came toward us. We expected her approach with impatience, to know who the stranger was and what news she brought us. Soon we were relieved from our uncertainty by the appearance of Mr. Hunt, who informed us that the ship was called the *Albatross* and was commanded by Captain Smith.

It will be remembered that Mr. Hunt had sailed from Astoria on board the *Beaver* on the

4th of August of the preceding year, and should
have returned with that vessel in the month of
October of the same year. We testified to him our
surprise that he had not returned at the time
appointed, and expressed the fears which we
entertained in regard to his fate, as well as that
of the *Beaver* itself: and in reply he explained
to us the reasons why neither he nor Captain
Sowles had been able to fulfil the promise which
they had made us.

After having got clear of the river Columbia,
they had scudded to the north, and had repaired
to the Russian post of Chitka, where they had
exchanged a part of their goods for furs. They
had made with the governor of that establishment, Baranoff by name, arrangements to supply
him regularly with all the goods of which he had
need, and to send him every year a vessel for
that purpose, as well as for the transportation of
his surplus furs to the East Indies.[68] They had

[68]Russian interest in the Northwest Coast of America
dates from the reign of Peter the Great, early in the
eighteenth century. Threatened destruction of the fur-
bearing animals by indifferent hunters led to the organization in 1799 of a monopoly called the Russian Fur Company, which was chartered for twenty years. Under the
able leadership of the Company's Alaskan manager, Alexander Baranoff, a central station was established at Sitka,
where ships were built for trade and exploration southward, and Fort Ross, established on Bodega Bay in California, was maintained until 1841. Baranoff's agreement

then advanced still farther to the north, to the coast of Kamchatka; and being there informed that some Kodiak hunters had been left on some adjacent isles, called the islands of St. Peter and St. Paul, and that these hunters had not been visited for three years, they determined to go thither, and having reached those isles, they opened a brisk trade and secured no less than eighty thousand skins of the South Sea seal. These operations had consumed a great deal of time; the season was already far advanced; ice was forming around them, and it was not without having incurred considerable dangers that they succeeded in making their way out of those latitudes. Having extricated themselves from the frozen seas of the north, but in a shattered condition, they deemed it more prudent to run for the Sandwich Isles, where they arrived after enduring a succession of severe gales. Here Mr. Hunt disembarked, with the men who had accompanied him, and who did not form a part of the ship's crew; and the vessel, after undergoing the necessary repairs, set sail for Canton.

Mr. Hunt had then passed nearly six months at the Sandwich Islands, expecting the annual

with Astor contemplated that the latter would supply the Russians in Alaska with needed provisions, in return for furs which Astor would sell in Canton. The War of 1812, with Astor's resultant loss of Astoria, defeated the carrying out of the project.

ship from New York and never imagining that
war had been declared. But at last, weary of waiting so long to no purpose, he had bought a small
schooner of one of the chiefs of the isle of Owahou,
and was engaged in getting her ready to sail for
the mouth of the Columbia when four sails hove
in sight and presently came to anchor in Whytiti
Bay. He immediately went on board of one of
them and learned that they came from the Indies,
whence they had sailed precipitately to avoid the
English cruisers. He also learned from the captain
of the vessel he boarded that the *Beaver* had arrived in Canton some days before the news of the
declaration of war. This Captain Smith, moreover, had on board some cases of nankeens and
other goods shipped by Mr. Astor's agent at Canton for us. Mr. Hunt then chartered the *Albatross*
to take him with his people and the goods to the
Columbia. That gentleman had not been idle
during the time that he sojourned at Owahou: he
brought us 35 barrels of salt pork or beef, nine
tierces of rice, a great quantity of dried taro, and
a good supply of salt.

As I knew the channel of the river I went on
board the *Albatross* and piloted her to the old
anchorage of the *Tonquin* under the guns of the
Fort, in order to facilitate the landing of the goods.

Captain Smith informed us that in 1810, a year
before the founding of our establishment, he had

entered the river in the same vessel and ascended
it in boats as far as Oak Point; and that he had
attempted to form an establishment there; but
the spot which he chose for building, and on
which he had even commenced fencing for a garden, being overflowed in the summer freshet, he
had been forced to abandon his project and re-
embark. We had seen, in fact, at Oak Point some
traces of this projected establishment. The bold
manner in which this Captain had entered the
river was now accounted for.

Captain Smith had chartered his vessel to a
Frenchman named Demestre, who was then a passenger on board of her, to go and take a cargo of
sandal wood at the Marquesas, where that gentleman had left some men to collect it the year before. He could not, therefore, comply with the
request we made him to remain during the summer with us in order to transport our goods and
people, as soon as they could be got together, to
the Sandwich Islands.

Mr. Hunt was surprised beyond measure when
we informed him of the resolution we had taken
of abandoning the country: he blamed us severely for having acted with so much precipitation,
pointing out that the success of the late coasting
voyage and the arrangements we had made with
the Russians promised a most advantageous trade,
which it was a thousand pities to sacrifice and

lose the fruits of the hardships he had endured
and the dangers he had braved, at one fell swoop,
by this rash measure. Nevertheless, seeing the
partners were determined to abide by their first
resolution, and not being able, by himself alone,
to fulfil his engagements to Governor Baranoff,
he consented to embark once more, in order to
seek a vessel to transport our heavy goods and
such of us as wished to return by sea. He sailed,
in fact, on the *Albatross* at the end of the month.
My friend Clapp embarked with him: they were,
in the first instance, to run down the coast of
California, in the hope of meeting there some of
the American vessels which frequently visit that
coast to obtain provisions from the Spaniards.

Some days after the departure of Mr. Hunt the
old one-eyed chief Comcomly came to tell us that
an Indian of Gray's Harbor, who had sailed on
the *Tonquin* in 1811, and who was the only soul
that had escaped the massacre of the crew of that
unfortunate vessel, had returned to his tribe. As
the distance from the river Columbia to Gray's
Harbor was not great, we sent for this native. At
first he made considerable difficulty about following our people, but was finally persuaded. He arrived at Astoria and related to us the circumstances of that sad catastrophe nearly as follows:

"After I had embarked on the *Tonquin*," said
he, "that vessel sailed for Nootka. Having arrived

opposite a large village called Newitte, we dropped anchor. The natives having invited Mr. McKay to land, he did so and was received in the most cordial manner: they even kept him several days at their village and made him lie every night on a couch of sea-otter skins. Meanwhile, the Captain was engaged in trading with such of the natives as resorted to his ship: but having had a difficulty with one of the principal chiefs in regard to the price of certain goods, he ended by putting the latter out of the ship and in the act of so repelling him struck him on the face with the roll of furs which he had brought to trade. This act was regarded by that chief and his followers as the most grievous insult, and they resolved to take vengeance for it. To arrive more surely at their purpose they dissembled their resentment and came, as usual, on board the ship. One day, very early in the morning, a large pirogue containing about a score of natives came alongside: every man had in his hand a packet of furs, and held it over his head as a sign that they came to trade. The watch let them come on deck. A little after, arrived a second pirogue, carrying about as many men as the other. The sailors believed that these also came to exchange their furs and allowed them to mount the ship's side like the first. Very soon, the pirogues thus succeeding one another, the crew saw themselves surrounded by a multitude of savages, who came upon the deck from all sides. Becoming alarmed at the appearance of things, they went to apprize the Captain and Mr. McKay, who hastened to the poop. I was with them," said the narrator, "and fearing, from the great multitude of Indians whom I saw already on the deck and from the movements of those on shore, who were hurrying to embark in their canoes to approach the vessel, and from the women being left in charge of the canoes of those who had arrived, that some evil design was on foot, I communicated my suspicions to Mr. McKay, who himself spoke to the Captain. The latter affected an air of security and said that with the firearms on board, there was no reason to fear even a greater number of Indians. Meanwhile, these gentlemen had come on deck unarmed, without even their sidearms. The trade, nevertheless, did not advance; the Indians offered less than was asked, and pressing with their furs close to the Captain, Mr. McKay, and Mr. Lewis, repeated the word *Makoke! Makoke!* 'Trade! Trade!' I urged the gentlemen to put to sea, and the Captain, at last, seeing the number of Indians increase every moment, allowed himself to be persuaded: he ordered a part of the crew to raise the anchor and the rest to go aloft and unfurl the sails. At the same time he warned the natives to withdraw, as the ship was going to sea. A fresh breeze was then springing up and in a few moments more their prey would have escaped them; but immediately on receiving this notice, by a preconcerted signal the Indians, with a terrific yell, drew forth the knives and war-bludgeons they had concealed in their bundles of furs and rushed upon the crew of the ship. Mr. Lewis was struck, and fell over a bale of blankets. Mr. McKay, however, was the first victim whom they sacrificed to their fury. Two savages, whom, from the crown of the poop where I was seated, I had seen follow this gentleman step by step, now cast themselves upon him, and having given him a blow on the head with a *potumagan* (a kind of saber which is described a little below) felled him to the deck, then took him up and flung him into the sea, where the women left in charge of the canoes quickly finished him with their paddles. Another set flung themselves upon the Captain, who defended himself for a long time with his pocket-knife, but, overpowered by numbers, perished also under the blows of these murderers. I next saw (and that was the last occurrence of which I was witness before quitting the ship) the sailors who were aloft slip down by the rigging and get below through the steerage hatchway. They were five, I think, in number, and one of them in descending received a knife-stab in the back. I then jumped overboard to escape a similar fate to that of the Captain and

Mr. McKay. The women in the canoes, to whom I surrendered myself as a slave, took me in and bade me hide myself under some mats which were in the pirogues, which I did. Soon after, I heard the discharge of firearms, immediately upon which the Indians fled from the vessel and pulled for the shore as fast as possible, nor did they venture to go alongside the ship again the whole of that day. The next day, having seen four men lower a boat and pull away from the ship, they sent some pirogues in chase: but whether those men were overtaken and murdered, or gained the open sea and perished there, I never could learn. Nothing more was seen stirring on board the *Tonquin*; the natives pulled cautiously around her and some of the more daring went on board; at last, the savages, finding themselves absolute masters of the ship, rushed on board in a crowd to pillage her. But very soon, when there were about four or five hundred either huddled together on deck or clinging to the sides, all eager for plunder, the ship blew up with a horrible noise. I was on the shore," said the Indian, "when the explosion took place, saw the great volume of smoke burst forth in the spot where the ship had been, and high in the air above, arms, legs, heads, and bodies flying in every direction. The tribe acknowledged a loss of over two hundred of their people on that occasion.

As for me, I remained their prisoner, and have been their slave for two years. It is but now that I have been ransomed by my friends. I have told you the truth, and hope you will acquit me of having in any way participated in that bloody affair.'"[69]

Our Indian having finished his discourse, we made him presents proportioned to the melancholy satisfaction he had given us in communicating the true history of the sad fate of our former companions and to the trouble he had taken in coming to us; so that he returned apparently well satisfied with our liberality.

According to the narrative of this Indian, Captain Thorn, by his abrupt manner and passionate temper, was the primary cause of his own death and that of all on board his vessel. What appears certain, at least, is that he was guilty of unpardonable negligence and imprudence in not causing the boarding netting to be rigged, as is the custom of all the navigators who frequent this coast, and in suffering (contrary to his instructions) too great a number of Indians to come on board at once.

[69]Both Franchère and Alexander Ross (*First Settlers on the Oregon,* 172–80) assume to give the Indian's story in his own words. Ross's version, however, is more detailed than Franchère's and the two accounts, as might be expected, differ in numerous respects. They afford the only first-hand record of the *Tonquin's* fate, and upon them all subsequent accounts are based.

Captain Smith of the *Albatross,* who had seen the wreck of the *Tonquin,* in mentioning to us its sad fate attributed the cause of the disaster to the rash conduct of a Captain Ayres of Boston. That navigator had taken off, as I have mentioned already, ten or a dozen natives of New-itte as hunters, with a promise of bringing them back to their country, which promise he inhumanly broke by leaving them on some desert islands in Sir Francis Drake's Bay. The countrymen of these unfortunates, indignant at the conduct of the American captain, had sworn to avenge themselves on the first white men who appeared among them. Chance willed it that our vessel was the first to enter that bay, and the natives but too well executed on our people their project of vengeance.

Whatever may have been the first and principal cause of this misfortune (for doubtless it is necessary to suppose more than one), seventeen white men and twelve Sandwich Islanders were massacred: not one escaped from the butchery to bring us the news of it, but the Indian of Gray's Harbor. The massacre of our people was avenged, it is true, by the destruction of ten times the number of their murderers; but this circumstance, which could perhaps gladden the heart of a savage, was a feeble consolation (if it was any) for civilized men. The death of Mr. Alexander McKay was an irreparable loss to the Company, which

would probably have been dissolved by the remaining partners but for the arrival of the ener-
getic Mr. Hunt. Interesting as was the recital of
the Indian of Gray's Harbor throughout, when
he came to the unhappy end of that estimable
man marks of regret were visibly painted on the
countenances of all who listened.

At the beginning of September, Mr. McKenzie
set off with Messrs. Wallace and Seton to carry
a supply of goods to the gentlemen wintering in
the interior, as well as to inform them of the
arrangements concluded with Mr. Hunt and to
enjoin them to send down all their furs and all
the Sandwich Islanders, that the former might be
shipped for America and the latter sent back to
their country.

Chapter XV
Surrender of Astoria

A FEW days after Mr. McKenzie left us we
were greatly surprised by the appearance of
two canoes bearing the British flag, with a third
between them carrying the flag of the United
States, all rounding Tongue Point. It was no
other than Mr. McKenzie himself, returning with
Messrs. J. G. McTavish and Angus Bethune of
the North West Company. He had met these
gentlemen near the first rapids, and had determined to return with them to the establishment
in consequence of information which they gave
him. Those gentlemen were in light canoes (i. e.,
without any lading) and formed the vanguard to
a flotilla of eight, loaded with furs, under the
conduct of Messrs. John Stuart and McMillan.

Mr. McTavish came to our quarters at the factory and showed Mr. McDougall a letter which
had been addressed to the latter by Mr. Angus
Shaw, his uncle, and one of the partners of the
North West Company. Mr. Shaw informed his
nephew that the ship *Isaac Todd* had sailed from
London with letters of marque in the month of
March, in company with the frigate *Phoebe,* having orders from the government to seize our establishment, which had been represented to the Lords

of the Admiralty as an important colony founded by the American government. The eight canoes left behind came up, meanwhile, and uniting themselves to the others they formed a camp of about seventy-five men at the bottom of a little bay or cove near our factory. As they were destitute of provisions we supplied them; but Messrs. McDougall and McKenzie affecting to dread a surprise from this British force under our guns, we kept strictly on our guard; for we were inferior in point of numbers, although our position was exceedingly advantageous.

As the season advanced and their ship did not arrive our new neighbors found themselves in a very disagreeable situation, without food, or merchandise wherewith to procure it from the natives; viewed by the latter with a distrustful and hostile eye, as being our enemies and therefore exposed to attack and plunder on their part with impunity; supplied with good hunters, indeed, but wanting ammunition to render their skill available. Weary, at length, of applying to us incessantly for food (which we furnished them with a sparing hand) unable either to retrace their steps through the wilderness or to remain in their present position, they came to the conclusion of proposing to buy of us the whole establishment.

Placed as we were in the situation of expecting, day by day, the arrival of an English ship-of-war to seize upon all we possessed, we listened to their propositions. Several meetings and discussions took place; the negotiations were protracted by the hope of one party that the long-expected armed force would arrive, to render the purchase unnecessary, and were urged forward by the other in order to conclude the affair before that occurrence should intervene; at length the price of the goods and furs in the factory was agreed upon, and the bargain was signed by both parties on the 23d of October. The gentlemen of the North West Company took possession of Astoria, agreeing to pay the servants of the Pacific Fur Company (the name which had been chosen by Mr. Astor) the arrears of their wages, to be deducted from the price of the goods which we delivered, to supply them with provisions, and give a free passage to those who wished to return to Canada overland. The American colors were hauled down from the factory and the British run up, to the no small chagrin and mortification of those who were American citizens.[70]

It was thus that after having passed the seas and suffered all sorts of fatigues and privations I lost in a moment all my hopes of fortune. I could not help remarking that we had no right to expect such treatment on the part of the British

[70] This sentence is not found in the Manuscript, nor in the 1820 edition.

government, after the assurances we had received from Mr. Jackson, His Majesty's *chargé d'affaires* previously to our departure from New York. But as I have just intimated, the agents of the North West Company had exaggerated the importance of the factory in the eyes of the British Ministry; for if the latter had known what it really was—a mere trading-post—and that nothing but the rivalry of the fur-traders of the North West Company was interested in its destruction, they would never have taken umbrage at it, or at least would never have sent a maritime expedition to destroy it. The sequel will show that I was not mistaken in this opinion.

The greater part of the servants of the Pacific Fur Company entered the service of the Company of the North West: the rest preferred to return to their country, and I was of the number of these last. Nevertheless, Mr. McTavish, after many ineffectual attempts to persuade me to remain with them, having intimated that the establishment could not dispense with my services as I was the only person who could assist them in their trade, especially for provisions, of which they would soon be in the greatest need, I agreed with them (without however relinquishing my previous engagement with Mr. Astor's agents) for five months, that is to say, till the departure of the expedition which was to ascend the Columbia in the spring, and reach Canada by way of the Rocky Mountains and the rivers of the interior.[71] Messrs. John Stuart and McKenzie set off about the end of this month for the interior in order that the latter might make over to the former the posts established on the Spokan and Okenakan.

On the 15th of November Messrs. Alexander Stuart and Alexander Henry,[72] both partners of the N. W. Company, arrived at the factory in a couple of bark canoes manned by sixteen voyageurs. They had set out from Fort William on Lake Superior in the month of July. They brought us Canadian papers, by which we learned that

[71]Alexander Ross states that Franchère was the only clerk who disclosed a willingness to join the North West Company. "He was a Canadian from Montreal, and in those days the North West stood high in Canada, and particularly in Montreal." *First Settlers on the Oregon,* 275. However, Ross himself remained with the Company, and its successor, the Hudson's Bay Company, for more than a decade, while Franchère persisted in his intention of leaving the Company and the Columbia country.

[72]Alexander Henry, frequently called "the younger," was a nephew of Alexander Henry of Montreal, whose *Travels and Adventures,* first published at New York in 1809, was reissued as the Lakeside Classics volume for 1921. Our present subject devoted his mature life to the fur trade as an employee of the North West Company. Throughout the entire period he kept a voluminous journal, maintained until the day before his death by drowning, May 22, 1814, in the mouth of the Columbia. The journal was published in 1897 by Elliott Coues (Ed.), entitled *New Light on the Early History of the Greater Northwest.*

the British arms so far had been in the ascend-
ant. They confirmed, also, the news that an English frigate was coming to take possession of our
quondam establishment; they were even surprised not to see the *Isaac Todd* lying in the road.

On the morning of the 30th we saw a large
vessel standing in under Cape Disappointment
(which proved in this instance to deserve its
name); and soon after that vessel came to anchor
in Baker Bay. Not knowing whether it was a
friendly or a hostile sail, we thought it prudent
to send on board Mr. McDougall in a canoe
manned by such of the men as had been previously in the service of the Pacific Fur Company,
with injunctions to declare themselves Americans
if the vessel was American, and Englishmen in
the contrary case. While this party was on its
way, Mr. McTavish caused all the furs which
were marked with the initials of the N. W. Company to be placed on board the two barges at the
Fort and sent them up the river above Tongue
Point, where they were to wait for a concerted
signal that was to inform them whether the new-
comers were friends or foes. Toward midnight
Mr. Halsey, who had accompanied Mr. McDougall to the vessel, returned to the Fort and announced to us that she was the British sloop-of-
war *Raccoon* of 26 guns, commanded by Captain
Black, with a complement of 120 men, fore and

aft. Mr. John McDonald, a partner of the N. W.
Company, was a passenger on the *Raccoon*, with
five voyageurs, destined for the Company's service. He had left England in the frigate *Phoebe*,
which had sailed in company with the *Isaac Todd*
as far as Rio Janeiro; but there falling in with the
British squadron, the admiral changed the des-
tination of the frigate, dispatching the sloops-of-
war *Raccoon* and *Cherub* to convoy the *Isaac Todd*,
and sent the *Phoebe* to search for the American
Commodore Porter, who was then on the Pacific
capturing all the British whalers and other trading vessels he met with.[73] These four vessels then

[73]David Porter (1780–1843) was one of the most notable
officers of the early American navy. Appointed a captain
July 2, 1812, he went to sea the next day, and during the
ensuing cruise captured nine British vessels, one of them
the first naval vessel taken in the War of 1812.

In November, 1812 Porter sailed in the *Essex* for the
Pacific, his vessel being the first American warship to visit
that ocean. His objective was the protection of American,
and the capture of British, whalers. Within six months he
had taken twelve of the latter, utilizing one as a store ship
and equipping another as a naval vessel. Upon learning of
the expected arrival of a British fleet in the Pacific, Porter
sailed for the Marquesas Islands, where he refitted his vessels in preparation for an attack upon the enemy. Sailing
for the coast of Chile, he was caught in Valparaiso harbor
by the *Phoebe* and the *Cherub*. On March 28, 1813, at-
tempting to run the blockade thus established, his vessel
was disabled in a squall and in the resultant battle was
overpowered, with losses to Porter of 155 of his total force
of 225 men. In 1823 Porter was given command of the
West India Squadron, whose chief function was the sup-

sailed in company as far as Cape Horn, where they parted, after agreeing on the island of Juan Fernandez as a rendezvous. The three ships-of-war met, in fact, at that island; but after having a long time waited in vain for the *Isaac Todd*, Commodore Hillier who commanded this little squadron, hearing of the injury inflicted by Commodore Porter on the British commerce, and especially on the whalers who frequent these seas, resolved to go in quest of him in order to give him combat; and retaining the *Cherub* to assist him, detailed the *Raccoon* to go and destroy the American establishment on the river Columbia, being assured by Mr. McDonald that a single sloop-of-war would be sufficient for that service.

Mr. McDonald had consequently embarked with his people on board the *Raccoon*. This gentleman informed us that they had experienced frightful weather in doubling the Cape, and that he entertained serious apprehensions for the safety of the *Isaac Todd*, but that if she was safe we might expect her to arrive in the river in two or three weeks. The signal gun agreed upon having been fired, for the return of the barges, Mr. McTavish came back to the Fort with the furs and was overjoyed to learn of the arrival of Mr. McDonald.

pression of piracy in West Indian waters. When he yielded his command two years later, the task had been chiefly accomplished.

On the 1st of December the *Raccoon*'s gig came up to the fort, bringing Mr. McDonald (surnamed *Bras Croche,* or crooked arm) and the first lieutenant, Mr. Sheriff. Both these gentlemen were convalescent from the effects of an accident which had happened to them in the passage between Juan Fernandez and the mouth of the Columbia. The Captain, wishing to clean the guns, ordered them to be scaled, that is, fired off: during this exercise one of the guns hung fire; the sparks fell into a cartridge tub and setting fire to the combustibles, communicated also to some priming horns suspended above; an explosion followed, which reached some twenty persons; eight were killed on the spot, the rest were severely burned; Messrs. McDonald and Sheriff had suffered a great deal; it was with difficulty that their clothes had been removed; and when the Lieutenant came ashore, he had not recovered the use of his hands. Among the killed was an American named Flatt, who was in the service of the North West Company and whose loss these gentlemen appeared exceedingly to regret.

As there were goods destined for the Company on board the *Raccoon,* the schooner *Dolly* was sent to Baker Bay to bring them up: but the weather was so bad and the wind so violent that she did not return till the 12th, bringing up, together with the goods, Captain Black, a lieutenant of marines, four soldiers, and as many sailors. We entertained our guests as splendidly as it lay in our power to do. After dinner the Captain caused firearms to be given to the servants of the Company and we all marched under arms to the square or platform, where a flag-staff had been erected. There the Captain took a British Union Jack, which he had brought on shore for the occasion, and caused it to be run up to the top of the staff; then, taking a bottle of Madeira wine, he broke it on the flag-staff, declaring in a loud voice that he took possession of the establishment and of the country in the name of His Britannic Majesty; and changed the name of Astoria to Fort George. Some few Indian chiefs had been got together to witness this ceremony and I explained to them in their own language what it signified. Three rounds of artillery and musketry were fired and the health of the king was drunk by the parties interested, according to the usage on like occasions.

The sloop being detained by contrary winds, the Captain caused an exact survey to be made of the entrance of the river, as well as of the navigable channel between Baker Bay and Fort George. The officers visited the fort, turn about, and seemed to me in general very much dissatisfied with their fool's errand, as they called it: they had expected to find a number of American vessels loaded with rich furs, and had calculated in advance their share in the booty of Astoria. They had not met a vessel, and their astonishment was at its height when they saw that our establishment had been transferred to the North West Company and was under the British flag. It will suffice to quote a single expression of Captain Black's in order to show how much they were deceived in their expectations. The Captain landed after dark; when we showed him the next morning the palisades and log bastions of the factory, he inquired if there was not another fort; on being assured that there was no other he cried out, with an air of the greatest astonishment: "What! is this the fort which was represented to me as so formidable! Good God! I could batter it down in two hours with a four-pounder!"

There were on board the *Raccoon* two young men from Canada who had been impressed at Quebec when that vessel was there some years before her voyage to the Columbia: one of them was named Parent, a blacksmith, and was of Quebec: the other was from Upper Canada, and was named McDonald. These young persons signified to us that they would be glad to remain at Fort George: and as there was among our men some who would gladly have shipped, we proposed to the Captain an exchange, but he would not consent to it. John Little, a boatbuilder from

New York, who had been on the sick list a long time, was sent on board and placed under the care of the sloop's surgeon, Mr. O'Brien, the Captain engaging to land him at the Sandwich Islands.[74] P. D. Jeremie also shipped himself as under clerk. The vessel hoisted sail and got out of the river on the 31st of December.[75]

From the account given in this chapter the reader will see with what facility the establishment of the Pacific Fur Company could have escaped capture by the British force. It was only necessary to get rid of the land party of the North West Company—who were completely in our power—then remove our effects up the river upon some small stream, and await the result. The sloop-of-war arrived, it is true; but as, in the case I suppose, she would have found nothing, she would have left, after setting fire to our deserted houses. None of their boats would have dared follow us, even if the Indians had betrayed to them our lurking-place. Those at the head of affairs had their own fortunes to seek, and

[74] "Captain Black was a gentleman of courteous and affable manners. He was never once heard to utter an oath or indecorous expression all the time he was in the river and there was a general and sincere regret felt when he left Fort George." Ross, *First Settlers on the Oregon.*

[75] The remaining portion of the chapter is not found in the 1820 edition, nor in the Manuscript. It represents, therefore, the statements of Mr. Huntington.

thought it more for their interest, doubtless, to act as they did, but that will not clear them in the eyes of the world, and the charge of treason to Mr. Astor's interests will always be attached to their characters.

Chapter XVI

Indian Treachery and Warfare

ON the 3d of January, 1814 two canoes laden with merchandise for the interior were dispatched under the command of Mr. Alexander Stuart and Mr. James Keith, with fifteen men under them. Two of the latter were charged with letters for the posts (of the North West Company) east of the mountains, containing instructions to the persons in superintendence there to have in readiness canoes and the requisite provisions for a large party intending to go east the ensuing spring. I took this opportunity of advising my friends in Canada of my intention to return home that season. It was the third attempt I had made to send news of my existence to my relatives and friends: the first two had miscarried and this was doomed to meet the same fate.

Messrs. J. Stuart and McKenzie, who (as was seen in a previous chapter) had been sent to notify the gentlemen in the interior of what had taken place at Astoria, and to transfer the wintering posts to the North West Company, returned to Fort George on the morning of the 6th. They stated that they had left Messrs. Clarke and D. Stuart behind with the loaded canoes, and also

154

that the party had been attacked by the natives above the Falls.

As they were descending the river toward evening, between the first and second portages, they had espied a large number of Indians congregated at no great distance in the prairie, which gave them some uneasiness. In fact, some time after they had encamped, and when all the people were asleep, except Mr. Stuart who was on guard, these savages had stealthily approached the camp and discharged some arrows, one of which had penetrated the coverlet of one of the men who was lying near the baggage and had pierced the cartilage of his ear; the pain made him utter a sharp cry, which alarmed the whole camp and threw it into an uproar. The natives, perceiving it, fled to the woods, howling and yelling like so many demons. In the morning our people picked up eight arrows round the camp: they could yet hear the savages yell and whoop in the woods: but notwithstanding, the party reached the lower end of the portage unmolested.

The audacity which these barbarians had displayed in attacking a party of from forty to forty-five persons made us suppose that they would much more probably attack the party of Mr. Stuart, which was composed of but seventeen men. Consequently I received orders to get ready forthwith a canoe and firearms in order to proceed to their relief. The whole was ready in the short space of two hours, and I embarked immediately with a guide and eight men. Our instructions were to use all possible diligence to overtake Messrs. Stewart and Keith, and to convey them to the upper end of the last portage; or to return with the goods, if we met too much resistance on the part of the natives. We travelled, then, all that day and all the night of the 6th, and on the 7th till evening. Finding ourselves then at a little distance from the Rapids, I came to a halt to put the firearms in order and let the men take some repose. About midnight I caused them to re-embark, and ordered the men to sing as they rowed, that the party whom we wished to overtake might hear us as we passed, if perchance they were encamped on some one of the islands of which the river is full in this part. In fact, we had hardly proceeded five or six miles when we were hailed by some one, apparently in the middle of the stream. We stopped rowing and answered, and were soon joined by our people of the expedition, who were all descending the river in a canoe. They informed us that they had been attacked the evening before and that Mr. Stuart had been wounded. We turned about and all proceeded in company toward the fort. In the morning, when we stopped

to breakfast, Mr. Keith gave me the particulars of
the affair of the day preceding.

Having arrived at the foot of the Rapids, they
commenced the portage on the south bank of the
river, which is obstructed with boulders over
which it was necessary to pass the effects. After
they had hauled over the two canoes and a part
of the goods the natives approached in great
numbers, trying to carry off something unob-
served. Mr. Stuart was at the upper end of the
portage (the portage being about six hundred
yards in length) and Mr. Keith accompanied the
loaded men. An Indian seized a bag containing
articles of little value and fled: Mr. Stuart, who
saw the act, pursued the thief and after some resistance on the latter's part succeeded in making
him relinquish his booty. Immediately he saw a
number of Indians armed with bows and arrows
approaching him: one of them bent his bow and
took aim; Mr. Stuart, on his part, levelled his
gun at the Indian, warning the latter not to
shoot, and at the same instant received an arrow
which pierced his left shoulder. He then drew
the trigger; but as it had rained all day the gun
missed fire and before he could re-prime another
arrow, better aimed than the first, struck him in
the left side and penetrated between two of his
ribs in the region of the heart, and would have
proved fatal, no doubt, but for a stone-pipe he

had fortunately in his side-pocket, and which was broken by the arrow; at the same moment his gun was discharged and the Indian fell dead. Several others then rushed forward to avenge the death of their compatriot; but two of the men came up with their loads and their gun (for these portages were made arms in hand) and seeing what was going forward one of them threw his pack on the ground, fired on one of the Indians, and brought him down. He got up again, however, and picked up his weapons, but the other man ran upon him, wrested from him his war-club, and dispatched him by repeated blows on the head with it. The other savages, seeing the bulk of our people approaching the scene of combat, retired and crossed the river. In the meantime, Mr. Stuart extracted the arrows from his body by the aid of one of the men: the blood flowed in abundance from the wounds and he saw that it would be impossible for him to pursue his journey; he therefore gave orders for the canoes and goods to be carried back to the lower end of the portage. Presently they saw a great number of pirogues full of warriors coming from the opposite side of the river. Our people then considered that they could do nothing better than to get away as fast as possible; they contrived to transport over one canoe in which they all embarked, abandoning the other and the goods to the natives. While the barbarians were plundering these effects, more precious in their estimation than the apples of gold in the garden of the Hesperides, our party retired and got out of sight. The retreat was, notwithstanding, so precipitate, that they left behind an Indian from the Lake of the Two Mountains who was in the service of the Company as a hunter.[76] This Indian had persisted in concealing himself behind the rocks, meaning, he said, to kill some of those thieves, and did not return in time for the embarkation. Mr. Keith regretted this brave man's obstinacy, fearing, with good reason, that he would be discovered and murdered by the natives.[77] We rowed all that day and night and reached the factory on the 9th at sunrise. Our first care, after having announced the misfortune of our people, was to dress the wounds of Mr. Stuart, which had been merely bound with a wretched piece of cotton cloth.

The goods which had been abandoned were of consequence to the Company, inasmuch as they could not be replaced. It was dangerous, besides, to leave the natives in possession of some fifty

[76]The Lake of the Two Mountains is an enlargement of the Ottawa River above Montreal. From early in the eighteenth century it was the site of an Indian mission.

[77] "Despite the insistence of Mr. Keith the canoe pushed off without taking this man, so precipitate was the retreat." Manuscript.

guns and a considerable quantity of ammunition, which they might use against us. The partners, therefore, decided to fit out an expedition immediately to chastise the robbers, or at least to endeavor to recover the goods. I went, by their order, to find the principal chiefs of the neighboring tribes, to explain to them what had taken place and invite them to join us, to which they willingly consented. Then, having got ready six canoes, we re-embarked on the 10th to the number of sixty-two men, all armed from head to foot, and provided with a small brass field-piece.

We soon reached the lower end of the first rapid: but the essential thing was wanting to our little force; it was without provisions; our first care then was to try to procure these. Having arrived opposite a village, we perceived on the bank about thirty armed savages who seemed to await us firmly. As it was not our policy to seem bent on hostilities, we landed on the opposite bank and I crossed the river with five or six men to enter into parley with them and try to obtain provisions. I immediately became aware that the village was abandoned, the women and children having fled to the woods, taking with them all the articles of food. The young men, however, offered us dogs, of which we purchased a score. Then we passed to a second village, where they were already informed of our coming. Here we bought forty-five dogs and a horse. With this stock we formed an encampment on an island called Strawberry Island.

Seeing ourselves now provided with food for several days, we informed the natives touching the motives which had brought us, and announced to them that we were determined to put them all to death and burn their villages if they did not bring back in two days the effects stolen on the 7th. A party was detached to the Rapids, where the attack on Mr. Stuart had taken place. We found the villages all deserted. Crossing to the north bank we found a few natives, of whom we made inquiries respecting the Nipissing Indian who had been left behind, but they assured us that they had seen nothing of him.*

Not having succeeded in recovering, above the Rapids, any part of the lost goods, the inhabitants

*This Indian returned some time after to the factory, but in a pitiable condition. After the departure of the canoe he had concealed himself behind a rock, and so passed the night. At daybreak, fearing to be discovered, he gained the woods and directed his steps toward the fort, across a mountainous region. He arrived at length at the bank of a little stream, which he was at first unable to cross. Hunger, in the meantime, began to urge him; he might have appeased it with game, of which he saw plenty, but unfortunately he had lost the flint of his gun. At last, with a raft of sticks, he crossed the river and arrived at a village, the inhabitants of which disarmed him and made him prisoner. Our people hearing where he was, sent to seek him, and gave some blankets for his ransom.   Bibaud.

all protesting that it was not they, but the villages below, which had perpetrated the robbery, we descended the river again and re-encamped on Strawberry Island. As the intention of the partners was to intimidate the natives, without (if possible) shedding blood, we made a display of our numbers and from time to time fired off our little field-piece to let them see that we could reach them from one side of the river to the other. The Indian Caalpo and his wife, who had accompanied us, advised us to make prisoner one of the chiefs. We succeeded in this design, without incurring any danger. Having invited one of the natives to come and smoke with us, he came accordingly: a little after, came another; at last, one of the chiefs, and he one of the most considered among them, also came. Being notified secretly of his character by Caalpo, who was concealed in the tent, we seized him forthwith, tied him to a stake, and placed a guard over him with a naked sword, as if ready to cut his head off on the least attempt being made by his people for his liberation. The other Indians were then suffered to depart with the news for his tribe that unless the goods were brought to us in twenty-four hours their chief would be put to death. Our stratagem succeeded: soon after we heard wailing and lamentation in the village and they presently brought us part of the guns, some brass kettles, and a variety of smaller articles, protesting that this was all their share of the plunder. Keeping our chief as a hostage, we passed to the other village and succeeded in recovering the rest of the guns and about a third of the other goods.

Although they had been the aggressors, yet as they had had two men killed and we had not lost any on our side we thought it our duty to conform to the usage of the country and abandon to them the remainder of the stolen effects, to cover, according to their expression, the bodies of their two slain compatriots. Besides, we began to find ourselves short of provisions, and it would not have been easy to get at our enemies to punish them if they had taken refuge in the woods, according to their custom when they feel themselves the weaker party. So we released our prisoner and gave him a flag, telling him that when he presented it unfurled we should regard it as a sign of peace and friendship: but if, when we were passing the portage, any one of the natives should have the misfortune to come near the baggage we would kill him on the spot. We re-embarked on the 19th and on the 22d reached the fort, where we made a report of our martial expedition. We found Mr. Stuart very ill of his wounds, especially of the one in the side, which was so much swelled that we had every reason to think the arrow had been poisoned.

If we did not do the savages as much harm as we might have done, it was not from timidity but from humanity, and in order not to shed human blood uselessly. For after all, what good would it have done us to have slaughtered some of these barbarians, whose crime was not the effect of depravity and wickedness, but of an ardent and irresistible desire to ameliorate their condition? It must be allowed also that the interest, well-understood, of the partners of the North West Company was opposed to too strongly marked acts of hostility on their part: it behooved them exceedingly not to make irreconciliable enemies of the populations neighboring on the portages of the Columbia, which they would so often be obliged to pass and repass in future. It is also probable that the other natives on the banks, as well as of the river as of the sea, would not have seen with indifference their countrymen too signally or too rigorously punished by strangers; and that they would have made common cause with the former to resist the latter, and perhaps even to drive them from the country.

I must not omit to state that all the firearms surrendered by the Indians on this occasion were found loaded with ball and primed, with a little piece of cotton laid over the priming to keep the powder dry. This shows how soon they would acquire the use of guns, and how careful traders should be in intercourse with strange Indians not to teach them their use.

Chapter XVII
Last Winter on the Columbia

THE new proprietors of our establishment, being dissatisfied with the site we had chosen, came to the determination to change it; after surveying both sides of the river they found no better place than the head-land which we had named Tongue Point. This Point, or to speak more accurately, perhaps, this Cape, extends about a quarter of a mile into the river, being connected with the main-land by a low, narrow neck over which the Indians in stormy weather haul their canoes in passing up and down the river, and terminating in an almost perpendicular rock of about 250 or 300 feet elevation. This bold summit was covered with a dense forest of pine trees; the ascent from the lower neck was gradual and easy; it abounded in springs of the finest water; on either side it had a cove to shelter the boats necessary for a trading establishment. This peninsula had truly the appearance of a huge tongue. Astoria had been built nearer the ocean, but the advantages offered by Tongue Point more than compensated for its greater distance. Its soil, in the rainy season, could be drained with little or no trouble; it was a better position to guard against attacks on the part of the natives and less exposed to that of civilized enemies by sea or land in time of war.

All the hands who had returned from the interior, added to those who were already at the Fort, consumed in an incredibly short space of time the small stock of provisions which had been conveyed by the Pacific Fur Company to the Company of the North West. It became a matter of necessity, therefore, to seek some spot where a part, at least, could be sent to subsist. With these views I left the fort on the 7th of February with a number of men belonging to the old concern, and who had refused to enter the service of the new one, to proceed to the establishment on the Wolamat River, under the charge of Mr. Alexander Henry,[78] who had with him a number of first-rate hunters. Leaving the Columbia to ascend the Wolamat, I found the banks on either side of that stream well wooded, but low and swampy, until I reached the first falls; having passed which, by making a portage, I commenced ascending a clear but moderately deep channel against a swift current. The banks on either side were bordered with forest trees, but behind that narrow belt, diversified with prairie, the landscape was magnificent; the hills were of moderate elevation and rising in

[78]Instead of Alexander Henry the post on the Willamette was in charge of William, a son of the elder Alexander and a cousin of Alexander Henry the Younger.

an amphitheater. Deer and elk are found here in great abundance; and the post in charge of Mr. Henry had been established with a view of keeping constantly there a number of hunters to prepare dried venison for the use of the factory. On our arrival at the Columbia, considering the latitude, we had expected severe winter weather, such as is experienced in the same latitudes east; but we were soon undeceived; the mildness of the climate never permitted us to transport fresh provisions from the Willamet to Astoria. We had not a particle of salt; and the attempts we made to smoke or dry the venison proved abortive.

Having left the men under my charge with Mr. Henry, I took leave of that gentleman and returned. At Oak Point I found Messrs. Keith and Pillet encamped, to pass there the season of sturgeon-fishing. They informed me that I was to stay with them.

Accordingly I remained at Oak Point the rest of the winter, occupied in trading with the Indians spread all along the river for some 30 or 40 miles above, in order to supply the factory with provisions. I used to take a boat with four or five men, visit every fishing station, trade for as much fish as would load the boat, and send her down to the fort. The surplus fish traded in the interval between the departure and return of the boat was cut up, salted, and barrelled for future use. The salt had been recently obtained from a quarter to be presently mentioned.

About the middle of March Messrs. Keith and Pillet both left me and returned to the fort. Being now alone, I began seriously to reflect on my position and it was in this interval that I positively decided to return to Canada. I made inquiries of the men sent up with the boats for fish concerning the preparations for departure, but whether they had been enjoined secrecy, or were unwilling to communicate, I could learn nothing of what was doing below.

At last I heard that on the 28th of February a sail had appeared at the mouth of the river. The gentlemen of the N. W. Company at first flattered themselves that it was the vessel they had so long expected. They were soon undeceived by a letter from Mr. Hunt which was brought to the fort by the Indians of Baker Bay. That gentleman had purchased at the Marquesas Islands a brig called the *Pedlar:* it was on that vessel that he arrived, having for pilot Captain Northrop, formerly commander of the ship *Lark.* The latter vessel had been outfitted by Mr. Astor and despatched from New York, in spite of the blockading squadron, with supplies for the *ci-devant* Pacific Fur Company; but unhappily she had been assailed by a furious tempest and capsized in lat. 16° N., and three or four hundred miles from the Sandwich

Islands. The mate, who was sick, was drowned in the cabin, and four of the crew perished at the same time. The captain had the masts and rigging cut away, which caused the vessel to right again, though full of water. One of the hands dived down to the sail-maker's locker and got out a small sail, which they attached to the bowsprit. He dived a second time and brought up a box containing a dozen bottles of wine. For thirteen days they had no other sustenance but the flesh of a small shark, which they had the good fortune to take, and which they ate raw, and for drink, a gill of the wine each man per diem. At last the trade winds carried them upon the island of Tohrahah, where the vessel went to pieces on the reef. The Islanders saved the crew, and seized all the goods which floated on the water. Mr. Hunt was then at Wahoo, and learned through some islanders from Morotoi that some Americans had been wrecked on the isle of Tohrahah.[79] He went immediately to take them off, and gave the pilotage of his own vessel to Captain Northrop.

[79]These are islands of the Hawaiian Island group. "Morotoi" is present-day Molokai, site of the celebrated leper Colony. "Wahoo" is Oahu, sixth of the Island chain in area but first in population and containing Honolulu, the capital. The Capitol, Iolani Palace, was once the seat of native kings. On Oahu, also, are the several military installations which constitute America's first line of defense in the Pacific.

It may be imagined what was the surprise of Mr. Hunt when he saw Astoria under the British flag, and passed into stranger hands. But the misfortune was beyond remedy and he was obliged to content himself with taking on board all the Americans who were at the establishment and who had not entered the service of the Company of the North West. Messrs. Halsey, Seton,[80] and Farnham were among those who embarked. I shall have occasion to inform the reader of the part each of them played, and how they reached their homes.

When I heard that Mr. Hunt was in the river, and knowing that the overland expedition was to set out early in April, I raised camp at Oak Point, and reached the fort on the 2d of that month. But the brig *Pedlar* had that very day got outside the

[80]Alfred Seton, member of a distinguished family of New York City. Although his father for many years held a commission in the British Army (beginning at the mature age of twelve), Alfred, who was a very young man at the time he joined the Astorian expedition (his parents were married March 20, 1792) was ardently patriotic, being one of the American youths at Astoria according to Washington Irving, "who manifested much grief and indignation at seeing the flag of their country hauled down." In 1830–31 Seton was one of the capitalists who financed the fur-trading enterprise of Captain Bonneville. Irving suggests that one of his motives for doing so may have been "the hope of seeing that flag once more planted on the shores of the Columbia." Data condensed from Monsignor Seton, *An Old Family or the Setons of Scotland and America* (New York, 1899), and Seton family sketches in *Dict. Am. Biog.*

river, after several fruitless attempts, in one of which she narrowly missed being lost on the bar.

I would gladly have gone in her, had I but arrived a day sooner. I found, however, all things prepared for the departure of the canoes, which was to take place on the 4th. I got ready the few articles I possessed and in spite of the very advantageous offers of the gentlemen of the N. W. Company and their reiterated persuasions, aided by the crafty McDougall, to induce me to remain at least one year more, I persisted in my resolution to leave the country.[81] The journey I was about to undertake was a long one: it would be accompanied with great fatigues and many privations and even by some dangers; but I was used to privations and fatigues; I had braved dangers of more than one sort; and even had it been otherwise, the ardent desire of revisiting my country, my relatives, and my friends, the hope of finding myself in a few months in their midst, would have made me overlook every other consideration.

I am about, then, to quit the banks of the river Columbia and conduct the reader through

[81]The remainder of this chapter was written by Bibaud, Editor of the 1820 edition. Chapters 18, 19, and 20 which follow were transferred by him to this place from the much earlier position they occupy in the Manuscript. In the latter, the opening sentence of Chapter 21 follows at this point.

the mountain passes, over the plains, the forests, and the lakes of our continent: but I ought first to give him at least an idea of the manners and customs of the inhabitants, as well as of the principal productions of the country that I now quit, after a sojourn of three years. This is what I shall try to do in the following chapters.*

*Some of my readers would, no doubt, desire some scientific details on the botany and natural history of this country. That is, in fact, what they ought to expect from a man who had travelled for his pleasure, or to make discoveries: but the object of my travels was not of this description; my occupations had no relation with science; and, as I have said in my preface, I was not, and am not now, either a naturalist or a botanist.

CHAPTER XVIII

Natural Resources of the Columbia

THE mouth of the Columbia River is situated in 46° 19′ north latitude, and 125° or 126° of longitude west of the meridian of Greenwich. The highest tides are very little over nine or ten feet at its entrance, and are felt up stream for a distance of twenty-five or thirty leagues.

During the three years I spent there the cold never was much below the freezing point; and I do not think the heat ever exceeded 76.° Westerly winds prevail from the early part of spring and during a part of the summer; that wind generally springs up with the flood tide, and tempers the heat of the day. The northwest wind prevails during the latter part of summer and commencement of autumn. This last is succeeded by a southeast wind, which blows almost without intermission from the beginning of October to the end of December or commencement of January. This interval is the rainy season, the most disagreeable of the year. Fogs (so thick that sometimes for days no object is discernible for five or six hundred yards from the beach) are also very prevalent.[82]

[82]These observations may be compared with the latest available data of the U.S. Weather Bureau on the climate

The surface of the soil consists (in the valleys) of a layer of black vegetable mould about five or six inches thick at most; under this layer is found another of gray and loose, but extremely cold earth; below which is a bed of coarse sand and gravel, and next to that pebble or hard rock. On the more elevated parts the same black vegetable mould is found, but much thinner, and under it is the trap rock. We found along the seashore south of Point Adams a bank of earth white as chalk, which we used for white-washing our walls. The natives also brought us several specimens of blue, red, and yellow earth or clay, which they said was to be found at a great distance south; and also a sort of shining earth resembling lead ore. We found no limestone although we burned several kilns, but never could get one ounce of lime.

We had brought with us from New York a variety of garden seeds, which were put in the ground in the month of May, 1811, on a rich piece of land laid out for the purpose on a slop-

of Astoria, which show an extreme annual variation in temperature from 10 to 101 degrees. The average monthly temperatures, however, varied only from 44.9 to 58.4 degrees. The rainy season is considerably longer than Franchère's statement indicates, the monthly rainfall being in excess of 5 inches from October through April. The more extreme precipitation, which Franchère may have had in mind, ranged from November to March, with monthly averages in excess of 8 inches.

ing ground in front of our establishment. The garden had a fine appearance in the month of August;
but although the plants were left in the ground
until December not one of them came to maturity, with the exception of the radishes, the turnips, and the potatoes. The turnips grew to a
prodigious size; one of the largest we had the curiosity to weigh and measure; its circumference
was thirty-three inches, its weight fifteen and a
half pounds. The radishes were in full blossom
in the month of December and were left in the
ground to perfect the seeds for the ensuing season, but they were all destroyed by the ground
mice, who hid themselves under the stumps which
we had not rooted out and infested our garden.
With all the care we could bestow on them during the passage from New York, only twelve potatoes were saved, and even these so shrivelled up
that we despaired of raising any from the few
sprouts that still gave signs of life. Nevertheless,
we raised one hundred and ninety potatoes the
first season and after sparing a few plants for our
inland traders we planted about fifty or sixty hills,
which produced five bushels the second year;
about two of these were planted, and gave us a
welcome crop of fifty bushels in the year 1813.

It would result from these facts that the soil on
the banks of the river as far as tide water, or for a
distance of fifty or sixty miles, is very little adapted

for agriculture; at all events, vegetation is very
slow. It may be that the soil is not everywhere so
cold as the spot we selected for our garden, and
some other positions might have given a better
reward for our labor: this supposition is rendered
more than probable when we take into consideration the great difference in the indigenous vegetables of the country in different localities.

The forest trees most common at the mouth of
the river and near our establishment were cedar,
hemlock, white and red spruce, and alder. There
were a few dwarf white and gray ashes; and here
and there a soft maple. The alder grows also to a
very large size; I measured some of twelve to fifteen inches diameter; the wood was used by us in
preference to make charcoal for the blacksmith's
forge. But the largest of all the trees that I saw in
the country was a white spruce: this tree, which
had lost its top branches and bore evident marks
of having been struck by lightning, was a mere
straight trunk of about eighty to one hundred
feet in height; its barks whitened by age, made it
very conspicuous among the other trees with
their brown bark and dark foliage, like a huge
column of white marble. It stood on the slope of a
hill immediately in the rear of our palisades.
Seven of us placed ourselves round its trunk and
we could not embrace it by extending our arms
and touching merely the tips of our fingers; we

measured it afterward in a more regular manner and found it forty-two feet in circumference. It kept the same size, or nearly the same, to the very top.

We had it in contemplation at one time to construct a circular staircase to its summit and erect a platform thereon for an observatory, but more necessary and pressing demands on our time made us abandon the project.

A short distance above Astoria the oak and ash are plentiful, but neither of these is of much value or beauty.

From the middle of June to the middle of October we had abundance of wild fruit; first, strawberries, almost white, small but very sweet; then raspberries, both red and orange color. These grow on a bush sometimes twelve feet in height: they are not sweet, but of a large size.

The months of July and August furnish a small berry of an agreeable, slightly acid flavor; this berry grows on a slender bush of some eight to nine feet high, with small round leaves; they are in size like a wild cherry: some are blue, while others are of a cherry red: the last being smaller; they have no pits, or stones in them, but seeds, such as are to be seen in currants.

I noticed in the month of August another berry growing in bunches or grapes like the currant on a bush very similar to the currant bush: the leaves of this shrub resemble those of the laurel: they are very thick and always green. The fruit is oblong and disposed in two rows on the stem: the extremity of the berry is open, having a little speck or tuft like that of an apple. It is not of a particularly fine flavor, but it is wholesome, and one may eat a quantity of it without inconvenience. The natives make great use of it; they prepare it for the winter by bruising and drying it; after which it is moulded into cakes according to fancy and laid up for use. There is also a great abundance of cranberries, which proved very useful as an antiscorbutic.

We found also the whortleberry, chokecherries, gooseberries, and black currants with wild crab-apples: these last grow in clusters, are of small size and very tart. On the upper part of the river are found blackberries, hazel-nuts, acorns, &c. The country also possesses a great variety of nutritive roots: the natives make great use of those which have the virtue of curing or preventing the scurvy. We ate freely of them with the same intention, and with the same success. One of these roots, which much resembles a small onion, serves them, in some sort, in place of cheese. Having gathered a sufficient quantity, they bake them with red-hot stones until the steam ceases to ooze from the layer of grass and earth with which the roots are covered; then they pound them into a paste and make the paste into loaves of five or six pounds weight: the taste is not unlike liquorice, but not of so sickly a sweetness. When we made our first voyage up the river the natives gave us square biscuits, very well worked and printed with different figures. These are made of a white root, pounded, reduced to paste, and dried in the sun. They called it Chapaleel: it is not very palatable nor very nutritive.

But the principal food of the natives of the Columbia is fish. The salmon-fishery begins in July: that fish is here of an exquisite flavor, but it is extremely fat and oily; which renders it unwholesome for those who are not accustomed to it, and who eat too great a quantity: thus several of our people were attacked with diarrhœa in a few days after we began to make this fish our ordinary sustenance; but they found a remedy in the raspberries of the country, which have an astringent property.

The months of August and September furnish excellent sturgeon. This fish varies exceedingly in size; I have seen some eleven feet long; and we took one that weighed, after the removal of the eggs and intestines, three hundred and ninety pounds. We took out nine gallons of roe. The sturgeon does not enter the river in so great quantities as the salmon.

In October and November we had salmon, too, but of a quite different species—lean, dry and insipid. It differs from the other sort in form also; having very long teeth and a hooked nose like the beak of a parrot. Our men termed it in derision "seven bark salmon," because it had almost no nutritive substance.

February brings a small fish about the size of a sardine. It has an exquisite flavor and is taken in immense quantities by means of a scoop net which the Indians, seated in canoes, plunge into the schools: but the season is short, not even lasting two weeks.

The principal quadrupeds of the country are the elk; the black and white tailed deer; four species of bear, distinguished chiefly by the color of the fur or poil, to wit, the black, brown, white and grizzly bear; the grizzly bear is extremely ferocious; the white is found on the seashore toward the north; the wolf, the panther, the catamount, the lynx, the raccoon, the ground hog, opossum, mink, fisher, beaver, and the land and sea otter. The sea otter has the handsomest fur that is known; the skin surpasses that of the land variety in size and in the beauty of the poil; the most esteemed color is the silver gray, which is highly prized in the Indies and commands a great price.

The most remarkable birds are the eagle, the turkey-buzzard, the hawk, pelican, heron, gull, cormorant, crane, swan, and a great variety of wild ducks and geese. The pigeon, woodcock, and pheasant are found in the forests as with us.

CHAPTER XIX
The Native Inhabitants

THE natives inhabiting on the Columbia from the mouth of that river to the falls, that is to say on a space extending about 250 miles from east to west, are generally speaking of low stature, few of them passing five feet six inches, and many not even five feet. They pluck out the beard, in the manner of the other Indians of North America; but a few of the old men only suffer a tuft to grow upon their chins. On arriving among them we were exceedingly surprised to see that they had almost all flattened heads. This configuration is not a natural deformity, but an effect of art, caused by compression of the skull in infancy. It shocks strangers extremely, especially at first sight; nevertheless, among these barbarians it is an indispensable ornament: and when we signified to them how much this mode of flattening the forehead appeared to us to violate nature and good taste, they answered that it was only slaves who had not their heads flattened. The slaves, in fact, have the usual rounded head, and they are not permitted to flatten the foreheads of their children, destined to bear the chains of their sires.[83] The natives of the Columbia procure these

[83]The name Flathead has been applied to many tribes which did not practice the custom which Franchère de-

slaves from the neighboring tribes, and from the interior, in exchange for beads and furs. They treat them with humanity while their services are useful, but as soon as they become incapable of labor neglect them and suffer them to perish of want. When dead, they throw their bodies, without ceremony, under the stump of an old decayed tree, or drag them to the woods to be devoured by the wolves and vultures.

The Indians of the Columbia are of a light copper color, active in body and, above all, excellent swimmers. They are addicted to theft, or rather they make no scruple of laying hands on whatever suits them in the property of strangers, whenever they can find an opportunity. The goods and effects of European manufacture are so precious in the eyes of these barbarians that they rarely resist the temptation of stealing them.

These savages are not addicted to intemperance, unlike, in that respect, the other American Indians, if we must not also except the Patagonians, who, like the Flatheads, regard intoxicating drinks as poisons and drunkenness as disgraceful. I will relate a fact in point: one of the sons of the chief Comcomly being at the establishment one day, some of the gentlemen amused

scribes. Oddly enough, the term was applied to tribes which did not practice the head-flattening custom, rather than to those of the lower Columbia which did, since in contrast with the latter their heads, left in their natural condition, were flat on top.

themselves with making him drink wine and he was very soon drunk. He was sick in consequence, and remained in a state of stupor for two days. The old Chief came to reproach us, saying that we had degraded his son by exposing him to the ridicule of the slaves, and besought us not to induce him to take strong liquors in future.

The men go entirely naked, not concealing any part of their bodies. Only in winter they throw over the shoulders a panther's skin, or else a sort of mantle made of the skins of wood-rats sewed together. In rainy weather I have seen them wear a mantle of rush mats, like a Roman toga or the vestment which a priest wears in celebrating mass; thus equipped, and furnished with a conical hat made from fibrous roots and impermeable, they may call themselves rain-proof. The women, in addition to the mantle of skins, wear a petticoat made of the cedar bark, which they attach round the girdle and which reaches to the middle of the thigh. It is a little longer behind than before, and is fabricated in the following manner: They strip off the fine bark of the cedar, soak it as one soaks hemp, and when it is drawn out into fibers, work it into a fringe; then, with a strong cord they bind the fringes together. With so poor a vestment they contrive to satisfy the requirements of modesty; when they stand it drapes them fairly enough; and when they squat down in their manner it falls between their legs, leaving nothing exposed but the bare knees and thighs. Some of the younger women twist the fibers of bark into small cords knotted at the ends, and so form the petticoat, disposed in a fringe like the first, but more easily kept clean and of better appearance.

Cleanliness is not a virtue among these females, who, in that respect, resemble the other Indian women of the continent. They anoint the body and dress the hair with fish oil, which does not diffuse an agreeable perfume. Their hair (which both sexes wear long) is jet black; it is badly combed, but parted in the middle, as is the custom of the sex everywhere, and kept shining by the fish-oil before-mentioned. Sometimes, in imitation of the men, they paint the whole body with a red earth mixed with fish-oil. Their ornaments consist of bracelets of brass, which they wear indifferently on the wrists and ankles; of strings of beads of different colors (they give a preference to the blue) and displayed in great profusion around the neck and on the arms and legs; and of white shells, called Haiqua, which are their ordinary circulating medium. These shells are found beyond the Straits of Juan de Fuca, and are from one to four inches long and about half an inch in diameter: they are a little curved and naturally perforated: the longest are most valued. The price of all commodities is reckoned in these shells; a fathom string of the largest of them is worth about ten beaver-skins.

Although a little less slaves than the greater part of the Indian women elsewhere, the women on the Columbia are, nevertheless, charged with the most painful labors; they fetch water and wood, and carry the goods in their frequent changes of residence; they clean the fish and cut it up for drying; they prepare the food and cook the fruits in their season. Among their principal occupations is that of making rush mats, baskets for gathering roots, and hats very ingeniously wrought. As they want little clothing they do not sew much, and the men have the needle in hand oftener than they.

The men are not lazy, especially during the fishing season. Not being hunters, and eating, consequently, little flesh-meat (although they are fond of it) fish makes, as I have observed, their principal diet. They profit, therefore, by the season when it is to be had, by taking as much as they can; knowing that the intervals will be periods of famine and abstinence, unless they provide sufficiently beforehand.

Their canoes are all made of cedar, and of a single trunk: we saw some which were five feet

wide at midships and thirty feet in length; these
are the largest, and will carry from 25 to 30
men; the smallest will carry but two or three.
The bows terminate in a very elongated point,
running out four or five feet from the water line.
It constitutes a separate piece, very ingeniously
attached, and serves to break the surf in landing,
or the wave on a rough sea. In landing they
put the canoe round, so as to strike the beach
stern on. Their oars or paddles are made of
ash and are about five feet long, with a broad
blade in the shape of an inverted crescent and
a cross at the top, like the handle of a crutch.
The object of the crescent shape of the blade is
to be able to draw it edge-wise through the
water without making any noise when they hunt
the sea-otter, an animal which can only be
caught when it is lying asleep on the rocks, and
which has the sense of hearing very acute. All
their canoes are painted red and fancifully decorated.

Their houses, constructed of cedar, are remarkable for their form and size: some of them
are one hundred feet in length by thirty or
forty feet in width. They are constructed as
follows: An oblong square of the intended size
of the building is dug out to the depth of two
or three feet; a double row of cedar posts is
driven into the earth about ten feet apart; be-

tween these the planks are laid, overlapping each
other to the requisite height. The roof is formed
by a ridge-pole laid on taller posts, notched to
receive it, and is constructed with rafters and
planks laid clapboard-wise and secured by cords
for want of nails. When the house is designed
for several families there is a door for each, and
a separate fireplace; the smoke escapes through
an aperture formed by removing one of the
boards of the roof. The door is low, of an oval
shape, and is provided with a ladder, cut out of
a log, to descend into the lodge. The entrance
is generally effected stern-foremost.

The kitchen utensils consists of plates of ash-
wood, bowls of fibrous roots, and a wooden kettle: with these they succeed in cooking their fish
and meat in less time than we take with the help
of pots and stewpans. See how they do it!
Having heated a number of stones red-hot, they
plunge them, one by one, in the vessel which is
to contain the food to be prepared; as soon as
the water boils, they put in the fish or meat, with
some more heated stones on top, and cover up
the whole with small rush mats to retain the
steam. In an incredibly short space of time
the article is taken out and placed on a wooden
platter, perfectly done and very palatable. The
broth is taken out also, with a ladle of wood
or horn.

It will be asked, no doubt, what instruments these savages use in the construction of their canoes and their houses. To cause their patience and industry to be admired as much as they deserve it will be sufficient for me to mention that we did not find among them a single hatchet: their only tools consisted of an inch or half-inch chisel, usually made of an old file, and of a mallet, which was nothing but an oblong stone. With these wretched implements, and wedges made of hemlock knots steeped in oil and hardened by the fire, they would undertake to cut down the largest cedars of the forest, to dig them out and fashion them into canoes, to split them and get out the boards wherewith to build their houses. Such achievements with such means are a marvel of ingenuity and patience.

CHAPTER XX

War, Matrimony, and Religion

THE politics of the natives of the Columbia are a simple affair: each village has its chief, but that chief does not seem to exercise a great authority over his fellow-citizens. Nevertheless, at his death they pay him great honors: they use a kind of mourning which consists in painting the face with black in lieu of gay colors; they chant his funeral song or oration for a whole month. The chiefs are considered in proportion to their riches: such a chief has a great many wives, slaves, and strings of beads—he is accounted a great chief. These barbarians approach in that respect to certain civilized nations, among whom the worth of a man is estimated by the quantity of gold he possesses.

As all the villages form so many independent sovereignties, differences sometimes arise whether between the chiefs or the tribes. Ordinarily these terminate by compensations equivalent to the injury. But when the latter is of a grave character, like a murder (which is rare) or the abduction of a woman (which is very common) the parties, having made sure of a number of young braves to aid them, prepare for war. Before commencing hostilities, however, they give no-

tice of the day when they will proceed to attack
the hostile village; not following in that respect
the custom of almost all other American Indians,
who are wont to burst upon their enemy un-
awares and to massacre or carry off men, women, and children; these people, on the contrary,
embark in their canoes, which on these occasions
are paddled by the women, repair to the hostile
village, enter into parley, and do all they can to
terminate the affair amicably: sometimes a third
party becomes mediator between the first two,
and of course observes an exact neutrality. If
those who seek justice do not obtain it to their
satisfaction, they retire to some distance and the
combat begins and is continued for some time
with fury on both sides; but as soon as one or
two men are killed, the party which has lost these
owns itself beaten and the battle ceases. If it is
the people of the village attacked who are
worsted, the others do not retire without receiving presents. When the conflict is postponed till
the next day (for they never fight but in open
daylight, as if to render nature witness of their
exploits) they keep up frightful cries all night
long, and when they are sufficiently near to understand each other, defy one another by men-
aces, railleries, and sarcasms, like the heroes of
Homer and Virgil. The women and children are
always removed from the village before the action.

Their combats are almost all maritime: for they fight ordinarily in their pirogues, which they take care to careen so as to present the broadside to the enemy, and half lying down, avoid the greater part of the arrows let fly at them.

But the chief reason of the bloodlessness of their combats is the inefficiency of their offensive weapons and the excellence of their defensive armor. Their offensive arms are merely a bow and arrow and a kind of double-edged saber about two and a half feet long and six inches wide in the blade: they rarely come to sufficiently close quarters to make use of the last. For defensive armor they wear a cassock or tunic of elkskin double, descending to the ankles, with holes for the arms. It is impenetrable by their arrows, which can not pierce two thicknesses of leather; and as their heads are also covered with a sort of helmet the neck is almost the only part in which they can be wounded. They have another kind of corselet, made like the corsets of our ladies, of splinters of hard wood interlaced with nettle twine. The warrior who wears this cuirass does not use the tunic of elk-skin; he is consequently less protected, but a great deal more free; the said tunic being very heavy and very stiff.

It is almost useless to observe that in their military expeditions, they have their bodies and faces daubed with different paints, often of the most extravagant designs. I remember to have seen a war-chief with one exact half of his face painted white and the other half black.

Their marriages are conducted with a good deal of ceremony. When a young man seeks a girl in marriage his parents make the proposals to those of the intended bride, and when it has been agreed upon what presents the future bridegroom is to offer to the parents of the bride, all parties assemble at the house of the latter, whither the neighbors are invited to witness the contract. The presents, which consist of slaves, strings of beads, copper bracelets, haiqua shells, &c., are distributed by the young man, who, on his part, receives as many, and sometimes more, according to the means or the munificence of the parents of his betrothed. The latter is then led forward by the old matrons and presented to the young man, who takes her as his wife, and all retire to their quarters.

The men are not very scrupulous in their choice, and take small pains to inform themselves what conduct a young girl has observed before her nuptials; and it must be owned that few marriages would take place, if the youth would only espouse maidens without reproach on the score of chastity; for the unmarried girls are by no means scrupulous in that particular, and their parents give them, on that head, full liberty. But once the marriage is contracted the spouses observe toward each other an inviolable fidelity; adultery is almost unknown among them, and the woman who should be guilty of it would be punished with death. At the same time the husband may repudiate his wife, and the latter may then unite herself in marriage to another man. Polygamy is permitted, indeed is customary; there are some who have as many as four or five wives; and although it often happens that the husband loves one better than the rest, they never show any jealousy, but live together in the most perfect concord.

There are charlatans everywhere, but they are more numerous among savages than anywhere else because among these ignorant and superstitious people the trade is at once more profitable and less dangerous. As soon as a native of the Columbia is indisposed, no matter what the malady, they send for the medicine man, who treats the patient in the absurd manner usually adopted by these impostors, and with such violence of manipulation that often a sick man, whom a timely bleeding or purgative would have saved, is carried off by a sudden death.

They deposit their dead in canoes on rocks sufficiently elevated not to be overflowed by the spring freshets. By the side of the dead are laid his bow, his arrows, and some of his fishing im-

plements; if it is a woman, her beads and bracelets: the wives, the relatives, and the slaves of the
defunct cut their hair in sign of grief, and for
several days, at the rising and setting of the sun,
go to some distance from the village to chant a
funeral song.

These people have not, properly speaking, a
public worship. I could never perceive, during
my residence among them, that they worshipped
any idol. They had, nevertheless, some small
sculptured figures; but they appeared to hold
them in light esteem, offering to barter them for
trifles.

Having travelled with one of the sons of the
chief of the Chinooks (Comcomly), an intelligent
and communicative young man, I put to him several questions touching their religious belief, and
the following is in substance what he told me
respecting it: Men, according to their ideas, were
created by a divinity whom they name Etalapass;
but they were imperfect, having a mouth that
was not opened, eyes that were fast closed, hands
and feet that were not moveable; in a word, they
were rather statues of flesh, than living men. A
second divinity, whom they call Ecannum, less
powerful, but more benign than the former, having seen men in their state of imperfection, took
a sharp stone and laid open their mouths and
eyes; he gave agility, also, to their feet, and mo-

tion to their hands. This compassionate divinity
was not content with conferring these first benefits; he taught men to make canoes, paddles, nets,
and, in a word, all the tools and instruments they
use. He did still more: he threw great rocks into
the river to obstruct the ascent of the salmon, in
order that they might take as many as they
wanted.

The natives of the Columbia further believe
that the men who have been good citizens, good
fathers, good husbands, and good fishermen, who
have not committed murder, &c., will be perfectly happy after their death and will go to a country
where they will find fish, fruit, &c. in abundance;
and that, on the contrary, those who have lived
wickedly will inhabit a country of fasting and
want, where they will eat nothing but bitter roots
and have nothing to drink but salt water.

If these notions in regard to the origin and
future destiny of man are not exactly conformed
to sound reason or to divine revelation, it will be
allowed that they do not offer the absurdities
with which the mythologies of many ancient nations abound. The article which makes skill in
fishing a virtue worthy of being compensated in
the other world does not disfigure the salutary
and consoling dogma of the immortality of the
soul and that of future rewards and punishments
so much as one is at first tempted to think; for if

we reflect a little we shall discover that the skilful fisherman, in laboring for himself labors also for society; he is a useful citizen, who contributes as much as lies in his power to avert from his fellow-men the scourge of famine; he is a religious man, who honors the divinity by making use of his benefits. Surely a great deal of the theology of a future life prevalent among civilized men does not excel this in profundity.

It is not to be expected that men perfectly ignorant, like these Indians, should be free from superstitions: one of the most ridiculous they have regards the method of preparing and eating fish. In the month of July, 1811, the natives brought us at first a very scanty supply of the fresh salmon, from the fear that we would cut the fish crosswise instead of lengthwise; being persuaded that if we did so, the river would be obstructed and the fishing ruined. Having reproached the chief on that account, they brought us a greater quantity, but all cooked, and which, not to displease them, it was necessary to eat before sunset. Re-assured at last by our solemn promises not to cut the fish crosswise, they supplied us abundantly during the remainder of the season.

In spite of the vices that may be laid to the charge of the natives of the Columbia, I regard them as nearer to a state of civilization than any

of the tribes who dwell east of the Rocky Mountains. They did not appear to me so attached to
their customs that they could not easily adopt
those of civilized nations: they would dress themselves willingly in the European mode, if they
had the means. To encourage this taste, we lent
pantaloons to the chiefs who visited us, when
they wished to enter our houses, never allowing
them to do it in a state of nudity. They possess
in an eminent degree the qualities opposed to indolence, improvidence, and stupidity: the chiefs,
above all, are distinguished for their good sense
and intelligence. Generally speaking, they have a
ready intellect and a tenacious memory. Thus old
Comcomly recognised the mate of the *Albatross*
as having visited the country sixteen years before, and recalled to the latter the name of the
captain under whom he had sailed at that period.

The Chinook language is spoken by all the nations from the mouth of the Columbia to the
Falls. It is hard and difficult to pronounce, for
strangers; being full of gutturals, like the Gaelic.
The combinations *thl,* or *tl,* and *lt,* are as frequent in the Chinook as in the Mexican.[84]

---

[84]In the 1820 edition this chapter concludes with a Chinook vocabulary which must have been supplied to Editor
Bibaud by Franchère. It is regrettable that Huntington did
not include it in the 1854 edition.

Chapter XXI
Return to Canada

WE quitted Fort George (or Astoria, if you please) on Monday morning, the 4th of April, 1814, in ten canoes, five of which were of bark and five of cedar wood, carrying each seven men as crew and two passengers, in all ninety persons, and all well armed. Messrs. J. G. McTavish, D. Stuart, J. Clarke, B. Pillet, W. Wallace, D. McGillis, D. McKenzie, &c. were of the party. Nothing remarkable occurred to us as far as the first falls, which we reached on the 10th. The portage was effected immediately, and we encamped on an island for the night. Our numbers had caused the greater part of the natives to take to flight, and those who remained in the villages showed the most pacific dispositions. They sold us four horses and thirty dogs, which were immediately slaughtered for food.

We resumed our route on the 11th at an early hour. The wind was favorable, but blew with violence. Toward evening the canoe in which Mr. McTavish was, in doubling a point of rock, was run under by its press of sail and sunk. Happily the river was not deep at this place; no one was drowned; and we succeeded in saving all the goods. This accident compelled us to camp at an early hour.

On the 12th we arrived at a rapid called the Dalles: this is a channel cut by nature through the rocks, which are here almost perpendicular: the channel is from 150 to 300 feet wide and about two miles long. The whole body of the river rushes through it with great violence and renders navigation impracticable. The portage occupied us till dusk. Although we had not seen a single Indian in the course of the day we kept sentinels on duty all night: for it was here that Messrs. Stuart and Reed were attacked by the natives.

On the 13th we made two more portages and met Indians, of whom we purchased horses and wood. We camped early on a sandy plain, where we passed a bad night; the wind, which blew violently, raised clouds of sand which incommoded us greatly and spoiled every mouthful of food we took.

On the 14th and 15th we passed what are called the Great Plains of the Columbia. From the top of the first rapid to this point the aspect of the country becomes more and more barren and disagreeable; one meets at first nothing but bare hills, which scarcely offer a few isolated pines at a great distance from each other; after that, the earth, stripped of verdure, does not afford you

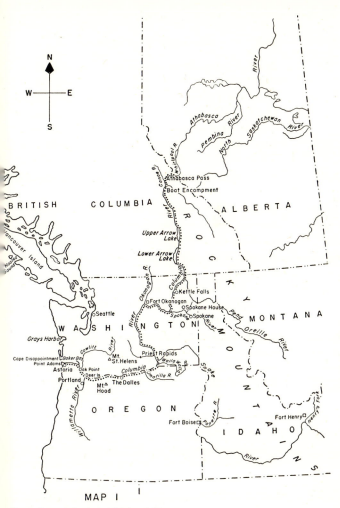

MAP I

Route from Astoria to Whirlpool River ············

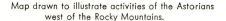

SCALE IN MILES

Map drawn to illustrate activities of the Astorians
west of the Rocky Mountains.

the sight of a single shrub; the little grass which grows in that arid soil appears burnt by the rigor of the climate. The natives who frequent the banks of the river for the salmon fishery have no other wood but that which they take floating down. We passed several rapids and a small stream called Utalah, which flows from the southeast.[85]

On the 16th we found the river narrowed; the banks rose on either side in elevations, without, however, offering a single tree. We reached the river Wallawalla, which empties into the Columbia on the southeast. It is narrow at its confluence and is not navigable for any great distance. A range of mountains was visible to the S. E., about fifty or sixty miles off. Behind these mountains the country becomes again flat and sandy, and is inhabited by a tribe called the Snakes. We found on the left bank of the Wallawalla an encampment of Indians consisting of about twenty lodges. They sold us six dogs and eight horses, the greater part extremely lean. We killed two of the horses immediately: I mounted one of the six that remained; Mr. Ross took another; and we drove the other four before us. Toward the de-

[85]The Umatilla, which rises in the Blue Mountains of northeastern Oregon and flows northwesterly to the Columbia. The town of Umatilla is at its mouth, Pendleton, the county seat of Umatilla County, is on this river.

cline of day we passed the river Lewis, called, in
the language of the country the Sha-ap-tin.[86] It
comes from the S. E. and is the same that Lewis
and Clark descended in 1805. The Sha-ap-tin
appeared to me to have little depth, and to be
about 300 yards wide at its confluence.

The country through which we were now passing was a mingling of hills, steep rocks, and valleys covered with wormwood; the stems of which
shrub are nearly six inches thick and might serve
for fuel. We killed six rattlesnakes on the 15th,
and on the 16th saw a great many more among
the rocks. These dangerous reptiles appeared to
be very numerous in this part of the country. The
plains are also inhabited by a little quadruped
only about eight or nine inches in length and approaching the dog in form. These animals have
the hair, or poil, of a reddish brown, and strong
fore-paws, armed with long claws which serve
them to dig out their holes under the earth. They
have a great deal of curiosity: as soon as they
hear a noise they come out of their holes and
bark. They are not vicious, but, though easily
tamed, can not be domesticated.[87]

[86]The Snake, to which Captain William Clark attached
the name Lewis in honor of his associate, Meriwether
Lewis.

[87]The prairie dog, whose characteristics were the subject of frequent comment by early travelers throughout
the western country.

The natives of the upper Columbia, beginning at the Falls, differ essentially in language, manners, and habits from those of whom I have spoken in the preceding chapters. They do not dwell in villages like the latter, but are nomads, like the Tartars and the Arabs of the desert: their women are more industrious, and the young girls more reserved and chaste than those of the populations lower down. They do not go naked, but both sexes wear habits made of dressed deerskin, which they take care to rub with chalk to keep them clean and white. They are almost always seen on horseback, and are in general good riders; they pursue the deer and penetrate even to the Missouri to kill buffaloes, the flesh of which they dry, and bring it back on their horses to make their principal food during the winter. These expeditions are not free from danger; for they have a great deal to apprehend from the Blackfeet, who are their enemies. As this last tribe is powerful and ferocious, the Snakes, the Pierced-noses or Sha-ap-tins, the Flatheads, &c., make common cause against them when the former go to hunt east of the mountains. They set out with their families and the cavalcade often numbers two thousand horses. When they have the good fortune not to encounter the enemy they return with the spoils of an abundant chase; they load a part of their horses with the hides and beef and return home to pass the winter in peace. Sometimes, on the contrary, they are so harassed by the Blackfeet, who surprise them in the night and carry off their horses, that they are forced to return light-handed, and then they have nothing to eat but roots all the winter.

These Indians are passionately fond of horse-races: by the bets they make on these occasions they sometimes lose all that they possess. The women ride as well as the men. For a bridle they use a cord of horse-hair, which they attach round the animal's mouth; with that he is easily checked, and by laying the hand on his neck is made to wheel to this side or that. The saddle is a cushion of stuffed deer-skin, very suitable for the purpose to which it is destined, rarely hurting the horse and not fatiguing the rider so much as our European saddles. The stirrups are pieces of hard wood, ingeniously wrought, and of the same shape as those which are used in civilized countries. They are covered with a piece of deer-skin, which is sewed on wet and in drying stiffens and becomes hard and firm. The saddles for women differ in form, being furnished with the antlers of a deer, so as to resemble the high pommelled saddle of the Mexican ladies.

They procure their horses from the herds of these animals which are found in a wild state in

the country extending between the northern latitudes and the Gulf of Mexico, and which sometimes count a thousand or fifteen hundred in a
troop. These horses come from New Mexico and
are of the Spanish race. We even saw some which
had been marked with a hot iron by Spaniards.
Some of our men who had been at the south told
me that they had seen among the Indians, bridles,
the bits of which were of silver. The form of the
saddles used by the females proves that they
have taken their pattern from the Spanish ones
destined for the same use. One of the partners
of the N. W. Company (Mr. McTavish) assured
us that he had seen among the Spokans an old
woman who told him that she had seen men
ploughing the earth; she told him that she had
also seen churches, which she made him understand by imitating the sound of a bell and the action of pulling a bell-rope; and further to confirm her account, made the sign of the cross.
That gentleman concluded that she had been
made prisoner and sold to the Spaniards on the
Del Norte;[88] but I think it more probable it was
nearer, in North California, at the mission of San
Carlos or San Francisco.[89]

[88]The Rio Grande.
[89]San Carlos Mission was in the vicinity of Monterey,
California. San Francisco Mission was on the site of the
present-day city of San Francisco. Both were founded in
the 1770's.

As the manner of taking wild horses would
not be generally known to my readers I will relate it here in few words. The Indian who wishes
to capture some horses mounts one of his fleetest
coursers, being armed with a long cord of horse-
hair, one end of which is attached to his saddle
and the other is a running noose. Arrived at the
herd, he dashes into the midst of it and flinging
his cord, or lasso, passes it dexterously over the
head of the animal he selects; then wheeling his
courser, draws the cord after him; the wild horse,
finding itself strangling, makes little resistance;
the Indian then approaches, ties his fore and
hind legs together, and leaves him till he has tak-
en in this manner as many as he can. He then
drives them home before him, and breaks them
in at leisure.

Chapter XXII

On the Upper Columbia

ON the 17th the fatigue I had experienced the
day before on horseback obliged me to re-
embark in my canoe. About eight o'clock we
passed a little river flowing from the N. W. We
perceived, soon after, three canoes, the persons
in which were struggling with their paddles to
overtake us. As we were still pursuing our way,
we heard a child's voice cry out in French—
"arrêtez donc, arrêtez, donc"—(stop! stop!). We
put ashore, and the canoes having joined us, we
perceived in one of them the wife and children of
a man named Pierre Dorion, a hunter who had
been sent on with a party of eight, under the command of Mr. J. Reed, among the Snakes, to join
there the hunters left by Messrs. Hunt and Crooks
near Fort Henry and to secure horses and provisions for our journey. This woman informed us,
to our no small dismay, of the tragical fate of all
those who composed that party. She told us that
in the month of January, the hunters being dispersed here and there setting their traps for the
beaver, Jacob Regner, Gilles Leclerc, and Pierre
Dorion, her husband, had been attacked by the
natives. Leclerc, having been mortally wounded,
reached her tent or hut, where he expired in a

few minutes, after having announced to her that her husband had been killed. She immediately took two horses that were near the lodge, mounted her two boys upon them, and fled in all haste to the wintering house of Mr. Reed, which was about five days' march from the spot where her husband fell. Her horror and disappointment were extreme when she found the house—a log cabin—deserted, and on drawing nearer was soon convinced by the traces of blood that Mr. Reed also had been murdered. No time was to be lost in lamentations, and she had immediately fled toward the mountains south of the Wallawalla, where, being impeded by the depth of the snow, she was forced to winter, having killed both the horses to subsist herself and her children. But at last, finding herself out of provisions, and the snow beginning to melt, she had crossed the mountains with her boys, hoping to find some more humane Indians, who would let her live among them till the boats from the fort below should be ascending the river in the spring, and so reached the banks of the Columbia, by the Wallawalla. Here, indeed, the natives had received her with much hospitality, and it was the Indians of Wallawalla who brought her to us. We made them some presents to repay their care and pains, and they returned well satisfied.

The persons who lost their lives in this unfortunate wintering party were Mr. John Reed (clerk), Jacob Regner, John Hubbough, Pierre Dorion (hunters), Gilles Leclerc, François Landry, J. B. Turcotte, André la Chapelle and Pierre De Launay (voyageurs).[90] We had no doubt that this massacre was an act of vengeance on the part of the natives in retaliation for the death of one of their people, whom Mr. John Clarke had hanged for theft the spring before.[91] This fact, the massacre on the *Tonquin,* the unhappy end of Captain Cook, and many other similar examples prove how carefully the Europeans, who have relations with a barbarous people, should abstain from acting in regard to them on the footing of too marked an inequality, and especially from punishing their offenses according to usages and codes in which there is too often an enormous disproportion between the crime and

[90]Chapelle's name is not included among the number listed by Franchère in the Manuscript. A footnote supplied by Bibaud at this point states that Turcotte died of the king's evil. De Launay was a half-breed of violent temper, who had taken an Indian wife. He left Reed in the autumn and was never again heard from.

[91]Both Alexander Ross and Ross Cox supply accounts of the execution to which Franchère here alludes. Cox, a member of Clarke's party, does not criticize the leader. Ross's narrative, however, is severely critical of Clarke's action. *First Settlers on the Oregon,* 230–35.

The remainder of the present paragraph is the work of Editor Bibaud; it is not found in the Manuscript.

the punishment. If these pretended exemplary punishments seem to have a good effect at first sight, they almost always produce terrible consequences in the sequel.

On the 18th, we passed Priest's Rapid, so named by Mr. Stuart and his people, who saw at this spot in 1811, as they were ascending the river, a number of savages, one of whom was performing on the rest certain aspersions and other ceremonies which had the air of being coarse imitations of the Catholic worship.[92] For our part, we met here some Indians of whom we bought two horses. The banks of the river at this place are tolerably high, but the country back of them is flat and uninteresting.

On the 20th we arrived at a place where the bed of the river is extremely contracted, and where we were obliged to make a portage. Messrs. J. Stuart and Clarke left us here to proceed on horseback to the Spokan trading house, to procure there the provisions which would be necessary for us in order to push on to the mountains.

On the 21st we lightened of their cargoes three canoes, in which those who were to cross the Continent embarked to get on with greater speed. We passed several rapids and began to see mountains covered with snow.

[92]Priest Rapids, still so called, is shown on modern maps at the northeastern corner of Yakima County, Washington.

On the 22d we began to see some pines on the ridge of the neighboring hills; and at evening we encamped under trees, a thing which had not happened to us since the 12th.

On the 23d toward 9 A.M. we reached the trading post established by D. Stuart at the mouth of the river Okenakan. The spot appeared to us charming, in comparison with the country through which we had journeyed for twelve days past: the two rivers here meeting, and the immense prairies covered with a fine verdure, strike agreeably the eye of the observer; but there is not a tree or a shrub to diversify the scene, and render it a little less naked and less monotonous. We found here Messrs. J. McGillivray and Ross, and Mr. O. de Montigny, who had taken service with the N. W. Company, and who charged me with a letter for his brother.[93]

Toward midday we re-embarked to continue our journey. After having passed several dangerous rapids without accident, always through a country broken by shelving rocks, diversified with hills and verdant prairies, we arrived on the 29th at the portage of the Chaudieres or Kettle

---

[93]Ross had accompanied the expedition from Astoria to this place. He left it here, to continue at various posts in the Columbia and Rocky Mountain area until 1825. In 1813 he married an Okanogan woman, by whom he had several children.

Joseph McGillivray was a son of William, for whom Fort William was named.

Falls. This is a fall where the water precipitates itself over an immense rock of white marble, veined with red and green, that traverses the bed of the river from N. W. to S. E. We effected the portage immediately and encamped on the edge of a charming prairie.

We found at this place some Indians who had been fasting, they assured us, for several days. They appeared, in fact, reduced to the most pitiable state, having nothing left but skin and bones and scarcely able to drag themselves along, so that not without difficulty could they even reach the margin of the river to get a little water to wet their parched lips. It is a thing that often happens to these poor people when their chase has not been productive; their principal nourishment consisting, in that case, of the pine moss, which they boil till it is reduced to a sort of glue or black paste, of a sufficient consistence to take the form of biscuit. I had the curiosity to taste this bread and I thought I had got in my mouth a bit of soap. Yet some of our people who had been reduced to eat this glue assured me that when fresh made it had a very good taste, seasoned with meat. We partly relieved these wretched natives from our scanty store.

On the 30th, while we were yet encamped at Kettle Falls, Messrs. J. Stuart and Clarke arrived from the post at Spokan. The last was mounted on the finest-proportioned gray charger, full seventeen hands high, that I had seen in these parts: Mr. Stuart had got a fall from his, in trying to urge him, and had hurt himself severely. These gentlemen not having brought us the provisions we expected, because the hunters who had been sent for that purpose among the Flatheads had not been able to procure any, it was resolved to divide our party, and that Messrs. McDonald, J. Stuart, and McKenzie should go forward to the post situated east of the mountains, in order to send us thence horses and supplies. These gentlemen quitted us on the 1st of May. After their departure we killed two horses and dried the meat; which occupied us the rest of that day and all the next. In the evening of the 2d, Mr. A. Stuart arrived at our camp. He had recovered from his wounds (received in the conflict with the natives, before related) and was on his way to his old wintering place on Slave Lake to fetch his family to the Columbia.

We resumed our route on the morning of the 3d of May, and went to encamp that evening at the upper end of a rapid, where we began to descry mountains covered with forests and where the banks of the river themselves were low and thinly timbered.

On the 4th, after having passed several considerable rapids, we reached the confluence of Flathead River.[94] This stream comes from the S. E. and falls into the Columbia in the form of a cascade: it may be one hundred and fifty yards wide at its junction.

On the morning of the 5th we arrived at the confluence of the Coutonois River.[95] This stream also flows from the south, and has nearly the same width as the Flathead. Shortly after passing it we entered a lake or enlargement of the river, which we crossed to encamp at its upper extremity. This lake may be thirty or forty miles long and about four wide at its broadest part: it is surrounded by lofty hills, which for the most part have their base at the water's edge and rise by gradual and finely-wooded terraces, offering a sufficiently pretty view.[96]

On the 6th, after we had run through a narrow strait or channel some fifteen miles long, we entered another lake, of less extent than the former but equally picturesque.[97] When we were nearly in the middle of it an accident occurred which, if not very disastrous, was sufficiently sin-

---

[94]Clark's Fork, or Pend Oreille River, which joins the Columbia close to the Washington-British Columbia boundary.

[95]The Kootenay, one of the principal affluents of the Columbia.

[96]Lower Arrow Lake in Kootenay District, British Columbia.

[97]Upper Arrow Lake.

gular. One of the men, who had been on the sick-list for several days, requested to be landed for an instant. Not being more than a mile from the shore we acceded to his request, and made accordingly for a projecting head-land; but when we were about three hundred or four hundred yards from the point, the canoe struck with force against the trunk of a tree which was planted in the bottom of the lake, and the extremity of which barely reached the surface of the water. It needed no more to break a hole in so frail a vessel; the canoe was pierced through the bottom and filled in a trice; and despite all our efforts we could not get off the tree, which had penetrated two or three feet within her; perhaps that was our good fortune, for the opening was at least a yard long. One of the men who was an expert swimmer, stripped, and was about to go ashore with an axe lashed to his back to make a raft for us, when the other canoe, which had been proceeding up the lake and was a mile ahead, perceived our signals of distress and came to our succor. They carried us to land, where it was necessary to encamp forthwith, as well to dry ourselves as to mend the canoe.

On the 7th Mr. A. Stuart, whom we had left behind at Kettle Falls, came up with us and we pursued our route in company. Toward evening we met natives camped on the bank of the river:

they gave us a letter from which we learned that Mr. McDonald and his party had passed there on the 4th. The women at this camp were busy spinning the coarse wool of the mountain sheep: they had blankets or mantles woven or platted of the same material, with a heavy fringe all round: I would gladly have purchased one of these, but as we were to carry all our baggage on our backs across the mountains, was forced to relinquish the idea. Having bought of these savages some pieces of dried venison we pursued our journey. The country began to be ascending; the stream was very rapid; and we made that day little progress.

On the 8th we began to see snow on the shoals or sand-banks of the river: the atmosphere grew very cold. The banks on either side presented only high hills covered to the top with impenetrable forests. While the canoes were working up a considerable rapid, I climbed the hills with Mr. McGillis and we walked on, following the course of the river, some five or six miles. The snow was very deep in the ravines or narrow gorges which are found between the bases of the hills. The most common trees are the Norway pine and the cedar: the last is here, as on the borders of the sea, of a prodigious size.

On the 9th and 10th, as we advanced but slowly, the country presented the same aspect as on

the 8th. Toward evening of the 10th we perceived ahead of us a chain of high mountains entirely covered with snow.[98] The bed of the river
was hardly more than sixty yards wide, and was
filled with dry banks composed of coarse gravel
and small pebbles.

[98]The Selkirk Range of the Rocky Mountains.

CHAPTER XXIII

Crossing the Rocky Mountains

O N the 11th, that is to say one month, day for
day, after our departure from the Falls, we
quitted the Columbia to enter a little stream to
which Mr. Thompson had given, in 1811, the
name of Canoe River, from the fact that it was on
this fork that he constructed the canoes which
carried him to the Pacific.[99]

The Columbia, which in the portion above the
Falls (not taking into consideration some local
sinuosities) comes from the N. N. E., takes a
bend here so that the stream appears to flow from
the S. E. Some boatmen, and particularly Mr.
Regis Bruguier, who had ascended that river to
its source, informed me that it came out of two
small lakes not far from the chain of the Rocky
Mountains, which at that place diverges considerably to the east.[100] According to Arrowsmith's
map, the course of the Tacoutche Tessé,[101] from

[99]See *ante*, p. 83. The Canoe River, northernmost trib-
utary of the Columbia, rises near the Fraser and flows in
a southerly direction to its junction with the Columbia at
the northernmost point attained by the latter.
[100]From this point to the paragraph break on page 219
the narrative seems to be the work of Bibaud. In the Manuscript the narrative resumes with the succeeding paragraph on page 288.
[101]The Columbia River.

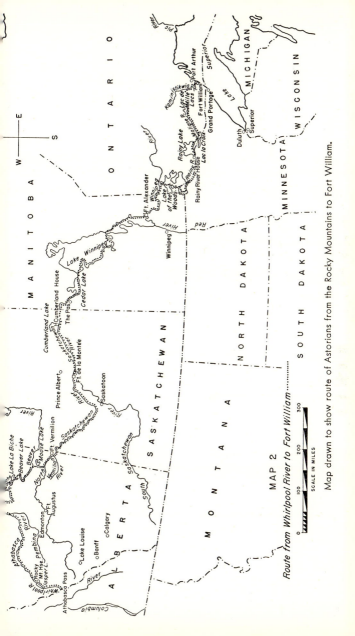

MAP 2

Route from Whirlpool River to Fort William

SCALE IN MILES
0   100   200   300

Map drawn to show route of Astorians from the Rocky Mountains to Fort William.

its mouth in the Pacific Ocean to its source in the Rocky Mountains is about twelve hundred English miles, or four hundred French leagues of twenty-five to a degree; that is to say, from two hundred and forty to two hundred and eighty miles from west to east from its mouth to the first falls: seven hundred and fifty miles nearly from S. S. W. to N. N. E. from the first rapids to the bend at the confluence of Canoe River; and one hundred and fifty or one hundred and eighty miles from that confluence to its source. We were not provided with the necessary instruments to determine the latitude, and still less the longitude, of our different stations; but it took us four or five days to go up from the factory at Astoria to the falls, and we could not have made less than sixty miles a day: and, as I have just remarked, we occupied an entire month in getting from the falls to Canoe River: deducting four or five days on which we did not travel, there remain twenty-five days' march; and it is not possible that we made less than thirty miles a day, one day with another.

We ascended Canoe River to the point where it ceases to be navigable and encamped in the same place where Mr. Thompson wintered in 1810–11.[102] We proceeded immediately to secure our canoes and to divide the baggage among the

[102]Apparently Franchère (or his Editor) is in error here. Boat Encampment, where Thompson encamped January

men, giving each fifty pounds to carry, including his provisions. A sack of pemican, or pounded meat, which we found in a cache where it had been left for us, was a great acquisition, as our supplies were nearly exhausted.

On the 12th we began our foot march to the mountains, being twenty-four in number, rank and file. Mr. A. Stuart remained at the portage to bestow in a place of safety the effects which we could not carry, such as boxes, kegs, camp-kettles, &c. We traversed first some swamps, next a dense bit of forest, and then we found ourselves marching up the gravelly banks of the little Canoe River. Fatigue obliged us to camp early.[103]

On the 13th we pursued our journey and entered into the valleys between the mountains, where there lay not less than four or five feet of snow. We were obliged to ford the river ten or a dozen times in the course of the day, sometimes with the water up to our necks. These frequent fordings were rendered necessary by abrupt and

17–April 17, 1811, was "at the very northernmost point" of the Columbia, and thus at the confluence of the Canoe with the greater river. The names Boat Encampment and Camp Creek, the latter a small stream, are still shown on modern maps at this point. See Elliott Coues, *New Light.* . . . II, 669.

[103]They were about to cross the main range of the Rockies from British Columbia to Alberta by way of Athabasca Pass.

steep rocks or bluffs, which it was impossible to get over without plunging into the wood for a great distance. The stream being very swift and rushing over a bed of stones, one of the men fell and lost a sack containing our last piece of salt pork, which we were preserving as a most precious treasure. The circumstances in which we found ourselves made us regard this as a most unfortunate accident. We encamped that night at the foot of a steep mountain and sent on Mr. Pillet and the guide, McKay, to hasten a supply of provisions to meet us.

On the morning of the 14th we began to climb the mountain which we had before us. We were obliged to stop every moment to take breath, so stiff was the ascent. Happily it had frozen hard the night before and the crust of the snow was sufficient to bear us. After two or three hours of incredible exertions and fatigues we arrived at the plateau or summit, and followed the footprints of those who had preceded us. This mountain is placed between two others a great deal more elevated, compared with which it is but a hill, and of which, indeed, it is only, as it were, the valley. Our march soon became fatiguing, on account of the depth of the snow, which, softened by the rays of the sun, could no longer bear us as in the morning. We were obliged to follow exactly the traces of those who had preceded us

and to plunge our legs up to the knees in the
holes they had made, so that it was as if we had
put on and taken off, at every step, a very large
pair of boots. At last we arrived at a good hard
bottom, and a clear space, which our guide said
was a little lake frozen over,[104] and here we
stopped for the night. This lake, or rather these
lakes (for there are two) are situated in the midst
of the valley or cup of the mountains.[105] On either
side were immense glaciers or ice-bound rocks,
on which the rays of the setting sun reflected the
most beautiful prismatic colors. One of these icy
peaks was like a fortress of rock; it rose perpen-
dicularly some fifteen or eighteen hundred feet
above the level of the lakes, and had the summit
covered with ice. Mr. J. Henry, who first discovered the Pass, gave this extraordinary rock the
name of McGillivray's Rock in honor of one of
the partners of the N. W. Company.[106] The lakes
themselves are not much over three or four hun-

[104]"Which we could not perceive since it was covered
with snow." Manuscript.

[105]The party had now attained the backbone of the Continent in the Athabasca Pass, discovered and traversed by
David Thompson in the month of January, 1811. For a
summary of his terrible experience in crossing it, see
Coues, *New Light. . . . ,* II, 668–69.

[106]At this point Editor Bibaud made a curious mistake,
which Huntington dutifully followed. Franchère wrote:
*Mr. Thompson donna a ce Roche le nom de M. McGilvrays
Roche.* Having so written, he crossed out "Thompson"
(all save the letter T) and wrote above it "Henry."
Although this is perfectly clear, Bibaud, misreading the

dred yards in circuit, and not over two hundred
yards apart. Canoe River, which, as we have already seen, flows to the west and falls into the
Columbia, takes its rise in one of them; while the
other gives birth to one of the branches of the
Athabasca, which runs first eastward, then northward, and which, after its junction with the
Unjighah north of the Lake of the Mountains,[107]
takes the name of Slave River as far as the lake of
that name, and afterward that of Mackenzie River
till it empties into, or is lost in, the Frozen
Ocean.[108] Having cut a large pile of wood, and
having by tedious labor for nearly an hour got
through the ice to the clear water of the lake on
which we were encamped, we supped frugally on
pounded maize, arranged our bivouac, and passed
a pretty good night, though it was bitterly cold.
The most common wood of the locality was cedar
and stunted pine. The heat of our fire made the
snow melt, and by morning the embers had

letter T, wrote "J. Henry," whose identity R. G. Thwaites
(in Early Western Travels Edition of Franchère) vainly
sought to surmise.

[107]The Unjighah was the Peace River and the Lake of
the Mountains was Lake Athabasca.

[108]Bibaud (followed by Huntington) here supplies considerable geographical information not found in the Manuscript, which reads: "The Canoe River rises in one of
these lakes while the other gives birth to the Athabasca
or La Béche River which runs east of the Mountains and
after becoming enlarged by several small tributaries empties by the Mackenzie River into the Frozen Ocean."

reached the solid ice: the depth from the snow surface was about five feet.

On the 15th we continued our route and soon began to descend the mountain. At the end of three hours we reached the banks of a stream— the outlet of the second lake above mentioned— here and there frozen over and then again tumbling down over rock and pebbly bottom in a thousand fantastic gambols; and very soon we had to ford it.[109] After a tiresome march by an extremely difficult path in the midst of woods we encamped in the evening under some cypresses. I had hit my right knee against the branch of a fallen tree on the first day of our march, and now began to suffer acutely with it. It was impossible, however, to flinch, as I must keep up with the party or be left to perish.[110]

On the 16th our path lay through thick swamps and forest; we recrossed the small stream we had forded the day before and our guide conducted us to the banks of the Athabasca, which we also forded. As this passage was the last to be made, we dried our clothes and pursued our journey through a more agreeable country than on the preceding days. In the evening we camped on the margin of a verdant plain, which the

[109]Whirlpool River, which the party descended to the Athabasca in the vicinity of Jasper Park.
[110]This sentence is not found in the Manuscript.

guide informed us was called Coro Prairie.[111] We had met in the course of the day several buffalo tracks, and a number of the bones of that quadruped bleached by time. Our flesh-meat having given out entirely, our supper consisted of some handfuls of corn, which we parched in a pan.

We resumed our route very early on the 17th and after passing a forest of trembling poplar or aspen we again came in sight of the river which we had left the day before. Arriving then at an elevated promontory or cape, our guide made us turn back in order to pass it at its most accessible point. After crossing it, not without difficulty, we soon came upon fresh horse-prints, a sure indication that there were some of those animals in our neighborhood. Emerging from the forest, each took the direction which he thought would lead soonest to an encampment. We all presently arrived at an old house which the traders of the N. W. Company had once constructed, but which had been abandoned for some four or five years.[112] The site of this trading post is the most

[111]In the Manuscript, *La Prairie de la Vache,* or Buffalo Prairie.
[112]They were now descending the valley of the Athabasca, which in this portion of its course is today paralleled by the Grand Trunk Railroad running westward to Yellowhead Pass of the Rockies. Elliott Coues locates the abandoned trading house at the junction of Miette and Athabasca Rivers. *New Light. . . .* II, 640.

charming that can be imagined: suffice to say that it is built on the bank of the beautiful river Athabasca and is surrounded by green and smiling prairies and superb woodlands. Pity there is nobody there to enjoy these rural beauties and to praise, while admiring them, the Author of Nature. [113] We found there Mr. Pillet and one of Mr. J. McDonald's party, who had had his leg broken by the kick of a horse. After regaling ourselves with pemican and some fresh venison we set out again, leaving two of the party to take care of the lame man, and went on about eight or nine miles farther to encamp.

On the 18th we had rain. I took the lead, and after having walked about ten or twelve miles on the slope of a mountain denuded of trees I perceived some smoke issuing from a tuft of trees in the bottom of a valley, and near the river. I descended immediately and reached a small camp, where I found two men who were coming to meet us with four horses. I made them fire off two guns as a signal to the rest of our people who were coming up in the rear, and presently we heard it repeated on the river, from which we were not far distant. We repaired thither and found two of the men, who had been left at the last ford and who, having constructed a bark

[113]Another reflection by Editor Bibaud, not found in the Manuscript.

canoe, were descending the river. I made one of them disembark and took his place, my knee being so painful that I could walk no farther. Meanwhile, the whole party came up; they loaded the horses, and pursued their route. In the course of the day my companion (an Iroquois) and I shot seven ducks. Coming at last to a high promontory called Rocher a Miette, we found some of our foot-travellers with Messrs. Stuart and Clarke, who were on horseback, all at a stand, doubting whether it would answer to wade round the base of the rock, which dipped in the water. We sounded the stream for them and found it fordable. So they all passed round, thereby avoiding the inland path, which is excessively fatiguing by reason of the hills which it is necessary perpetually to mount and descend. We encamped, to the number of seven, at the entrance of what at high water might be a lake, but was then a flat of blackish sand, with a narrow channel in the center. Here we made an excellent supper on the wild ducks, while those who were behind had nothing to eat.

Chapter XXIV
Descending the Athabasca

ON the 19th we raised our camp and followed the shore of the little dry lake along a smooth sandy beach, having abandoned our little bark canoe, both because it had become nearly unserviceable and because we knew ourselves to be very near the Rocky Mountain House.[114] In fact, we had not gone above five or six miles when we discerned a column of smoke on the opposite side of the stream. We immediately forded across and arrived at the post, where we found Messrs. McDonald, Stuart, and McKenzie, who had preceded us only two days.

The post of the Rocky Mountains, in English, Rocky Mountain House, is situated on the shore of the little lake I have mentioned, in the midst of a wood, and is surrounded, except on the water side, by steep rocks inhabited only by the mountain sheep and goat. Here is seen in the west the chain of the Rocky Mountains, whose

---

[114]Elliott Coues identifies five different establishments which were known at varying periods as Rocky Mountain House. The one Franchère's party had now reached, more commonly known as Jasper House, had been built about 1800 near the mouth of Moose Creek, which joins the Athabasca from the west between Jasper and Brulé Lakes. Coues, *New Light. . . .* II, 640–42.

summits are covered with perpetual snow. On the lake side, Le Rocher a Miette, of which I have spoken above, is in full view, of an immense height, and resembles the front of a huge church seen in perspective. The post was under the charge of a Mr. Decoigne. He does not procure many furs for the Company, which has only established the house as a provision depôt, with the view of facilitating the passage of the mountains to those of its employes who are repairing to, or returning from, the Columbia.[115]

People speak so often of the Rocky Mountains, and appear to know so little about them, that the reader will naturally desire me to say here a word on that subject. If we are to credit travellers and the most recent maps these mountains extend nearly in a straight line from the 35th or 36th degree of north latitude to the mouth of the Unjighah, or Mackenzie River, in the Arctic Ocean, in latitude 65° or 66°N. This distance of thirty degrees of latitude, or seven hundred and fifty leagues, equivalent to two thousand two hundred and fifty English miles or thereabouts, is, however, only the mean side of a right-angled triangle, the base of which occupies twenty-six

---

[115]From this point to the first paragraph break on page 232 the composition is the work of Editor Bibaud, who, however, apparently drew, in part, upon data found elsewhere in the Manuscript.

degrees of longitude, in latitude 35° or 36°, that is to say, is about sixteen hundred miles long, while the chain of mountains forms the hypotenuse; so that the real, and as it were diagonal, length of the chain across the continent, must be very near three thousand miles from S. E. to N. W. In such a vast extent of mountains the perpendicular height and width of base must necessarily be very unequal. We were about eight days in crossing them; whence I conclude, from our daily rate of travel, that they may have, at this point, i. e., about latitude 54°, a base of two hundred miles.

The geographer Pinkerton is assuredly mistaken when he gives these mountains an elevation of but three thousand feet above the level of the sea; from my own observations I would not hesitate to give them six thousand; we attained, in crossing them, an elevation probably of fifteen hundred feet above the valleys, and were not, perhaps, nearer than half way of their total height, while the valleys themselves must be considerably elevated above the level of the Pacific, considering the prodigious number of rapids and falls which are met in the Columbia, from the first falls to Canoe River. Be that as it may, if these mountains yield to the Andes in elevation and extent they very much surpass in both respects the Appalachian Chain, regarded until recently as the principal mountains of North America: they give rise, accordingly, to an infinity of streams, and to the greatest rivers of the continent.

They offer a vast and unexplored field to natural history: no botanist, no mineralogist, has yet examined them. The first travellers called them the Glittering Mountains, on account of the infinite number of immense rock crystals which they say cover their surface, and which, when they are not covered with snow, or in the bare places, reflect to an immense distance the rays of the sun. The name of Rocky Mountains was given them, probably, by later travellers, in consequence of the enormous isolated rocks which they offer here and there to the view. In fact, Le Rocher a Miette, and McGillivray's above all, appeared to me wonders of nature. Some think that they contain metals and precious stones.

With the exception of the mountain sheep and goat, the animals of the Rocky Mountains, if these rocky passes support any, are not better known than their vegetable and mineral productions. The mountain sheep resort generally to steep rocks, where it is impossible for men or even for wolves to reach them: we saw several on the rocks which surround the Mountain House. This animal has great curved horns, like those of the domestic ram: its wool is long, but coarse;

that on the belly is the finest and whitest. The Indians who dwell near the mountains make blankets of it, similar to ours, which they exchange with the Indians of the Columbia for fish and other commodities. The ibex, or mountain goat, frequents, like the sheep, the top and the declivities of the rocks: it differs from the sheep in having hair instead of wool, and straight horns projecting backward instead of curved ones. The color is also different. The natives soften the horns of these animals by boiling, and make platters, spoons, &c. of them in a very artistic manner.

Mr. Decoigne had not sufficient food for us, not having expected so many people to arrive at once. His hunters were then absent on Smoke River[116] (so called by some travellers who saw in the neighborhood a volcanic mountain belching smoke) in quest of game. We were therefore compelled to kill one of the horses for food. We found no birch bark either to make canoes, and set the men to work constructing some of wood. For want of better materials we were obliged to use poplar. On the 22d the three men whom we had left at the old house arrived in a little canoe made of two elk-skins sewed together and stretched like a drum on a frame of poles.

On the 24th, four canoes being ready, we fastened them together two and two and embarked

[116]Boucane River in 1820 edition.

to descend the river to an old post called Hunter's Lodge, where Mr. Decoigne, who was to return with us to Canada, informed us that we should find some bark canoes *en cache*, placed there for the use of the persons who descend the river. The water was not deep, and the stream was rapid; we glided along, so to speak, for ten or a dozen leagues and encamped, having lost sight of the mountains. In proportion as we advanced, the banks of the river grew less steep and the country became more agreeable.

On the 25th, having only a little pemican left, which we wished to keep, we sent forward a hunter in the little elk-skin canoe to kill some game. About ten o'clock we found him waiting for us with two moose that he had killed. He had suspended the hearts from the branch of a tree as a signal. We landed some men to help him in cutting up and shipping the game. We continued to glide safely down. But toward two o'clock P. M., after doubling a point, we got into a considerable rapid, where by the maladroitness of those who managed the double pirogue in which I was we met with a melancholy accident. I had proposed to go ashore, in order to lighten the canoes, which were loaded to the water's edge; but the steersman insisted that we could go down safe, while the bow-man was turning the head of the pirogue toward the beach; by this maneuver we were brought athwart the stream, which was carrying us fast toward the falls; just then our frail bark struck upon a sunken rock; the lower canoe broke amid-ships and filled instantly, and the upper one being lighted, rolled over, precipitating us all into the water. Two of our men, Olivier Roy Lapensée and André Bélanger, were drowned; and it was not without extreme difficulty that we succeeded in saving Messrs. Pillet and Wallace, as well as a man named J. Hurteau. The latter was so far gone that we were obliged to have recourse to the usual means for the resuscitation of drowned persons. The men lost all their effects; the others recovered but a part of theirs; and all our provisions went. Toward evening, in ascending the river (for I had gone about two miles below to recover the effects floating down) we found the body of Lapensée. We interred it as decently as we could and planted at his grave a cross, on which I inscribed with the point of my knife his name and the manner and date of his death.[117] If anything could console the shades of

---

[117] ". . . . on which I carved with the point of my knife the unfortunate fate of these two young Canadians," Manuscript. In 1825 Alexander Ross saw and copied the inscription: "Olivie Lapensée, from Lachine, drowned here in May, 1814."

The reflections which follow at this point (to end of first paragraph on page 235) represent the meditations of Bibaud and are not found in the Manuscript. Huntington,

the departed for a premature and unfortunate
end it would be, no doubt, that the funeral rites
have been paid to their remains and that they
themselves have given their names to the places
where they perished: it is thus that the shade of
Palinurus rejoiced in the regions below, at learning from the mouth of the Sibyl that the promontory near which he was drowned would hence-
forth be called by his name: *gaudet cognomine
terra.* The rapid and the point of land where the
accident I have described took place will bear,
and bears already, probably, the name of Lapensée.

On the 26th a part of our people embarked in
the three canoes which remained and the others
followed the banks of the river on foot. We saw in
several places some veins of bituminous coal on
the banks between the surface of the water and
that of the plain, say thirty feet below the latter;
the veins had a dip of about 25°. We tried some
and found it to burn well. We halted in the evening near a small stream, where we constructed
some rafts to carry all our people.

On the 27th I went forward in the little canoe
of skins with the two hunters. We soon killed an
elk, which we skinned and suspended the hide,
besmeared with blood, from the branch of a tree
at the extremity of a point in order that the peo-

not aware of this, bases a somewhat curious note upon
them, which we do not undertake to reprint.

ple behind, as they came up, might perceive and take in the fruit of our chase. After fortifying ourselves with a little food we continued to glide down and encamped for the night near a thick wood where our hunters, from the tracks they observed, had hopes of encountering and capturing some bears. This hope was not realized.

On the 28th a little after quitting camp we killed a swan. While I was busy cooking it, the hunters having plunged into the wood, I heard a rifle-shot which seemed to me to proceed from a direction opposite to that which they had taken. They returned very soon running and were extremely surprised to learn that it was not I who had fired it. Nevertheless, the canoes and rafts having overtaken us, we continued to descend the river. Very soon we met a bark canoe containing two men and a woman, who were ascending the river and bringing letters and some goods for the Rocky Mountain House. We learned from these letters, addressed to Mr. Decoigne, several circumstances of the war, and among others the defeat of Captain Barclay on Lake Erie.[118] We arrived that evening at Hunter's Lodge, where we found four new birch-bark canoes. We got ready two of them and resumed

[118]The Battle of Lake Erie, fought Sept. 10, 1813. From the Manuscript we learn that the letter was dated Oct. 14, 1813; Decoigne received it on May 28, 1814.

our journey down on the 31st. Mr. Pillet set out before us with the hunters at a very early hour. They killed an elk, which they left on a point and which we took in. The country through which we passed that day is the most charming possible; the river is wide, handsome, and bordered with low outjutting points, covered with birch and poplar.

On the 1st of June in the evening we encamped at the confluence of the river Pembina. This stream comes from the south and takes its rise in one of the spurs of the great chain of the Rocky Mountains; ascending it for two days and crossing a neck of land about seventy-five miles, one reaches Fort Augustus, a trading post on the Saskatchawin River.[119] Messrs. McDonald and McKenzie had taken this route, and had left for us half a sack of pemican in a cache at the mouth of the river Pembina.[120] After landing that evening Mr. Stuart and I amused ourselves with angling, but took only five or six small fish.

[119]On the site of present-day Edmonton, Alberta. This was "new" Fort Augustus, not to be confused with "old" Fort Augustus, which stood on the left bank of the Saskatchewan a short distance above the mouth of Sturgeon River and some 20 miles, air-line, north-east of Edmonton. It was destroyed by the Blackfeet between July, 1809 and July, 1810. Elliott Coues, *New Light. . . .* , II, 566.

[120]There are several Pembina rivers. This one, the largest southern affluent of the Athabasca, was discovered and explored by David Thompson in 1799.

On the 2d we passed the confluence of Little
Slave Lake River. At eight o'clock in the morning
we met a band or family of Indians of the Knisteneaux tribe. They had just killed a buffalo, which
we bought of them for a small brass kettle. We
could not have had a more seasonable rencounter
for our provisions were all consumed.

On the 3d we reached La Biche River, which
we began to ascend, quitting the Athabasca, or
Great Red Elk. This stream was very narrow in
its channel and obstructed with boulders: we
were obliged to take to the shore while some of
the men dragged along the canoes. Their method
was to lash poles across, and wading themselves,
lift the canoes over the rocks—a laborious and
infinitely tedious operation. The march along the
banks was not less disagreeable: for we had to
traverse points of forest where the fire had passed,
and which were filled with fallen trees.

Wallace and I having stopped to quench our
thirst at a rill, the rest got in advance of us; and
we lost our way in a labyrinth of buffalo tracks
which we mistook for the trail, so that we wandered about for three hours before we came up
with the party, who began to fear for our safety
and were firing signal-guns to direct us. As the
river now grew deeper we all embarked in the
canoes and about evening overtook our hunters,
who had killed a moose and her two calves.

We continued our journey on the 4th, sometimes seated in our canoes sometimes marching along the river on foot, and encamped in the evening excessively fatigued.

Chapter XXV

Down the Saskatchewan

THE 5th of June brought us to the beautiful sheet of water called Lac la Biche, irregular in shape, dotted with islands, and about forty miles in length by thirty in its greatest width. We met about the middle of it a small canoe conducted by two young women. They were searching for gull and duck eggs on the islands, this being the season of laying for those aquatics. They told us that their father was not far distant from the place where we met them. In fact, we presently saw him appear in a canoe with his two boys, rounding a little isle. We joined him and learned that his name was Antoine Desjarlais; that he had been a guide in the service of the North West Company, but had left them since 1805. On being made acquainted with our need of provisions he offered us a great quantity of eggs and made one of our men embark with his two daughters in their little canoe to seek some more substantial supplies at his cabin, on the other side of the lake. He himself accompanied us as far as a portage of about twenty-five yards formed at the outlet of the lake by a beaver dam. Having performed the portage and passed a small pond or marsh, we encamped to await

the return of our man. He arrived the next
morning with Desjarlais, bringing us about fifty
pounds of dried venison and from ten to twelve
pounds of tallow. We invited our host to breakfast with us: it was the least we could do after
the good offices he had rendered us. This man
was married to an Indian woman, and lived with
his family on the produce of his chase; he appeared quite contented with his lot. Nobody, at
least, disputed with him the sovereignty of Red
Deer Lake, of which he had, as it were, taken
possession. He begged me to read for him two
letters which he had had in his possession for
two years, and of which he did not yet know the
contents. They were from one of his sisters, and
dated at Varennes, in Canada. I even thought
that I recognized the handwriting of Mr. L. G.
Labadie, teacher of that parish. At last, having
testified to this good man in suitable terms our
gratitude for the services he had rendered us, we
quitted him and prosecuted our journey.

After making two portages we arrived on the
banks of Beaver River, which was here but a riv-
ulet. It is by this route that the canoes ordinarily
pass to reach Little Slave Lake and the Athabasca
country, from the head of Lake Superior, via
Cumberland House on English River. We were
obliged by the shallowness of the stream to drag
along our canoes, walking on a bottom or beach

of sand where we began to feel the importunity of the mosquitoes. One of the hunters scoured the woods for game but without success. By-and-by we passed a small canoe turned bottom up and covered with a blanket. Soon after we came to a cabin or lodge where we found an old Canadian hunter named Nadeau. He was reduced to the last stage of weakness, having had nothing to eat for two days. Nevertheless, a young man who was married to one of his daughters came in shortly after with the good news that he had just killed a buffalo; a circumstance which determined us to encamp there for the night. We sent some of our men to get in the meat. Nadeau gave us half of it and told us that we should find thirty miles lower down at the foot of a pine tree a cache, where he had deposited ten swan-skins and some of martin, with a net, which he prayed us to take to the next trading-post. We quitted this good fellow the next morning and pursued our way. Arriving at the place indicated, we found the cache and took the net, leaving the other articles. A short distance farther we came to Moose River, which we had to ascend in order to reach the lake of that name. The water in this river was so low that we were obliged entirely to un-load the canoes and to lash poles across them, as we had done before, that the men might carry them on their shoulders over the places where they could not be floated. Having distributed the baggage to the remainder of the hands, we pursued our way through the woods under the guidance of Mr. Decoigne.

This gentleman, who had not passed here for nineteen years, soon lost his way and we got separated into small parties in the course of the afternoon, some going one way and some another in search of Moose Lake. But as we had outstripped the men who carried the baggage and the small stock of provisions that old Nadeau had given us, Mr. Wallace and I thought it prudent to retrace our steps and keep with the rear-guard. We soon met Mr. Pillet and one of the hunters. The latter, ferreting the woods on both sides of a trail that he had discovered, soon gave a whoop to signify that we should stop. Presently emerging from the underwood, he showed us a horse-whip which he had found, and from which and from other unmistakable signs he was confident the trail would lead either to the lake or a navigable part of the river. The men with the baggage then coming up, we entered the thicket single file and were conducted by this path in a very short time to the river, on the banks of which were visible the traces of an old camping ground. The night was coming on, and soon after the canoes arrived, to our great satisfaction, for we had begun to fear that they had already passed. The splashing of their paddles was a welcome sound, and we who had been wise enough to keep behind all encamped together.

Very early on the 8th I set out accompanied by one of the hunters in quest of Messrs. D. Stuart, Clarke, and Decoigne, who had gone on ahead the night previous. I soon found MM. Clarke and M'Gillis encamped on the shore of the lake. The canoes presently arrived and we embarked; MM. Stuart and Decoigne rejoined us shortly after, and informed us that they had bivouacked on the shore of Lac Puant, or Stinking Lake, a pond situated about twelve miles E. N. E. from the lake we were now entering. Finding ourselves thus reunited, we traversed the latter, which is about eighteen miles in circuit and has very pretty shores. We encamped very early on an island in order to use old Nadeau's fishing net. I visited it that evening and brought back three carp and two water-hens. We left it set all night and the next morning found in it twenty white-fish. Leaving camp at an early hour, we gained the entrance of a small stream that descends between some hills of moderate elevation and there stopped to breakfast. I found the white-fish more delicious in flavor even than the salmon. We had again to foot it, following the bank of this little stream. It was a painful task as we were obliged to open a path through thick underbrush, in the midst of a rain that lasted all day and kept us drenched. Two men being left in each canoe, conveyed them up the river about thirty miles, as far as Long Lake—a narrow pond, on the margin of which we spent the night.

On the 10th we got through this lakelet[121] and entered another small stream which it was necessary to navigate in the same manner as the preceding, and which conducted us to Bridge Lake. The latter received its name from a sort of bridge or causeway formed at its southern extremity, and which is nothing more than a huge beaver dam. We found here a lodge, where were a young man and two women who had charge of some horses appertaining to one of the Hudson's Bay trading houses. We borrowed of them half a dozen pack horses and crossed the bridge with them. After surmounting a considerable hill we reached an open, level, and dry prairie which conducted us in about two hours to an ancient trading-post on the banks of the Sascatchawin. Knowing that we were near a factory, we made our toilets as well as we could before arriving. Toward sundown we reached Fort Vermilion,

---

[121] "made a portage of half a league" occurs at this point in the Manuscript.

which is situated on the bank of a river at the foot of a superb hill.[122]

We found at this post some ninety persons, men, women, and children; these people depend for subsistence on the chase and fishing with hooks and lines, which is very precarious. Mr. Hallet, the clerk in charge, was absent, and we were dismayed to hear that there were no provisions on the place, a very disagreeable piece of news for people famished as we were. We had been led to suppose that if we could only reach the plains of the Saskatchawin, we should be in the land of plenty. Mr. Hallet, however, was not long in arriving: he had two quarters of buffalo meat brought out, which had been laid in ice, and prepared us supper. Mr. Hallet was a polite, sociable man, loving his ease passably well and desirous of living in these wild countries as people do in civilized lands. Having testified to him our surprise at seeing in one of the buildings a large cariole like those of Canada, he informed us that, having horses, he had had this carriage made in order to enjoy a sleighride; but that the workmen having forgot to take the measure of the doors of the building before constructing it, it was found when finished much too large

[122]On the Saskatchewan, opposite the mouth of Vermilion River, which joins the Saskatchewan from the south several miles west of West Longitude 110°.

for them, and could never be got out of the room where it was; and it was like to remain there a long time, as he was not disposed to demolish the house for the pleasure of using the cariole.

By the side of the factory of the North West Company is another belonging to the Company of Hudson's Bay. In general these trading-houses are constructed thus, one close to the other and surrounded with a common palisade, with a door of communication in the interior for mutual succor in case of attack on the part of the Indians. The latter, in this region, particularly the Blackfeet, Gros Ventres, and those of the Yellow River, are very ferocious: they live by the chase, but bring few furs to the traders; and the latter maintain these posts principally to procure themselves provisions.

On the 11th, after breakfasting at Fort Vermilion we resumed our journey, with six or seven pounds of tallow for our whole stock of food. This slender supply brought us through to the evening of the third day, when we had for supper two ounces of tallow each.

On the 14th in the morning we killed a wild goose, and toward midday collected some flag-root and *choux-gras* a wild herb, which we boiled with the small game: we did not forget to throw into the pot the little tallow we had left, and made a delicious repast. Toward the decline of day we had the good luck to kill a buffalo.

On the 15th, MM. Clarke and Decoigne having landed during our course to hunt, returned presently with the agreeable intelligence that they had killed three buffaloes. We immediately encamped and sent the greater part of the men to cut up the meat and jerk it. This operation lasted till the next evening, and we set forward again in the canoes on the 17th with about six hundred pounds of meat half cured. The same evening we perceived from our camp several herds of buffaloes, but did not give chase, thinking we had enough meat to take us to the next post.[123]

The river Sascatchawin flows over a bed composed of sand and marl, which contributes not a little to diminish the purity and transparency of its waters, which, like those of the Missouri, are turbid and whitish. Except for that it is one of the prettiest rivers in the world. The banks are perfectly charming, and offer in many places a scene the fairest, the most smiling, and the best diversified that can be seen or imagined: hills in

[123]The rhapsody which follows, to the end of the present chapter, was chiefly composed by Bibaud, although Franchère afforded the inspiration for it by his own brief description of the Saskatchewan.

varied forms, crowned with superb groves; valleys, agreeably embrowned at evening and
morning by the prolonged shadow of the hills
and of the woods which adorn them; herds of
light-limbed antelopes, and heavy colossal buffalo
—the former bounding along the slopes of the
hills, the latter trampling under their heavy feet
the verdure of the plains; all these champaign
beauties reflected and doubled as it were by the
waters of the river; the melodious and varied song
of a thousand birds, perched on the tree-tops;
the refreshing breath of the zephyrs; the serenity
of the sky; the purity and salubrity of the air;
all, in a word, pours contentment and joy into
the soul of the enchanted spectator. It is above
all in the morning when the sun is rising, and
in the evening when he is setting, that the spec-
tacle is really ravishing. I could not detach my
regards from that superb picture till the nascent
obscurity had obliterated its perfection. Then, to
the sweet pleasure that I had tasted succeeded a
triste, not to say a somber, melancholy. How comes
it to pass, I said to myself, that so beautiful a
country is not inhabited by human creatures?
The songs, the hymns, the prayers of the laborer
and the artisan, shall they never be heard in
these fine plains? Wherefore, while in Europe,
and above all in England, so many thousands of
men do not possess as their own an inch of

ground, and cultivate the soil of their country
for proprietors who scarcely leave them whereon
to support existence; wherefore do so many
millions of acres of apparently fat and fertile
land, remain uncultivated and absolutely useless?
Or, at least, why do they support only herds of
wild animals? Will men always love better to
vegetate all their lives on an ungrateful soil than
to seek afar fertile regions, in order to pass in
peace and plenty at least the last portion of their
days? But I deceive myself; it is not so easy as
one thinks for the poor man to better his condition: he has not the means of transporting
himself to distant countries, or he has not those
of acquiring a property there; for these untilled
lands, deserted, abandoned, do not appertain to
whoever wishes to establish himself upon them
and reduce them to culture; they have owners,
and from these must be purchased the right of
rendering them productive! Besides, one ought
not to give way to illusions: these countries, at
times so delightful, do not enjoy a perpetual
spring; they have their winter, and a rigorous
one; a piercing cold is then spread through the
atmosphere; deep snows cover the surface; the
frozen rivers flow only for the fish; the trees are
stripped of their leaves and hung with icicles;
the verdure of the plains has disappeared; the
hills and valleys offer but a uniform whiteness;

Nature has lost all her beauty; and man has enough to do to shelter himself from the injuries of the inclement season.[124]

[124]Pierre Radisson, to whose pen we owe our first description of the primitive Wisconsin wilderness, indulged in strikingly similar reflections over a century and a half in advance of Bibaud. Lake Michigan, he declared, was "the delightfulest lake in the world;" Wisconsin was "so pleasant, so beautiful and so fruitfull" as to move him to grief over the reflection that the world could not discover "such inticing countrys" to live in. "What conquest would that be at little or no cost; what laborinth of pleasure should millions of people have, instead that millions [in Europe] complaine of misery and poverty. . . . Its true, I confesse, that the accesse [to that country] is difficult . . . but we ought [to remember] that virtue is not acquired without labour and taking great pains."

In the autumn of 1923 David Lloyd George, viewing for the first time the relatively untenanted plains of western Canada, expressed substantially the same thought to which Radisson and Bibaud had given earlier utterance.

CHAPTER XXVI

Lake Winnipeg and Rainy Lake

O N the 18th of June we re-embarked at an early hour: and the wind rising, spread sail, a thing we had not done before since we quitted the river Columbia. In the afternoon the clouds gathered thick and black and we had a gust, accompanied with hail, but of short duration; the weather cleared up again and about sundown we arrived at Fort de la Montée, so called on account of its being a depôt where the traders going south leave their canoes and take packhorses to reach their several posts. [125] We found here, as at Fort Vermilion, two trading-houses joined together to make common cause against the Indians; one belonging to the Hudson's Bay Company, the other to the Company of the North West: the Hudson's Bay house being then under the charge of a Mr. Prudent, and the N. W. Company's under a Mr. John McLean. Mr. de Rocheblave, one of the partners of the last Company having the superintendence of this district, where he had wintered, had gone to Lake Superior to attend

[125]Fort de la Montée was on the North Saskatchewan some miles above its junction with the South Saskatchewan. Latter-day Hudson's Bay Company's Fort Carlton, or Carlton House, occupies the site of the former Fort de la Montée.

the annual meeting of the partners.[126] There were cultivated fields around the house; the barley and peas appeared to promise an abundant harvest. Mr. McLean received us as well as circumstances permitted; but that gentleman having no food to give us and our buffalo meat beginning to spoil, we set off the next morning to reach Cumberland House as quick as possible. In the course of the day we passed two old forts, one of which had been built by the French before the conquest of Canada.[127] According to our guide it was the most distant western post that the French traders ever had in the northwestern wilderness. Toward evening we shot a moose. The aspect of the country changes considerably since leaving La Montée; the banks of the river rise more boldly and the country is covered with forests.

[126]Pierre de Rocheblave was a nephew of the Sieur de Rocheblave whom George Rogers Clark captured at Kaskaskia in 1778. The younger Rocheblave devoted his career to the fur trade, in which he rose to prominence in the North West Company.

[127]Fort Nippewean and Fort La Corne. Fort Nippewean was on the main Saskatchewan below the Forks of the river, on the site of present-day Prince Albert.

Fort La Corne was founded in 1753 by St. Luc de la Corne. It was about twelve miles "air-line" below Fort Nippewean, but much more by the bends of the river. For the sites and history of these forts see Elliott Coues (Ed.). *New Light. . . .*, II, 481–84.

On the 20th we saw some elms—a tree that I had not seen hitherto since my departure from Canada. We reached Fort Cumberland a little before the setting of the sun.[128] This post, called in English Cumberland House, is situated at the outlet of the Saskatchawin, where it empties into English Lake, between the 53d and 54th degrees of north latitude. It is a depot for those traders who are going to Slave Lake or the Athabasca, or are returning thence, as well as for those destined for the Rocky Mountains. It was under the orders of Mr. J. D. Campbell, who having gone down to Fort William, however, had left it in charge of a Mr. Harrison. There are two factories, as at Vermilion and La Montée. At this place the traders who resort every year to Fort William leave their half-breed or Indian wives and families, as they can live here at little expense, the lake abounding in fish. Messrs. Clarke and Stuart, who were behind, arrived on the 22d and in the evening we had a dance. They gave us four sacks of pemican and we set off again on the 23d at

[128]Cumberland House was established by Samuel Hearne as a Hudson's Bay Company post in 1774. Twenty years later the North West Company established a post close by the older one. This was one of the chief fur trade centers of the Far Northwest, since it was at the junction of the routes of the Athabasca and Saskatchewan brigades. For Alexander Henry's account of his visit to it in 1775 see his *Travels and Adventures* . . . , the Lakeside Classics volume for 1921, pp. 251–53.

eight A. M. We crossed the lake and entered a small river, and having made some eighty or ninety miles under sail encamped on a low shore where the mosquitoes tormented us horribly all night.

On the 24th we passed Muddy Lake and entered Lake Bourbon,[129] where we fell in with a canoe from York Factory under the command of a Mr. Kennedy, clerk of the Hudson's Bay Company.[130] We collected some dozens of gull eggs, on the rocky islands of the lake: and stopping on one of the last at night, having a little flour left, Mr. Decoigne and I amused ourselves in making fritters for the next day's breakfast: an occupation, which despite the small amount of materials, employed us till we were surprised by the daybreak; the night being but brief at this season in that high latitude.

[129]Muddy Lake is better known as Cedar Lake. In Franchère's time it was commonly regarded as the outlet of the Saskatchewan, instead of Lake Winnipeg. The French, who established Fort Bourbon here in 1749, called it Lake Bourbon. On the confusion of names, sites, and geography of the region see Elliott Coues (Ed.), *New Light. . . .* , II, 465–68.

[130]York Factory, on Hudson Bay at the mouth of Hayes River, was built in 1682, and from this time forward was one of the most important posts of the Hudson's Bay Company. Its ownership changed often from French to English hands, the last time in 1782 when La Perouse captured the place, only to have it restored to the English by the Treaty of Paris in 1783.

At sunrise on the 25th we were again afloat, passed Lake Travers or Cross Lake, which empties into Lake Winnipeg by a succession of rapids; shot down these cascades without accident and arrived toward noon at the great rapid Ouénipic or Winnipeg, which is about four miles long. We disembarked here and the men worked down the canoes. At the foot of this rapid, which is the inlet of Winnipeg, we found an old Canadian fisherman who called himself King of the lake. He might fairly style himself king of the fish, which are abundant and which he alone enjoyed. Having made a boil and regaled ourselves with excellent sturgeon, we left this old man and entered the great Lake Winnipeg, which appeared to me like a sea of fresh water. This lake is now too well known to need a particular description: I will content myself with saying that it visibly yields in extent only to Lake Superior and Great Slave Lake: it has for tributaries several large rivers, and among others the Sascatchawin, the Winnipeg, in the east; and Red River in the south; and empties into Hudson Bay by the Nelson, N. N. E., and the Severn, E. N. E. The shores which it bathes are generally very low; it appears to have little depth, and is dotted with a vast number of islands lying pretty close to land.[131] We reached one called Egg Island, whence it was necessary

[131]The canoe route led down the western shore of Lake Winnipeg to the mouth of Sturgeon Bay; thence across to

to cross to the south to reach the main; but the
wind was so violent that it was only at decline of
day that we could perform the passage. We profited by the calm to coast along all day and a part
of the night of the 26th; but to pay for it, remained in camp on the 27th till evening, the
wind not suffering us to proceed. The wind having appeared to abate somewhat after sunset, we
embarked, but were soon forced to land again.
On the 28th we passed the openings of several
deep bays and the isles of St. Martin, and camped
at the bottom of a little bay, where the mosquitoes did not suffer us to close our eyes all night.
We were rejoiced when dawn appeared, and were
eager to embark to free ourselves from these in-
convenient guests. A calm permitted us that day
to make good progress with our oars and we
camped at Buffalo Strait. We saw that day two
Indian wigwams, the first we had seen since leaving the Athabasca River.

The 30th brought us to Winnipeg River, which
we began to ascend, and about noon reached
Fort Bas de la Rivière.[132] This trading post had
more the air of a large and well-cultivated farm

the narrows and down the eastern coast to the outlet of
Winnipeg River. The Saint Martin Islands lie to the southward of Reindeer Island. All the mid-portion of Lake Winnipeg is much indented, particularly on the western coast,
and is liberally strewn with islands.

[132]Shown on modern maps as Fort Alexander, on the
Winnipeg River a short distance above its outlet.

than of a fur traders' factory: a neat and elegant
mansion, built on a slight eminence and surrounded with barns, stables, storehouses, &c.
and by fields of barley, peas, oats, and potatoes
reminded us of the civilized countries which we
had left so long ago. Messrs. Crébassa and Kennedy, who had this post in charge, received us
with all possible hospitality and supplied us with
all the political news which had been learned
through the arrival of canoes from Canada.

They also informed us that Messrs McDonald
and Rocheblave had passed a few days before our
arrival, having been obliged to go up Red River
to stop the effusion of blood, which would probably have taken place but for their intervention,
in the colony founded on that river by the Earl of
Selkirk.[133] Mr. Miles McDonnell, the Governor of
that colony, or rather of the Assiniboyne district,
had issued a proclamation forbidding all persons
whomsoever to send provisions of any kind out

[133]At the present-day city of Winnipeg. Here Alexander
Ross passed his later years. In 1856, just at the close of his
life, he published a history entitled The *Red River Settlement, Its Rise, Progress, and Present State*. Franchère's narrative provides a short account of the troubles then current between the settlers sent out by Lord Selkirk and the
traders of the Hudson's Bay and North West companies.
They led to the massacre of Governor Semple and about
twenty of his followers by a party of Northwesters and Indians in 1816, and eventually to the absorption of the
North West by the Hudson's Bay Company in 1821.

of the district. The Hudson's Bay traders had conformed to this proclamation, but those of the North West Company paid no attention to it, thinking it illegal, and had sent their servants, as usual, to get provisions up the river. Mr. McDonnell having heard that several hundred sacks of pemican* were laid up in a storehouse under the care of a Mr. Pritchard, sent to require their surrender: Pritchard refused to deliver them, whereupon Mr. McDonnell had them carried off by force. The traders who winter on Little Slave Lake, English River, the Athabasca Country, &c., learning this and being aware that they would not find their usual supply at Bas de la Rivière, resolved to go and recover the seized provisions by force, if they were not peaceably given up. Things were in this position when Messrs. Rocheblave and McDonald arrived. They found the

---

*Pemican, of which I have already spoken several times, is the Indian name for the dried and pounded meat which the natives sell to the traders. About fifty pounds of this meat is placed in a trough (*un grand vaisseau fait d'un tronc d'arbre*), and about an equal quantity of tallow is melted and poured over it; it is thoroughly mixed into one mass and when cold is put up in bags made of undressed buffalo hide, with the hair outside, and sewed up as tightly as possible. The meat thus impregnated with tallow hardens and will keep for years. It is eaten without any other preparation; but sometimes wild pears or dried berries are added, which render the flavor more agreeable.—Bibaud.

Canadian voyageurs in arms and ready to give
battle to the colonists, who persisted in their re-
fusal to surrender the bags of pemican. The two
peacemakers visited the Governor and having explained to him the situation in which the traders
of the North West Company would find themselves by the want of necessary provisions to enable them to transport their peltries to Fort William, and the exasperation of their men, who saw
no other alternative for them but to get possession of those provisions or to perish of hunger,
requested him to surrender the same without delay. Mr. McDonnell, on his part, pointed out the
misery to which the colonists would be reduced
by a failure in the supply of food. In consequence
of these mutual representations it was agreed that
one-half of the pemican should be restored and
the other half remain for the use of the colonists.
Thus was arranged without bloodshed the first
difficulty which occurred between the rival companies of the North West, and of Hudson's
Bay.

Having spent the 1st of July in repairing our
canoes, we re-embarked on the 2d and continued
to ascend Ouenìpic River, called also White
River on account of the great number of its cascades, which being very near each other offer to
the sight an almost continuous foam.[134] We made

[134]The Winnipeg River.

that day twenty-seven portages, all very short. On the 3d and 4th we made nine more and arrived on the 5th at the Lake of the Woods. This lake takes its name from the great number of woody islands with which it is dotted. Our guide pointed out to me one of these isles, telling me that a Jesuit father had said mass there, and that it was the most remote spot to which those missionaries had ever penetrated.[135] We encamped on one of the islands. The next day the wind did not allow us to make much progress. On the 7th we gained the entrance of Rainy Lake River. I do not remember ever to have seen elsewhere so many mosquitoes as on the banks of this river. Having landed near a little rapid to lighten the canoes, we had the misfortune, in getting through the brush, to dislodge these insects from under the leaves where they had taken refuge from the rain of the night before; they attached themselves to us, followed us into the canoes, and tormented us all the remainder of the day.

[135]This is an interesting instance of the persistence of local memory. Father Aulneau came from France to Quebec in 1734 and after a year there devoted to completing his theological study was sent in 1735 to open a mission at Fort St. Charles, Lake of the Woods. In the spring of 1736 he joined a party of twenty Frenchmen bound for Mackinac, which was surprised and all of its number massacred by Sioux Indians a short distance from the fort. See R. G. Thwaites (Ed.), *The Jesuit Relations* LXVIII, 331; Grace Lee Nute, *Rainy River Country* (St. Paul, 1950), p. 9.

On the 8th at sunset we reached Rainy Lake House. This fort is situated about a mile from a considerable rapid. We saw here cultivated fields and domestic animals, such as horses, oxen, cows, &c. The post is a depôt for the wintering parties of the Athabasca and others still more remote, who bring to it their peltries and return from it with their outfits of merchandise. Mr. John Dease, to whose charge the place had been confided, received us in the most friendly manner possible; and after having made an excellent supper we danced a part of the evening.[136]

We took leave of Mr. Dease on the 10th, well provided for the journey, and passing around Rainy Lake Falls and then traversing the lake itself, which I estimated to be forty miles long, we encamped at the entrance of a small river. On the next day we pursued our way, now traversing little lakes, now passing straits where we scarcely found water to float our canoes. On the 13th we encamped near Dog Portage (Portage des Chiens), where, from not having followed the advice of Mr. Dease who had counselled us to take

[136]For the various forts and trading posts established in the Rainy River region see Grace Lee Nute, *Rainy River Country, passim*. The North West Company's Rainy River House was established prior to 1787, when Alexander Mackenzie visited the place. It was maintained until the absorption of the Company by the Hudson's Bay Company in 1821.

along a bag of pemican, we found ourselves absolutely without food.[137]

[137]Grand Portage, at the beginning of the Pigeon River-
Rainy River route from Lake Superior to Lake Winnipeg,
was the favorite trade route followed throughout the
French and British periods. Following the discovery that
Grand Portage lay south of the International Boundary,
and hence under the control of the United States, the
North West Company established Fort William at the
mouth of the Kaministikwia River and reached Rainy Lake
by ascending this stream and crossing by way of Lac Mille
Lacs, Sturgeon River, and other connecting waters until
the route joined the one from Pigeon River at Lac La Croix.
Franchère's party, eastward bound, followed the route
from Lac La Croix to the Kaministikwia and Fort William.
For an account of these divergent routes, together with
map, see Grace L. Nute, The *Voyageur's Highway* (St.
Paul, 1941). Alexander Henry the elder traveled from
Lake Superior to Lake Winnipeg and beyond in 1775–76,
being one of the earliest British traders to visit the country
beyond Lake Superior. For an account of the journey from
Lake Superior to Lake Winnipeg see his *Travels and Adventures*, the Lakeside Classics volume for 1921, Chap. 8.

Chapter XXVII
Arrival at Fort William

STARVING men are early risers. We set out on the 14th before day and effected the portage, which is long and difficult. At the foot of the rapid we found a sort of restaurant or cabaret, kept by a man named Boucher. We treated the men to a little *eau de vie* and breakfasted on some detestable sausages, poisoned with salt.

After this wretched repast we set out again and passed, toward noon, the Mountain Portage. Here the river Kaministikwia flings itself over a rock of immense height and forms a fall scarcely less curious to see than that of Niagara. Below, the succession of falls and rapids is constant, so that we made no fewer than thirty-six portages in the course of the day. Nevertheless, we pursued our laborious way with good cheer and without a murmur from our Canadian boatmen, who kept their spirits up by singing their voyageur songs. At last, at about nine o'clock in the evening we arrived at Fort William.[138]

[138]For the history of Fort William see Nute, The *Voyageur's Highway*. Duluth had established a post here in 1678 and although the site was long abandoned, another post built in 1717 was occupied until the close of the French period. Fort William was established on the site by the North West Company during the years 1802–1805.

Fort William is situated on Lake Superior, at the mouth of the Kaministikwia River, about forty-five miles north of old Grand Portage. It was built in 1805, when the two rival Canadian companies were united, and was named in honor of Mr. (now the Honorable) William McGillivray, principal agent of the North West Company. The proprietors, perceiving that the old fort of Grand Portage was on the territory claimed by the American government, resolved to demolish it and build another on the British territory. No site appeared more advantageous than the present for the purposes intended; the river is deep, of easy access, and offers a safe harbor for shipping. It is true they had to contend with all the difficulties consequent on a low and swampy soil; but by incredible labor and perseverance they succeeded in draining the marshes and reducing the loose and yielding soil to solidity.

Fort William has really the appearance of a fort, with its palisade fifteen feet high, and that of a pretty village, from the number of edifices it encloses. In the middle of a spacious square rises a large building elegantly constructed, though of

For many years it was the rendezvous of the "wintering" partners from the interior and those who resided in Montreal, and each season was the scene of great activity and rude revelry. Following the union of the Hudson's Bay and the North West companies in 1821 Fort William was abandoned and allowed to fall into decay.

wood, with a long piazza or portico, raised about
five feet from the ground and surmounted by a
balcony extending along the whole front. In the
center is a saloon or hall sixty feet in length by
thirty in width decorated with several pieces of
painting and some portraits of the leading partners. It is in this hall that the agents, partners,
clerks, interpreters, and guides take their meals
together at different tables. At each extremity of
the apartment are two rooms; two of these are
destined for the two principal agents; the other
two to the steward and his department. The
kitchen and servants' rooms are in the basement.
On either side of this edifice is another of the
same extent, but of less elevation; they are each
divided by a corridor running through its length
and contain each a dozen pretty bed-rooms. One
is destined for the wintering partners, the other
for the clerks. On the east of the square is another building similar to the last two and intended for the same use, and a warehouse where
the furs are inspected and repacked for shipment.
In the rear of these are the lodging-house of the
guides, another fur-warehouse, and finally, a
powder magazine. The last is of stone and has a
roof covered with tin. At the angle is a sort of bastion or look-out place commanding a view of the
lake. On the west side is seen a range of buildings, some of which serve for stores and others

for workshops; there is one for the equipment of the men, another for the fitting out of the canoes, one for the retail of goods, another where they sell liquors, bread, pork, butter, &c. and where a treat is given to the travellers who arrive. This consists in a white loaf, half a pound of butter, and a gill of rum. The voyageurs give this tavern the name of *Cantine salope.* Behind all this is another range, where we find the counting-house, a fine square building, and well-lighted; another storehouse of stone, tin-roofed; and a jail, not less necessary than the rest. The voyageurs give it the name of *pot au beurre*—the butter-tub. Beyond these we discover the shops of the carpenter, the cooper, the tinsmith, the blacksmith, &c.; and spacious yards and sheds for the shelter, reparation, and construction of canoes. Near the gate of the fort, which is on the south, are the quarters of the physician and those of the chief clerk. Over the gate is a guard-house.

As the river is deep at its entrance the Company has had a wharf constructed, extending the whole length of the fort, for the discharge of the vessels which it keeps on Lake Superior, whether to transport its furs from Fort William to the Saut Ste. Marie or merchandise and provisions from Saut Ste. Marie to Fort William. The land behind the fort and on both sides of it is cleared and under tillage. We saw barley, peas, and oats, which had a very fine appearance. At the end of the clearing is the burying-ground. There are also, on the opposite bank of the river, a certain number of log houses, all inhabited by old Canadian voyageurs, worn out in the service of the Company without having enriched themselves. Married to women of the country and incumbered with large families of half-breed children, these men prefer to cultivate a little Indian corn and potatoes and to fish for a subsistence, rather than return to their native districts to give their relatives and former acquaintance certain proofs of their misconduct or their imprudence.

Fort William is the grand depôt of the North West Company for their interior posts, and the general rendezvous of the partners. The agents from Montreal and the wintering partners assemble here every summer to receive the returns of the respective outfits, prepare for the operations of the ensuing season, and discuss the general interests of their association. The greater part of them were assembled at the time of our arrival. The wintering hands who are to return with their employers pass also a great part of the summer here; they form a great encampment on the west side of the fort, outside the palisades. Those who engage at Montreal to go no farther than Fort William or Rainy Lake, and who do not winter, occupy yet another space on the east side. The winterers, or *hivernants,* give to these last the name of *mangeurs de lard,* or pork-eaters. They are also called comers-and-goers. One perceives an astonishing difference between these two camps, which are composed sometimes of three or four hundred men each; that of the pork-eaters is always dirty and disorderly, while that of the winterers is clean and neat.

To clear its land and improve its property the Company inserts a clause in the engagement of all who enter its service as canoe-men that they shall work for a certain number of days during their stay at Fort William. It is thus that it has cleared and drained the environs of the fort and has erected so many fine buildings. But when a hand has once worked the stipulated number of days he is for ever after exempt, even if he remain in the service twenty or thirty years and should come down to the fort every summer.

They received us very courteously at Fort William and I perceived by the reception given to myself in particular that, thanks to the Chinook dialect of which I was sufficiently master, they would not have asked better than to give me employment on advantageous terms. But I felt a great deal more eagerness to arrive in Montreal, than desire to return to the river Columbia.

A few days after we reached Fort William Mr. Keith made his appearance there from Fort George, or Astoria, with the news of the arrival of the *Isaac Todd* in the Columbia River. This vessel, which was a dull sailer, had been kept back a long time by contrary winds in doubling Cape Horn and had never been able to rejoin the vessels-of-war, her consorts, from which she was then separated. When she reached the rendez-vous at the island of Juan Fernandez, finding that the three ships-of-war had sailed, the Captain and passengers, as they were short of provisions, de-termined to range the coast. Entering the harbor of Monterey on the coast of California in order to obtain provisions, they learned that there was an English vessel-of-war in distress, in the bay of San Francisco. They repaired thither accord-ingly, and found, to their great surprise, that it was the sloop *Raccoon*. This vessel, in getting out of the river Columbia, had touched on the bar with such violence that a part of her false keel was carried away; and she had with difficulty made San Francisco with seven feet of water in the hold, although her crew had been constantly at the pumps. Captain Black, finding it impossi-ble to repair his ship, had decided to abandon her and to cross the continent to the Gulf of Mexico, thence to reach some of the British West India Islands. However, on the arrival of the

Isaac Todd means were found to careen the vessel and repair the damage. The *Isaac Todd* then pursued her voyage and entered the Columbia on the 17th of April, thirteen months after her departure from England.

Chapter XXVIII

From Fort William to Montreal

ON the 20th of July in the evening Mr. D. Stuart notified me that he should start the next morning for Montreal in a light canoe. I immediately wrote to my relatives, but the next morning Mr. Stuart told me that I was to be myself the bearer of my letters by embarking with him. I got ready my effects and toward evening we quitted Fort William, with fourteen stout voyageurs to man our large canoe and were soon floating on the bosom of the largest body of fresh water on the surface of the globe. We counted six passengers, namely, Messrs. D. Stuart, D. McKenzie, J. McDonald, J. Clarke, myself, and a little girl of eight or nine years, who came from Kildonan, on Red River. We passed the first night on one of the islands in Thunder Bay, so named on account of the frequent storms, accompanied with lightning and thunder, which burst over it at certain seasons of the year. On the 22d and 23d we continued to range the northern coast of Lake Superior. The navigation of this superb lake would be extremely agreeable but for the thick fogs which reign during a part of the day, and do not permit a rapid progress. On the 24th we dined at a small trading estab-

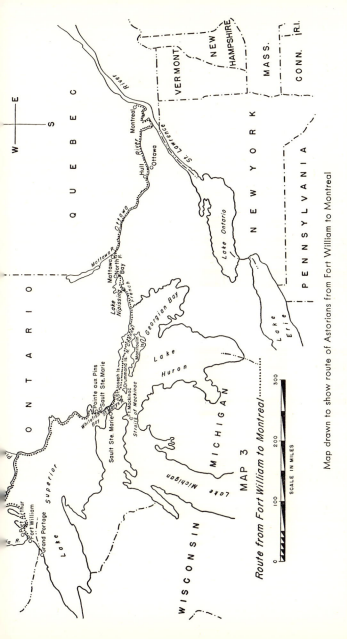

MAP 3

Route from Fort William to Montreal

SCALE IN MILES

0   100   200   300

Map drawn to show route of Astorians from Fort William to Montreal

lishment called Le Pic, where we had excellent fish.[139]

On the 26th we crossed Michipicoton Bay, which at its entrance may be nine miles wide. As we were nearing the eastern point we met a small canoe, having on board Captain McCargo and the crew of one of the schooners owned by the Company. Mr. McCargo informed us that he had just escaped from Saut Ste. Marie, whither the Americans had sent a detachment of one hundred and fifty men; and that having been obliged to abandon his schooner he had set fire to her. In consequence of this news it was resolved that the canoe on which we were proceeding should return to Fort William. I embarked with Mr. Stuart and two men in Captain McCargo's canoe, while he and his crew took our places. In the haste and confusion of this exchange, which was made on the lake, they gave us a ham, a little tea and sugar, and a bag containing about twenty-five pounds of flour, but forgot entirely a kettle, knives, forks, and so on, all articles which Mr. McCargo had not time to take when he left Saut Ste. Marie. We subsisted miserably, in consequence, for two days and a half that we continued to coast the lake before reaching any post.

[139]At the mouth of Pic River, where the North West Company maintained a trading post. It was more important than Franchère's brief statement implies.

We moistened in the bag a little flour, and having kneaded it made cakes which we baked on flat stones by our camp fire.

On the 29th we reached Batchawainon, where we found some women who prepared us food and received us well. It is a poor little post, situated at the bottom of a sandy cove which offers nothing agreeable to the eye. Mr. Frederic Goedike, who resided here, was gone to see what had taken place at Saut Ste. Marie. He returned the next day and told us that the Americans had come with a force of one hundred and fifty men, under the command of Major Holmes; and that after having pillaged all that they considered worth taking of the property of the N. W. Company and that of a Mr. Johnston they had set fire to the houses, warehouses, &c. belonging to the Company and to that gentleman and retired without molesting any other person.[140] Our canoe

[140]As the opening act of the War of 1812 a British force from Fort Saint Joseph surprised and captured Mackinac on July 17. The attacking force comprised the small British regular garrison of Fort Saint Joseph, a much larger number of Indians from the Lake Superior area, and a large number of voyageurs, marshaled and led by North West Company traders from Saint Joseph and by John Johnston of Sault Sainte Marie, who, although not a Northwester, and despite the fact that he had for many years lived on American soil and held office under the American Government, now conducted himself as a British subject. When, in 1814, an American fleet and army

arrived from Fort William in the evening, with that of Mr. McGillivray; and on the morrow we all repaired to Saut Ste. Marie, where we saw the ruins which the enemy had left. The houses, stores, and saw-mills of the Company were still smoking. The schooner was at the foot of the rapids; the Americans had run her down, but she grounded on a ledge of rocks whence they could not dislodge her and so they had burned her to the water's edge.

Le Saut de Ste. Marie, or as it is shortly called, Saut Ste. Marie, is a rapid at the outlet of Lake Superior, and may be five hundred or six hundred yards wide; its length may be estimated at three-quarters of a mile and the descent of the water at about twenty feet. At the lower extremity the river widens to about a mile, and here there are a certain number of houses. The north bank belongs to Great Britain; the southern to the United States. It was on the American side that Mr. Johnston lived. Before the war he was Collector of the Port for the American govern-

was dispatched from Detroit to recover Mackinac, John-ston and his voyageurs again journeyed to Mackinac to share in the British defense. Meanwhile, a detachment from the American army was dispatched to the Sault, with results which are described by Franchère above. After all this, Johnston, having vainly sought compensation from the British Government for the losses he had sustained, had the assurance to seek payment from the American Government.

ment. On the same side resided a Mr. Nolin with
his family. He was an old Indian trader and his
house and furniture showed signs of his former
prosperity. On the British side we found Mr.
Charles Ermatinger, who had a pretty establishment: he dwelt temporarily in a house that belonged to Nolin, but he was building another of
stone, very elegant, and had just finished a grist
mill. He thought that the last would lead the
inhabitants to sow more grain than they did.
These inhabitants are principally old Canadian
boatmen, married to half-breed or Indian women.
The fish afford them subsistence during the greater
part of the year and provided they secure potatoes enough to carry them through the remainder they are content. It is to be regretted that
these people are not more industrious, for the
land is very fertile.

On the 1st of August an express was sent to
Michilimackinac (Mackinaw) to inform the com-
mandant thereof what had happened at Saut Ste.
Marie. While expecting the return of the messen-
ger we put ourselves in a state of defense, in case
that by chance the Americans should make another
irruption. The thing was not improbable, for according to some expressions which fell from one
of their number who spoke French their object
was to capture the furs of the North West Com-

pany, which were expected to arrive shortly from the interior. We invited some Indians who were camped on Pine Point, at some distance from the Saut, to help us in case of need; which they promised to do. Meanwhile, we had no provisions, as everything had been carried off by the American forces, and were obliged to subsist on such brook trout as we could take with hook and line and on wild raspberries.

On the 4th the express returned without having been able to accomplish his mission. He had found the island of Mackinac so completely blockaded by the enemy that it was impossible to reach it without running the greatest risk of being made prisoner.

On the 12th we heard distinctly the discharges of artillery which our people were firing off at Michilimackinac, although the distance was nearly ninety miles.[141] We thought it was an attempt of the enemy to retake that post, but we afterward learned that it was only a royal salute in honor of the birthday of the Prince Regent. We learned, however, during our stay at Saut Ste. Marie, that the Americans had really made a descent upon

[141]The distance from Saint Ignace to Sault Sainte Marie by U.S. Highway No. 2, substantially an air-line route, is 52 miles. Although the 1854 edition, which we reprint, says "nearly sixty miles," the Manuscript clearly says *pas de 30 lieues*.

the Island, but were compelled to retire with a considerable loss.[142]

On the 19th Messrs. McGillivray and McLeod, two partners of the North West Company, arrived from Fort William, preceding the flotilla which was coming down richly laden with furs. They sent on Mr. Decoigne in a light canoe with letters to Montreal to order provisions to meet this brigade.

On the 21st the canoe in which I was a passenger was sent to the mouth of French River to observe the motions of the enemy. This river comes from the north and empties into Lake Huron about 120 miles from Sault Ste. Marie. We remained at the entrance of the river till the evening of the 25th, when the fleet of 44 loaded and 3 light canoes arrived there. The value of the furs which they carried could not be estimated at less than a million of dollars:[143] an impor-

[142]The American army landed on the back side of the Island (from the fort) with a view to taking the place in the rear. This plan proved sadly faulty, since it afforded the Indian allies of the British the advantage of fighting in the woods which intervened between the landing place and the fort. Major Holmes, leader of the raid on Sault Sainte Marie, was killed in the battle of August 4, and the attack was abandoned. Major Holmes' body was carried back to Detroit for burial. Many years later an old resident related that it was trailed in a hollow log in the water the entire distance from Mackinac.

[143]200,000 louis in Manuscript; 200,000 pounds in 1820 edition.

tant prize for the Americans, if they could have laid their hands upon it. We were three hundred and twenty-five men, all well armed; a large camp was formed with a breast-work of fur-packs, and we kept watch all night. The next morning we began to ascend French River, and were soon out of reach of the dreaded foe.[144] We reached Lake Nipissing, of which it is the outlet, the same evening and encamped. We crossed that lake on the 27th, made a number of portages, and encamped again, not far from Mattawan.

On the 28th we entered, at an early hour, the river Ottawa, and encamped in the evening at the Portage des Joachims. On the 29th we passed Fort Coulange where Mr. Goddin resides, and after passing a great number of portages caused by the rapids and falls which obstruct the navigation of this river we arrived on the evening of the 31st at the Chaudière or Hull, where Mr. Wright has a fine establishment and a large number of men employed in cultivating the land

[144]From Georgian Bay the route led up the French River to Lake Nipissing, across that lake to the Mattawa River, down the latter to its confluence with the Ottawa and down the latter river to Montreal. This was the famous Ottawa River route from Lower Canada to the Upper Lakes, followed from the time of Champlain early in the seventeenth century onward. For one somewhat detailed description of it see Alexander Henry's *Travels and Adventures*, the Lakeside Classics volume for 1921, Chapter 2.

and in cutting timber, in which he conducts an extensive trade.

The rock which here arrests the course of the Ottawa extends from shore to shore and so completely cuts off the waters that at the time we passed none was seen falling over, but sinking by subterranean channels or fissures in the rock, it boiled up below from seven or eight different openings not unlike water in a huge caldron, whence the first explorers of the country gave it the name of Chaudière or Caldron Falls.

We left the Chaudière a little before sunset, and passed very soon the confluence of the Rideau or Curtain River.[145] This river, which casts itself into the Ottawa over a rock twenty-five by thirty feet high, is divided in the middle of the fall by a little island which parts the waters into two white sheets, resembling a double curtain open in the middle and spreading out below. The *coup d'œil* is really picturesque; the rays of the setting sun, which struck the waters obliquely as we passed, heightened exceedingly their beauty and rendered it worthy of a pencil more skilful than mine.

We traveled a great part of the night and passed several habitations. Toward midnight we stopped to let our men have a little rest. They had

[145]Nearby is the city of Ottawa, capital of the Dominion of Canada.

much need of it, for when a war is going on two hours' rest each night is the custom when traveling express in a light canoe. At two o'clock we re-embarked and at sunrise on the 1st September we reached Long Saut, where, having procured guides, we passed that dangerous rapid, and set foot on shore near the dwelling-house of a Mr. McDonell, who sent us milk and fruits for our breakfast. Toward noon we passed the Lake of the Two Mountains, where I began to see the mountain of my native isle. About two o'clock we passed the rapids of St. Ann. Soon after we came opposite Saut St. Louis and aided by a good wind we passed this last rapid and landed at Montreal a little before sunset, after an absence of four years, one month and six days.

I hastened to the paternal roof, where the family were not less surprised than overjoyed at beholding me. Not having heard of me since I had sailed from New York, they had believed, in accordance with the common report, that I had been murdered by the savages with Mr. McKay and the crew of the *Tonquin:* and certainly it was by the goodness of Providence that I found myself thus safe and sound in the midst of my relations and friends, at the end of a voyage accompanied by so many perils and in which so many of my companions had met with an untimely death.

CHAPTER XXIX

In Retrospect

THE last chapter closes the original French narrative of my travels around and across the continent, as published thirty-three years ago. The translation follows that narrative as exactly as possible, varying from it only in the correction of a few not very important errors of fact. It speaks of places and persons as I spoke of them then. I would not willingly lose the verisimilitude of this natural and unadorned description in order to indulge in any new turns of style or more philosophical reflections.

But since that period many changes have occurred in the scenes which I so long ago visited and described. Though they are well known, I may be pardoned for alluding to them.

The natives of the Sandwich Islands, who were in a state of paganism at that time, have since adopted a form of Christianity, have made considerable progress in imitating the civilization of Europe, and even, at this moment, begin to entertain the idea of annexation to the United States.[146] It appears, however, that the real na-

---

[146]Before and following the Mexican War of 1846–48 the idea of the "Manifest Destiny" of the United States to acquire additional territory was widely popular. President

tives are rapidly dwindling away by the effects of their vices, which an exotic and ill-assimilated civilization has rather increased than diminished, and to which religion has not succeeded in applying a remedy.

At the mouth of the Columbia whole tribes, and among them the Clatsops, have been swept away by disease. Here again licentious habits universally diffused spread a fatal disorder through the whole nation, and undermining the constitutions of all, left them an easy prey to the first contagion or epidemic sickness. But missionaries of various Christian sects have labored among the Indians of the Columbia also; not to speak of the missions of the Catholic Church, so well known by the narrative of Father De Smet and others;[147] and numbers have been taught to cultivate the soil, and thus to provide against the

Pierce and Secretary of State Marcy (1853–57) interpreted it to include the annexation of the Hawaiian Islands, an act not actually accomplished until July 7, 1898. By Act of April 30, 1900 Hawaii became a Territory and this status is still (1954) retained, despite a long-continued struggle to achieve admission to statehood.

[147]Father Pierre Jean De Smet (1801–73) was one of the most notable missionaries to the Indians in American history. Beginning about 1840 he labored in the Oregon country, presently extending his activities to practically the entire Great Plains, Rocky Mountain, and Pacific Coastal areas. He won the confidence of red men and white men alike, and some of his most notable achievements were performed as a mediator between the two races.

famines to which they were formerly exposed from their dependence on the precarious resources of the chase; while others have received, in the faith of Christ, the true principle of national permanence, and a living germ of civilization which may afterward be developed.

Emigration has also carried to the Oregon the axe of the settler as well as the canoe and pack of the fur-trader. The fertile valleys and prairies of the Willamet, once the resort of the deer, the elk, and the antelope, are now tilled by the industrious husbandman. Oregon City, so near old Astoria, whose first log fort I saw and described, is now an Archiepiscopal See, and the capital of a Territory which must soon be a state of the Union.

Of the regions east of the mountains described in my itinerary little can be said in respect to improvement: they remain in the same wild state. The interest of the Hudson's Bay Company as an association of fur-traders is opposed to agricultural improvements, whose operation would be to drive off and extinguish the wild animals that furnish their commerce with its object. But on Lake Superior steamboats have supplanted the birch-bark canoe of the Indian and the fur-trader, and at Sault Ste. Marie, especially on the American side, there is now every sign of prosperity. How remote and wild was the region beyond through which I passed may be estimated by the fact that in thirty-eight years the onward-rolling wave of our population has but just reached its confines.

Canada, although it has not kept pace with the United States, has yet wonderfully advanced in forty years. The valley of the Ottawa, that great artery of the St. Lawrence, where I thought it worth while to notice the residence of an enterprising farmer and lumber merchant, is now a populous district, well cultivated, and sprinkled with villages, towns, and cities.

The reader, in perusing my first chapter, found a description of the city of New York in 1810, and of the neighboring village of Brooklyn. It would be superfluous to establish a comparison at this day. At that time, it will be observed, the mere breaking out of war between America and England was thought to involve the sacrifice of an American commercial establishment on the Pacific, on the ground of its supplies being necessarily cut off (it was supposed), and of the United States Government being unable to protect it from hostile attack. At present it suffices to remark that while New York, then so inconsiderable a port, is now perhaps the third city in the world, the United States, also, are undoubtedly a first-rate power, unassailable at home and formidable abroad to the greatest nations.

As in my preface I alluded to Mr. Irving's
Astoria as reflecting, in my opinion unjustly,
upon the young men engaged in the first expedition to the mouth of the Columbia, it may suffice
here to observe, without entering into particulars,
that my narrative, which I think answers for its
own fidelity, clearly shows that some of them, at
least, did not want courage, activity, zeal for the
interests of the Company while it existed, and patient endurance of hardship. And although it
forms no part of the narrative or my voyage, yet as
subsequent visits to the West and an intimate
knowledge of St. Louis enable me to correct Mr.
Irving's poetical rather than accurate description
of that place, I may well do it here. St. Louis
now bids fair to rival ere long the "Queen of the
West;"[148] Mr. Irving describes her as a small trading place where trappers, half-breeds, gay,
frivolous Canadian boatmen, &c., &c., congregated and revelled, with that lightness and buoy-
ancy of spirit inherited from their French fore-
fathers; the indolent Creole of St. Louis caring
for little more than the enjoyment of the present
hour; a motley population, half-civilized, half-
barbarous, thrown, on his canvas, into one
general, confused (I allow highly picturesque)
mass, without respect of persons: but it is fair

[148]The allusion is to Cincinnati, for several decades the
foremost city of the western country.

to say, with due homage to the talent of the
sketcher, who has verged slightly on caricature
in the use of that humor-loving pencil admired
by all the world, that St. Louis even then con-
tained its noble, industrious, and I may say
princely merchants; it could boast its Chouteaus,
Soulands, Céré, Chéniers, Vallées, and La Croix,
with other kindred spirits whose descendants
prove the worth of their sires by their own, and
are now among the leading business men, as their
fathers were the pioneers, of the flourishng St.
Louis.

With these remarks, which I make simply as
an act of justice in connection with the general
subject of the founding of Astoria, but in which
I mean to convey no imputation on the inten-
tional fairness of the accomplished author to
whom I have alluded, I take a respectful leave
of my readers.

APPENDIX[149]

Errors of Washington Irving

IN Chapter XVII I promised the reader to give him an account of the fate of some of the persons who left Astoria before and after its sale or transfer to the British. I will now redeem that pledge.

Messrs. Ramsay Crooks, R. McClellan, and Robert Stuart, after enduring all sorts of fatigue, dangers, and hair-breadth escapes with their lives —all which have been so graphically described by Washington Irving in his *Astoria*, finally reached St. Louis and New York.

Mr. Clapp went to the Marquesas Islands, where he entered into the service of his country in the capacity of midshipman under Commodore Porter—made his escape from there in company with Lieutenant Gamble of the Marine Corps, by directions of the Commodore, was captured by the British, landed at Buenos Ayres, and finally reached New York.

D. McDougall, as a reward for betraying the trust reposed in him by Mr. Astor, was made a

[149]We have thought it best to give this Appendix, excepting some abbreviations rendered necessary to avoid repetition of what has been stated before, in Mr. Franchère's own words, particularly as a specimen of his own English style may be justly interesting to the reader.—Huntington.

partner of the North West Company, crossed the mountains, and died a miserable death at Bas de la Rivière, Winnipeg. Donald McKenzie, his co-adjutor, went back to the Columbia River, where he amassed a considerable fortune, with which he retired, and lived in Chautauqua County in this State, where he died a few years since unknown and neglected: he was a very selfish man, who cared for no one but himself.

It remains only to speak of Messrs. J. C. Halsey, Russell Farnham, and Alfred Seton, who, it will be remembered, embarked with Mr. Hunt on the *Pedlar,* in February 1814.

Leaving the River about the 1st of April, they proceeded to the Russian establishment at Sitka, Norfolk Sound, where they fell in with two or three more American vessels, which had come to trade with the natives or to avoid the British cruisers. While there, a sail under British colors appeared, and Mr. Hunt sent Mr. Seton to ascertain who she was. She turned out to be the *Forester,* Captain Pigott, a repeating signal ship and letter-of-marque, sent from England in company of a fleet intended for the South Seas. On further acquaintance with the Captain, Mr. Seton (from whom I derive these particulars) learned a fact which has never before been published, and which will show the solicitude and perseverance of Mr. Astor. After despatching the *Lark* from

New York, fearing that she might be intercepted by the British, he sent orders to his correspondent in England to purchase and fit out a British bottom and despatch her to the Columbia to relieve the establishment.

When Mr. Hunt learned this fact he determined to leave Mr. Halsey at Sitka, and proceeding himself northward, landed Mr. Farnham on the coast of Kamchatka, to go overland with despatches for Mr. Astor. Mr. Farnham accomplished the journey, reached Hamburg, whence he sailed for the West Indies, and finally arrived at New York, having made the entire circuit of the globe.

The *Pedlar* then sailed to the southeast, and soon reached the coast of California, which she approached to get a supply of provisions. Nearing one of the harbors, they descried a vessel at anchor inside, showing American colors. Hauling their wind, they soon came close to the stranger, which, to their surprise, turned out to be the Spanish corvette *Santa Barbara* which sent boats alongside the *Pedlar* and captured her, and kept possession of the prize for some two months, during which they dropped down to San Blas. Here Mr. Hunt proposed to Mr. Seton to cross the Continent and reach the United States the best way he could. Mr. Seton, accordingly, went to the Isthmus of Darien, where he was detained several months by sickness, but finally reached Carthagena, where a British fleet was lying in the roads to take off the English merchants, who in consequence of the revolutionary movements going on sought shelter under their own flag. Here Mr. Seton, reduced to the last stage of destitution and squalor, boldly applied to Captain Bentham, the commander of the squadron, who, finding him to be a gentleman, offered him every needful assistance, gave him a berth in his own cabin, and finally landed him safely on the Island of Jamaica, whence he, too, found his way to New York.

Of all those engaged in the expedition there are now but four survivors—Ramsay Crooks, Esq., the late President of the American Fur Company; Alfred Seton, Esq., Vice-president of the Sun Mutual Insurance Company; both of New York City; Benjamin Pillet of Canada; and the author, living also in New York. All the rest have paid the debt of nature, but their names are recorded in the foregoing pages.

Notwithstanding the illiberal remarks made by Captain Thorn on the persons who were on board the ill-fated *Tonquin*, and reproduced by Mr. Irving in his *Astoria*—these young men who were represented as "Bar keepers or Billiard markers, most of whom had fled from Justice, &c." I feel it a duty to say that they were for the most part of good parentage, liberal education, and in every way were qualified to discharge the duties of their respective stations. The remarks on the general character of the voyageurs employed as boat-men and mechanics, and the attempt to cast ridicule on their "braggart and swaggering manners" come with a bad grace from the author of *Astoria*, when we consider that in that very work Mr. Irving is compelled to admit their indomitable energy, their fidelity to their employers, and their cheerfulness under the most trying circumstances in which men can be placed.

With respect to Captain Thorn, I must confess that though a stern commander and an irritable man he paid the strictest attention to the health of his crew. His complaints of the squalid appearance of the Canadians and mechanics who were on board can be abated of their force by giving a description of the accommodation of these people. The *Tonquin* was a small ship; its forecastle was destined for the crew performing duty before the mast. The room allotted for the accommodation of the twenty men destined for the Establishment was abaft the forecastle; a bulk-head had been let across, and a door led from the forecastle into a dark, unventilated, unwholesome place, where they were all heaped together, without means of locomotion and consequently deprived of that exercise of the body so necessary to health.

Add to that, we had no physician on board. In view of these facts, can the complaints of the gallant Captain be sustained? Of course Mr. Irving was ignorant of these circumstances, as well as of many others which he might have known had some one suggested to him to ask a few questions of persons who were within his reach at the time of his publication. I have (I need scarcely say) no personal animosity against the unfortunate Captain; he always treated me, individually, as well as I could expect; and if, in the course of my narrative I have been severe on his actions, I was impelled by a sense of justice to my friends on board, as well as by the circumstance that such explanations of his general deportment were requisite to convey the historical truth to my readers.

The idea of a conspiracy against him on board is so absurd that it really does not deserve notice. The threat, or rather the proposal made to him by Mr. McKay, in the following words—"if you say fight, fight it is"—originated in a case where one of the sailors had maltreated a Canadian lad, who came to complain to Mr. McKay. The Captain would not interpose his authority, and said in my presence: "Let them fight out their own battles." It was upon that answer that Mr. McKay gave vent to the expression quoted above. I might go on with a long list of inaccuracies, more

or less grave or trivial, in the beautifully written
work of Mr. Irving, but it would be tedious to go
through the whole of them. The few remarks to
which I have given place above will suffice to
prove that the assertion made in the preface was
not unwarranted. It is far from my intention to
enter the lists with a man of the literary merit and
reputation of Mr. Irving, but as a narrator of
events of which I was an eyewitness, I felt bound
to tell the truth, although that truth might im-
pugn the historical accuracy of a work which
ranks as a classic in the language. At the same
time I entirely exonerate Mr. Irving from any intention of prejudicing the minds of his readers,
as he doubtless had only in view to support the
character of his friend: that sentiment is worthy
of a generous heart, but it should not be gratified,
nor would he wish to gratify it, I am sure, at the
expense of the character of others.

NOTE BY THE EDITOR.

Perhaps even contrary to the wish of Mr. Franchère I
have left the above almost word for word as he wrote it. It
is a part of the history of the affairs related as well in Mr.
Irving's *Astoria* as in the present volume, that the recla-
mations of one of the clerks on that famous and unfortunate voyage of the *Tonquin* against the disparaging description of himself and his colleagues given in the former
work should be fairly recorded. At the same time I can
not help stating my own impression that a natural sus-
ceptibility, roused by those slighting remarks from Captain Thorn's correspondence to which Mr. Irving as an

historian gives currency, has somewhat blinded my excellent friend to the tone of banter so characteristic of the chronicler of the Knickerbockers, in which all these particulars are given more as traits of the character of the stern old Sea-Captain, with his hearty contempt for land-lubbers and literary clerks, than as a dependable account of the persons on board his ship, some of whom might have been, and as we see by the present work, were, in fact, very meritorious characters, for whose literary turn and faithful journalizing (which seems to have especially provoked the Captain's wrath), now at the end of more than forty years we have so much reason to be thankful. Certainly Mr. Irving himself, who has drawn frequently on Mr. Franchère's narrative, could not, from his well-known taste in such matters, be insensible to the Defoe-like simplicity thereof, nor to the picturesque descriptions, worthy of a professional pen, with which it is sprinkled.— Huntington.

Index

INDEX

Ottawa River Route, history, 279.
Ottawa River Valley, progress, 285.
Owahou Island. See Oahu Island.

Pacific Fur Company, sale of property, 142–43.
Peace (Unjighah) River, 223.
Pedlar, voyages, 168–70, 289–90.
Pelton, Archibald, story of, 109–10.
Pembina River, Astorians pass, 237.
Pemican, Astorians find, 220; as food supply, 233, 237, 254, 262–63; controversy over, 258–60; method of making, 259.
Pend Oreille (Flathead, Clark's Fork) River, Astorians pass, 213–14.
Penguins, described, 20–21.
Perrault, Guilleaume, falls overboard, 28.
Perrault, —, clerk, LIII.
Phoebe, naval activities, 141–43, 147–48.
Pillet, Benjamin, member of Astorian expedition, XXIII; of searching party, 65; of party which founds Fort Okanogan, 84, 91–92; of Cowlitz River expedition, 101; of Spokane River expedition, 117; conducts sturgeon fishery, 167–68; on journey from Astoria to Montreal, 199, 221, 226, 237, 243; later years, 291.
Point Adams, named, 56.
Point George, Astoria established on, 68–69.
Point Hancock, named, 56.
Point Vancouver, named, 76.
Pork-eaters. See *Mangeurs de lard*.
Portage des Joachims, Astorians camp, 279.
Porter, Kenneth, work cited, XVI.
Porter, Commodore David, naval operation, 147–48, 288.
Potatoes, raised, 175.
Prairie dogs, described, 202.
Prevost, Jean B., drowned, 108.
Priest Rapids, named, 210.
Prince, John S., stepson of Franchère, XXI–XXII.
Prince, Mrs. —, wife of Franchère, XXI–XXII.

Index

The Lakeside Classics